THE
ER
COMPANION

THE

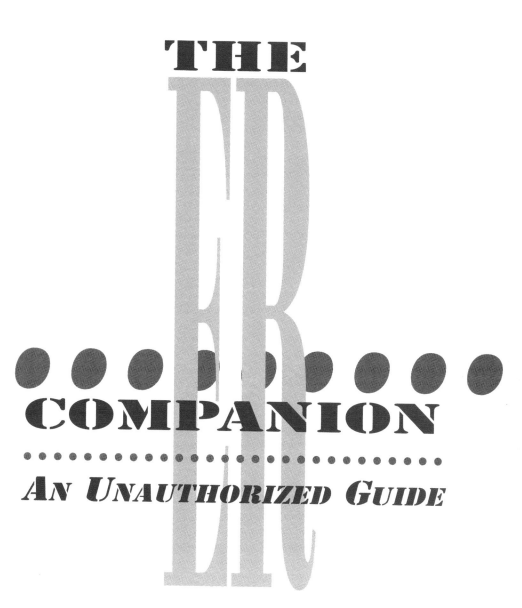

COMPANION

AN UNAUTHORIZED GUIDE

Stephen J. Spignesi

A SIGNET BOOK

SIGNET

Published by the Penguin Group
Penguin Books Ltd, 27 Wrights Lane, London W8 5TZ, England
Penguin Books USA Inc., 375 Hudson Street, New York, New York 10014, USA
Penguin Books Australia Ltd, Ringwood, Victoria, Australia
Penguin Books Canada Ltd, 10 Alcorn Avenue, Toronto, Ontario, Canada M4V 3B2
Penguin Books (NZ) Ltd, 182–190 Wairau Road, Auckland 10, New Zealand

Penguin Books Ltd, Registered Offices: Harmondsworth, Middlesex, England

First published in the USA by Citadel Press 1996
First published in Great Britain in Signet 1996
1 3 5 7 9 10 8 6 4 2

Printed and bound in Great Britain by
Butler & Tanner Ltd, Frome and London

This book is dedicated with thanks to

Cheryl Monde, R. T. R.
Annie Pantalena, R.N.
and
Lori Zuccaro, R.N.

three dear friends who took the time to explain,
and who made this book better
than I could have made it by myself.

CONTENTS

"WELCOME TO HELL"

"I never really showed much interest in what my parents

did until it came time for me to make use of it. But my

mother and I rekindled a really nice friendship

where I now get to call her up and say,

'How do I pronounce tach-y-car-di-a?'"

—Noah Wyle (John Carter), in *Cosmopolitan*, talking about
his post-*ER* relationship with his mother, who is head
orthopedic nurse at a Los Angeles hospital

"I melded together two nurses I met in ERs, Janis and Sue—

I don't even know their last names. One seemed like

someone who could juggle while standing very still,

she was so calm. The other was very good

but kind of over the job, and over doctors telling her stuff she already knew."

—Julianna Margulies (Carol Hathaway), in *Entertainment Weekly*, talking about how she prepared for her role on *ER*

"I'm a terrible patient, and I find that doctors can be very condescending. . . . I wanted [Susan Lewis] to be someone who walks in, says, 'You're having trouble, these are the problems, we're going to run these tests'—someone who tells you the truth."

—Sherry Stringfield (Dr. Susan Lewis), in *Entertainment Weekly*, talking about her hopes for her character on *ER*

"You get to cover a wide range of emotions. There's humor at the strangest times; and pathos and pain. At the other end of that, we have an opportunity here to present high drama that is very much something that people can relate to."

—Eriq La Salle (Dr. Peter Benton), in an interview on NBC, talking about the popularity of *ER*

"When we had about nine shows in the can and they picked us up for the total of twenty-six hours in the season, we started going, 'Okay, I can afford to spend some money now.' Everyone bought something except for Tony [Edwards]. He's got all he needs."

—**George Clooney (Dr. Doug Ross), in *GQ***

"I'm the same height as [my character Mark Greene]. I'm not as smart as he is. George stole that line from me. He steals all my best stuff!"

—**Anthony Edwards (Dr. Mark Greene), in *Entertainment Weekly***

Two words sum up the *ER* experience: drama and trauma.

ER burst on the 1994 TV scene like one of its own gurneys smashing through the Emergency Department doors.

Originally conceived as a feature film, *ER*'s two-hour debut episode, "24 Hours," had an impressive lineage. It was written by none other than Michael Crichton (who had a killer year that included scripting the films *Jurassic Park* and *Disclosure* in addition to *ER*) and boasted no less than forty-five guest stars and, perhaps more important, the stories and treatment histories of thirty-one ER patients.

The "ER" Companion takes you through the entire, pulse-pounding first season of *ER* and provides complete details on the dramatic lives of the ER staff—Mark, Doug, Peter, Carol, Susan, Carter, Haleh, Malik, Jerry, Lydia, and all the others—and also allows you to peak into the medical records of over five hundred ER patients treated in the show's first twenty-five episodes.

One of the most powerful elements of *ER* is its medical authenticity: The tests, drugs, procedures, and traumas are all as genuine as those that exist in the real-world ERs. Thus, the Patient Histories included in each chapter of this book meticulously record every CBC (complete blood count), Chem 7, and pneumothorax performed or diagnosed on the show in medically precise detail. Reading these histories is like having access to a stranger's private medical records.

The "ER" Companion also includes a trivia quiz, "What's Your ER I.Q.? and a Medical Glossary that will help explain some of the bewildering jargon Mark or Susan or Peter throws around so glibly while wheeling a gurney at breakneck speed through the halls of the hospital.

Who said going to the hospital wasn't any fun?

Stephen Spignesi
November 1995
New Haven, Connecticut

I

THE *ER* HALL OF FAME

THE ER
HALL OF FAME

This Hall of Fame catalogs some of the more interesting and intriguing *ER* cases and patients.

You can browse this list and then look up the patients of interest, or you can read *The "ER" Companion* in the order the episodes were aired for total immersion in the entire *ER* experience!

[NOTE: The episode number and patient number are provided in parentheses following the name of the patient, e.g., "14.265" means this patient's history can be found in chapter 14 and that he is Patient 265 in *The "ER" Companion*.]

Funniest Patients
- The Lobster Man (2.42)
- The guy with the arrow in his head (14.265)
- Mr. Connolly (15.272)
- The Viking woman (15.279)
- Louie (20.374)

Most Obnoxious Patients
- Mr. Luck (9.146)
- Mr. Desmond (13.247)
- Mr. DeNardo (20.391)

Most Unusual Emergencies
- The guy with the cigarette lighter embedded in his chest (10.179)

- Jorge the body packer (13.240)
- Gus (17.316)
- Mr. Longét, the Tattoo Man (19.358)
- Santi (23.476)
- The old man who swallowed his dentures (24.496)

Most Tragic Cases
- Henry Carlton (9.147)
- Mr. Vennerbeck (12.222)
- Jody O'Brien (19.359)

Most Disgusting Patients
- Velma Zevallo (4.65)
- Gilbert McCabe (12.215)
- Evoldo (13.237)
- The lice case (20.379)
- Palmer and six other Ranger Scouts with diarrhea (24.482–24.488)

Stupidest Patients
- The drunk burglar (20.394)
- Dumb and Dumber (23.474 and 23.475)

Drunkest Patient
- Daniel Quinn (5.93)

Most "Unsick" Patient
- Mrs. Raskin (1.18)

Most Unexpected Patients
- Carol Hathaway (1.24)
- Dr. Kayson (14.266)

Craziest Patients
- Regina (10.178)
- Mr. Halgrim (17.315)
- Marty (a.k.a. John Koch) (18.346)

Horniest Patient
- Liz (1.28)

Most Violent Patients
- The PCP Gurney Man (20.372)
- The girl whose ear was cut off by Rosario (24.501)

Favorite Nonhuman Patient
- Bill the dog (16.290)

Most Imaginary Patients
- Doug's nonexistent six-year-old tetralogy of Fallot (15.285)

- Dr. Swift's fictitious third-degree-burn patients (20.390)
- The patient with ptosis, myosis, and hidrosis (20.392)

Most Violent Injuries
- Lorenzo and Pauly Renzetti (16.300 and 16.301

Cutest Patients
- The little girls in Valentine's Day heart costumes (16.302–16.307)

Most Miraculous Recovery
- Murray Valerio (11.196)

Funniest Student Patients
- The cheerleaders on acid (16.293–16.295)
- The Popsicle pledges (20.384–20.387)

Patients With the Most
- The abused baby boy (1.27)

Detestable Parents
- The baby who "fell" out of a second-floor window (17.324)
- Bonnie Howe (18.343)
- The baby in the trash bag (20.395)

Oddest Student Patient
- The drug test subject (18.336)

Most Devious Patients
- Art Moss (a.k.a. Sam Hart; a.k.a. Gene Finch) (18.344)
- "Dr." Lyle Strong (22.432)

Tragic AIDS Cases
- Terry (14.264)
- Tatiana (16.287)
- Timmy Falco (20.380)
- Thomas Allison (25.507)

Most Entrepreneurial Patient
- Kovalev (23.447)

Most Prestigious Patient
- Howard Davis (23.454)

Weirdest Patients
- Arlena the astrologer (20.382)
- Mr. Talbott the werewolf (20.393)

Kinkiest Patients
- Neal Shearer (4.71)
- Eddie (16.308)

Most Uncooperative Patients
- Harry Stopeck (4.67)
- The wrestler (8.134)

Sexiest Patients
- The blonde in the waitress uniform (1.25)
- Priscilla (4.72)

Most Appreciative Patient
- Bob Brickley (4.75)

Most Bewildering Emergencies
- Kanesha Freeman (6.96)
- Michael Carson (7.127)

Patient in the Most Denial
- Samantha (22.429)

Most Senile Patient
- Mrs. Hayden (16.309)

Most Loathsome Patient
- The Skinhead (17.330)

Unluckiest Patient
- Caleb Hahn (25.506)

Most Emotionally Distraught Patient
- Jamie Hendricks (8.133)

Most Uncommon Emergency
- Leslie Nesbitt (22.445)

Saddest Deaths
- Sam Gasner (5.87)
- Kathleen Horne (14.252)
- Grace Holsten (15.277)

Friendliest Patient
- Patrick (7.110)

Most Poignant Cases
- Ben Gather (13.241)
- Alan the color guy (13.244)
- Tatiana (16.287)

Most Talented Patient
- Mary Cavanaugh (3.50)

Most Obsessed Patient
- Donny (Donald) Costanza (23.453)

THE
LEGEND
BEGINS

· · · · · · · · · · · · · · · · ·

ER's First Season

ER THE STAFF

This section lists all the recurring characters in the first season of *ER*.

Any *ER* character that appeared in more than one episode is included here.

Characters other than the main cast are organized by ER Staff, Hospital Staff, EMTs and Medical Support Personnel, Visitors to the ER, and Family Members of ER and Hospital Staff.

MAIN CHARACTERS

Dr. Mark Greene, ER Chief Resident—*Anthony Edwards*
Dr. Doug Ross, Pediatrics Resident—*George Clooney*
Dr. Peter Benton, Second-Year Surgical Resident—*Eriq La Salle*
Dr. Susan Lewis, Second-Year Resident—*Sherry Stringfield*
Carol Hathaway, ER Head Nurse—*Julianna Margulies*
John Carter, Medical Student—*Noah Wyle*

REGULAR CHARACTERS

ER STAFF
Haleh, ER R.N.—*Yvette Freeman*
Lydia Wright,* ER R.N.—*Ellen Crawford*

---

*This character was known as Lydia Woodward in the two-hour pilot episode.

Wendy Goldman, ER Student Nurse—*Vanessa Marquez*
Conni Oligario, ER R.N.—*Conni Marie Brazelton*
Jerry, Emergency Service Coordinator—*Abraham Benrubi*
Malik, R.N. Aide—*Deezer D.*
Dr. Morgenstern, Chief of Surgery—*William Macy*
Dr. John Tagliari, Staff Orthopedist—*Rick Rossovich*
Dr. Div Cvetic, Staff Psychiatrist—*John Terry*
Dr. William "Wild Willy" Swift, Chief of Surgery—*Michael Ironside*
Dr. Sara Langworthy, Attending Physician—*Tyra Ferrell*
Dr. Jack Kayson, Cardiologist—*Sam Anderson*
Dr. Angela Hicks, ER Attending Surgeon—*CCH Pounder*
"Bob" Bighdonovichski, Polish Vascular Surgeon—*Malgoscha Gebel*
Deb Chen, Medical Student—*Ming-Na Wen*
Timmy, ER Aide—*Glenn Plummer*
Mookie James, ER Aide—*Christian Coleman*
Rolando, Emergency Service Coordinator—*Rolando Molina*

● ●

HOSPITAL STAFF
Dr. Steve Flint, Radiologist—*Scott Jaeck*
Jeannie Boulet, Physical Therapist—*Gloria Reuben*
Dr. Nancy Coburn—*Amy Aquino*
Diane Leeds, Hospital Risk Management Administrator—*Lisa Zane*
Perez—*Petra Porras*
Lily Jarvic—*Lily Mariye*
O.R. and Scrub Nurse—*Suzanne Carney*
Pickman—*Emily Wagner*
Shirley—*Dinah Lenney*

● ●

EMTS* AND MEDICAL SUPPORT PERSONNEL
Camacho, EMT—*Rick Marzan*
Mrs. McGillis, Children and Family Services Administrator—*Valeri Ross*
Scott, EMT—*Lee R. Sellars*
Jagman—*Todd Merrill*
Del Torre—*Javi Mulero*
Zadro—*Monte Russell*
Swanson—*Julie Fulton*

*EMT is the abbreviation for Emergency Medical Technician.

VISITORS TO THE ER

Linda Farrell, Pharmaceutical Representative—*Andrea Parker*

Mary Cavanaugh (Madame X)—*Rosemary Clooney*

Ivan Gregor—*John La Motta*

Patrick—*Kevin Michael Richardson*

Regina—*Pamela Gordon*

Liz (a.k.a. Persephone)—*Liz Vassey*

Officer Grabarsky—*Mike Genovese*

Tatiana Hall—*Eda Reiss Merin*

● ●

FAMILY MEMBERS OF ER AND HOSPITAL STAFF

Chloe Lewis, Dr. Lewis's sister—*Kathleen Wilhoite*

Jenn Greene, Dr. Greene's attorney wife—*Christine Harnos*

Rachel Greene, Dr. Greene's daughter—*Yvonne Zima*

Jake Leeds, Diane Leed's son—*Zachary Browne*

Mrs. Benton, Dr. Benton's mother—*Beah Richards*

Walt, Dr. Benton's brother-in-law—*Ving Rhames*

Jackie, Dr. Benton's sister—*Khandi Alexander*

Cookie Lewis, Dr. Lewis and Chloe's mother—*Valerie Perrine*

Helen, Carol Hathaway's mother—*Giorgi Tarlian*

Jesse, Jackie and Walt's son—*Christopher Richardson*

Steven, Jackie and Walt's son—*Marc Dakota Robinson*

● ●

NOTABLE FIRST SEASON GUEST STARS

Lance Gentile, M.D.—*Jimmy (Episode 1)*

Alan Rosenberg—*Sam Gasner (Episode 5)*

Vondie Curtis-Hall—*Henry Carlton/Miss Carlton (Episode 9)*

Garrett Morris—*Mr. Luck (Episode 9)*

Linda Kelsey—*Grace Holsten (Episode 15)*

Bobcat Goldthwaite—*Mr. Connolly (Episode 15)*

Meg Foster—*Mrs. Hall (Episode 16)*

Robert Carradine—*Marty [a.k.a. John Koch] (Episode 18)*

Valerie Perrine—*Cookie Lewis (Episode 24)*

ER 1

"24 HOURS"

*"We work thirty-six hours on, eighteen off,
which is ninety hours a week, fifty-two weeks a year,
and for that we are paid $23,739 before taxes,
and we also have to make the coffee?"*

—**Dr. Peter Benton**

"My heart is breaking."

—**Carol Hathaway, R.N.**

"24 Hours," the two-hour pilot episode of *ER* opens (and closes, for that matter), with Dr. Mark Greene sleeping. He is first awakened by Lydia, an ER nurse, who insists that he handle a certain patient, who we soon learn is Dr. Doug Ross, the ER's resident pediatrician. Doug is drunk as a skunk and Mark has to handle him, which he does with dextrose and aspirin. We learn that Doug frequently does this on his nights off, and his drinking problem, while never actually discussed, is obviously being alluded to.

Mark goes back to sleep and Lydia wakes him again to ask if a patient can have more Demerol for her pain.

12

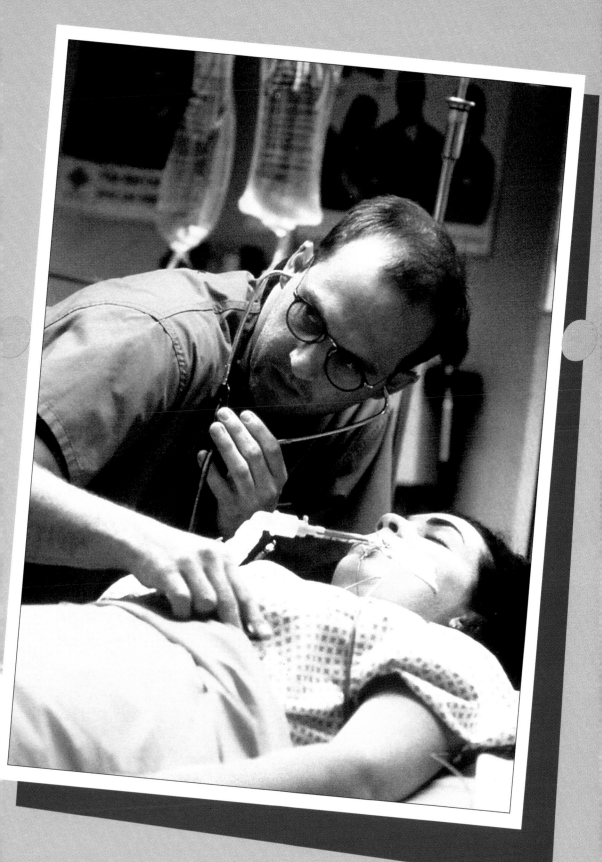

The night shift ends and another day in the ER begins. Dr. Susan Lewis and Dr. Peter Benton come on duty; Mark continues his eighteen-hour shift.

The staff gets the news that there has been a building collapse in the Loop, and that there were twelve injuries, seven of which are critical. They gear up for multiple trauma victims. (Mark even rescinds a bunch of orders he was giving to an intern in order to prepare for the wounded.)

The patients begin arriving: Mr. Wilson's hand is hanging by a thread; Mr. Jackson has a bleeding chest wound; Jeff Barr has facial injuries; Mr. Canelli has a heart attack; and, while all this is going on, an elderly woman Doug Ross is attending to goes into cardiac arrest.

The patients are attended to (including one horny young guy who makes a pass at Susan) and, from madness and confusion, the ER suddenly transforms into a quiet and orderly place.

Mark meets his wife Jenn and daughter Rachel in the cafeteria, and we get the first hints that there might be trouble in the Greene marriage. Jenn really wants Mark to take a plush job with a prestigious medical group. Mark wants to stay in the ER.

Medical student John Carter (*ER* creator Michael Crichton's alter ego) arrives and is assigned to Dr. Peter Benton, who takes him on a whirlwind, meant-to-intimidate tour of the Emergency Department. Carter meets *ER* head nurse Carol Hathaway, who later that evening will be brought into the ER comatose from a deliberate drug overdose. Carter also meets Dr. Morgenstern, the chief of surgery and head of the ER, and is told that the chief "eats students for lunch."

Doug Ross also welcomes a medical student. She's a young, overconfident beauty named Tracy Young, and when Doug immediately comes on to her, she buries him with a blistering retort.

We then learn that Carol and Doug were recently an item, and that he wants to start up again, an idea Carol completely rejects (she calls him a fool). Shortly thereafter, Carter sees his first unplanned emergency delivery.

Mark goes on his job interview and, later, he and Doug talk about it. Doug also tries to get Mark to admit that he's fooling around on his wife, which he most definitely is not. This exchange gives us some insight into Doug's Lothario personality and begins to explain why he drinks and why he has racked up so many failed relationships.

The patients continue to stream into the ER. The shift ends, and we see people leaving. We also see Carol Hathaway rummaging in the narcotics cabinet before she leaves for the day.

Susan and Mark have coffee together and discuss Mark's job offer. He expresses the feeling that the group practice is "not like real medicine." He gets beeped, and they both learn that Carol is being brought in for a drug overdose that is an undeniable suicide attempt.

It doesn't look good as they work on Carol and Mark demands the staff stop gawking and proceed with business as usual in their care of her. As other ER patients continue to arrive, Mark discusses Carol's case with Dr. Morgenstern. Doug looks on as they work on Carol, and it is clear he is devastated. She is not expected to survive.

The day winds down as patients come and go, and finally Mark has a chance to get some rest. Jerry asks Peter to look at his sore throat, but the surgical resident blows him off. Jerry also asks Dr. Greene to examine him, but to no avail.

Mark writes "Wake at 6:30" on a piece of tape and sticks it to an examination room door. It is five in the morning when he lies down and turns off the light. Immediately, Lydia opens the door and says, "6:30." Mark just says, "Wow."

PATIENT HISTORIES

● ●

1.1. Dr. Doug Ross

Dr. Ross came to the ER on his night off, exhibiting signs of intoxication, including slurred speech, excessive and inappropriate affectionate behavior, and the singing (badly) of "Oh Danny Boy" in the halls.

Dr. Greene was on duty and was awakened by ER nurse Lydia Woodward. Mark placed Doug in one of the ER's examination rooms and administered via IV a 2,000 cc drip of 5 percent dextrose in normal saline and 600 milligrams ASA (aspirin).

Dr. Ross was then left to sleep it off.

1.2. Mrs. Williston

Mrs. Williston was in the ER for an unknown but painful complaint. R.N. Lydia Woodward awakened Dr. Greene to ask if Mrs. Williston could have more Demerol since she was complaining of pain. Dr. Greene ordered 50 milligrams IM (intrasmuscular).

Later Dr. Greene canceled a CBC (complete blood count) he had ordered for Mrs. Williston after being told that the ER was about to receive multiple injured from a building collapse.

1.3. The man in 5

This unnamed patient was exhibiting myocardial infarction symptoms, and Dr. Greene ordered a cardiac enzyme test.

1.4. Mr. Wilson

Mr. Wilson presented at the ER with a partial amputation of his right hand after having been caught in the building collapse. Dr. Benton ordered his blood typed and crossmatched, a CBC, an EKG (electrocardiogram), X-rays of his chest and hand, and a hematocrit level (which came back at 32.5). He also ordered IV (intravenous) administration of 500 ccs of normal saline.

Mr. Wilson was then referred to an orthopedic surgeon for reattachment surgery.

1.5. Jeff Barr

Jeff Barr presented with facial bruising after he fell on his face during the building collapse. Dr. Lewis ordered X-rays of his facial bones and resisted his amorous advances.

1.6. The elderly female

This patient presented with abdominal pain and vomiting of blood. While being examined by Dr. Ross, she experienced a total loss of blood pressure and went into cardiac arrest.

Dr. Benton assisted Doug and ordered the patient's blood typed and cross-matched for 10 units and a hematocrit reading. (It was 23.0.) Peter also ordered two large bore IVs of saline wide open, 4 units of O-negative blood, an ampule of epinephrine, and the administration of 100 milligrams of lidocaine. An IV was started, an NG (nasogastric) tube was inserted, and the patient was defibrillated three times. External heart massage was also performed.

The patient was admitted to the hospital.

1.7. The male with the broken arm

This patient presented with an open fracture of the arm and knee trauma. Dr. Greene ordered a tetanus shot and 5 milligrams of morphine. The patient was later operated on to repair his broken arm.

1.8. Mr. Canelli

Mr. Canelli had a heart attack when he was caught in the building collapse in the Loop. He went into full cardiac arrest at the ER. Defibrillation was administered, but to no avail.

The patient died, and Dr. Greene got the job of informing his son, who broke down in tears in the waiting room.

1.9. The woman with a hand laceration

This middle-aged patient presented with a laceration of her right hand, sustained when she broke a breakfast dish. Dr. Benton began the suturing and then made Carter complete it. Lidocaine was used to anesthetize the laceration.

1.10. The woman who delivered in a cab

This woman arrived at the ER in a cab with her baby crowning. Carter and Dr. Greene wheeled her into the ER, where she delivered immediately. Doug Ross examined the baby, and Carter stood there in awe at witnessing (and assisting in) his first birth.

1.11. Jonathan Martin

This middle-aged cop shot himself in the right calf during an argument with his wife. Carter started an IV (after a couple of botched attempts), and the patient's leg was X-rayed. The radiologist's report was as follows:

> Anterior and lateral right lower extremity; femur articulating, patella, tibia, fibula all appear normal. There is a radioluscent density in the soft tissue superficial to the mid-shaft of the fibula. There is no apparent fragmentation of the foreign body; distal, tibia, and fibula all appear within normal limits. IMPRESSION: Foreign body in the right lower extremity consistent with possible bullet.

Officer Martin was operated on and the bullet was successfully removed.

1.12. Billy

Eight-year-old Billy was brought to the ER by his mother because he was vomiting blood. Tracy Young began the examination under the supervision of Dr. Ross. Tracy had a problem with Billy's mother when she tried to convince her to leave the examination room.

Dr. Ross stepped in and placated the mother, and Tracy learned a little something about bedside manner and the furious protectiveness of mothers. Dr. Ross diagnosed Billy as having an ulcer and noted that this was the first eight-year-old ulcer patient he had ever seen.

1.13. Mr. Ervin

Mr. Ervin presented with double vision (transient diplopia). He had no pain, weakness, or headache. Dr. Greene examined him and suggested that he go home and return if his symptoms reoccured.

Mr. Ervin became angry and suggested that Dr. Greene was dismissing him because he was black. Dr. Greene explained that he was aware that Mr. Ervin had no medical insurance and that a consultation with a neurologist would cost him an additional $200.

Mr. Ervin then asked Mark if he was Jewish.

Dr. Greene then ordered a neuro consult and told Lydia to bill Mr. Ervin.

1.14. The man with a fractured ankle

This patient presented with a fractured ankle and was mainly interested in whether or not he'd be able to collect worker's compensation.

He changed his tune when a sheet was pulled up over the head of an elderly patient in the bed next to him.

1.15. "Tiger"

This child was brought to the ER by his mother. The baby's ear was red, and he was crying. Dr. Ross diagnosed otitis media (a middle-ear infection) and ordered Haleh to administer 250 milligrams of oral Amoxicillin.

1.16. The GSW (gunshot wound)

This patient, a crack dealer, was brought to the ER with five gunshot wounds from an Uzi. Dr. Susan Lewis initially saw him, but quickly called in Malik, a male R.N., to restrain him, and then Dr. Benton for assistance.

1.17. Mr. Parker

Mr. Parker, age forty, presented at the ER with symptoms that included coughing blood and weight loss. He smoked two to three packs of cigarettes a day. Dr. Lewis ordered chest X-rays.

The X-rays showed a density in his right middle lobe. Susan told the patient that the density could be an infiltrate, a dense area of tissue from an old infection; an inhaled foreign body; or a granuloma of some sort. She recommended bronchoscopy and possibly exploratory surgery.

Mr. Parker suspected that he had lung cancer, and when he confronted Dr. Lewis and asked how long he had, she told him six months to a year, and that even the six months estimate was not certain. But Susan also attempted to reassure him by telling him, "If there's one thing you learn in my job, it's that nothing is certain—nothing that seems very bad and nothing that seems very good. Nothing is certain. Nothing." Mr. Parker was not comforted, however, and sardonically remarked that now he wouldn't have to quit smoking.

He then embraced Dr. Lewis, thanking her for being honest with him, and left the hospital.

1.18. Mrs. Raskin
Mrs. Raskin presented at the ER with a hangnail.

When informed by Dr. Greene that excising it would cost $180, she thanked him for being willing to take the time to help her. He escorted her into the lab, where he informed Malik that was he was about to excise her hangnail. Malik replied, "I'll stand back."

The fur-clad Mrs. Raskin was a regular visitor to the ER. [This patient was taken from Michael Crichton's book, *Five Patients*, which was originally published in 1970. Back then, the fee to excise a hangnail was $14.]

1.19. The lady in 3
This unseen patient was suffering from pulmonary edema and was being treated with Lasix and a nitro drip.

1.20. The guy in 5
This unseen patient was being seen for a questionable pulmonary embolism.

1.21. Suzanne
Teenager Suzanne presented at the ER with a lacerated foot. Her injuries were sustained in a motor vehicle accident during which she totaled her father's new Cadillac Seville (which had power steering and air conditioning, and which was the first new car her father had ever owned).

John Carter sutured her foot. Suzanne's father was somewhat upset upon learning what she had done to his new car.

1.22. Jimmy
Jimmy, who looked to be about six years old, was brought to the ER by his mother after he swallowed her one and only house key. Dr. Ross ordered a chest X-ray, on which the key could clearly be seen.

Doug told Jimmy's mother to watch Jimmy's stools for the key and assured her that the boy should have no trouble passing it. Jimmy's mother, however, was more concerned about how she was going to get into her house.

This is the admitting desk. If you need someone paged or a chart called up, you do it here. This is Timmy. Don't shake his hand, he's afraid of disease. This is the way to the lab. We do crits, counts, spindowns. Chemistries are marked with D slips and left at the front desk. Mark everything STAT whether you want it fast or not. The chem lab is 7022, the hem lab is 6944. Memorize them. Everybody gets an IV the minute they walk through the door. Use an angiocath with a 16 needle. You need a large bore in case they're bleeding and you need to transfuse them. Now the best way to do this is to pull the skin tight so the veins don't roll and go in low. Once you're in, pull the gizmo out and hook it up to here. Now what you wanna do is tape it, moderate flow, two or three drips per second. That's it. That's all there is to it, okay?

—Dr. Benton's speech to med student John Carter
on Carter's first day in the ER

A Description of the Compensation Package Offered to Dr. Mark Greene During His Interview With the Harris Medical Group

Because he would be a new partner, Mark would have to handle all calls and week-ends for one year. For this, he was offered the following:

●

1. $120,000 a year to start plus bonuses

●

2. A plush and luxurious office

●

3. Use of the group's condos in Aspen and Jamaica

●

4. Attendance at all the annual medical conferences (past conferences were in Maui, Paris, and Rome).

Jimmy and Doug had a good laugh over this.

1.23. Miss Murphy

Miss Murphy, age thirteen, presented at the ER with pain in her lower left quadrant. John Carter questioned her about the possibility that she might be pregnant, concerned that she could be suffering from an ectopic pregnancy. Miss Murphy repeatedly insisted that she was not pregnant. Carter then called in Dr. Benton to consult on the case.

Dr. Benton asked Miss Murphy when she had had her last menstrual period, and she replied it was sometime after Christmas. Since it was St. Patrick's Day, Benton got her to admit that it had been a few months since her last period. He then asked her point-blank if she had had sexual intercourse. She sheepishly admitted that she had, much to Carter's amazement.

Dr. Benton then made the diagnosis of an ectopic pregnancy and instructed Carter to order ultrasound and surgery.

Carter's lesson? Ask patients specific, to-the-point questions. (Miss Murphy kept insisting, "I'm not pregnant, I'm not pregnant," in complete denial of the truth. It was only when Dr. Benton asked her if she had had sex that she admitted that pregnancy was a possibility.)

1.24. Carol Hathaway, ER charge nurse

Head ER nurse Carol Hathaway was brought to the ER by ambulance after her room-mate found her unconscious. Carol had attempted suicide by taking a large quantity of short-acting barbiturates with alcohol.

Dr. Greene began treatment immediately. He ordered a drug screen and the administration of 2 milligrams of Narcan. He also ordered an amp of D50 and decided to pump her stomach. Additional tests included blood gases and electrolytes, and a main arterial line was inserted (Mark ordered an "arterial stick"). Carol's Babinski's reflex was positive, and they administered 15 liters of oxygen and kept it running. Her serum barbiturate level (repeated twice) was 45 micrograms per milliliter. Her pupils were midrange and sluggish. Her blood pressure was 90/70.

Dr. Morgenstern arrived and consulted with Dr. Greene. Morgenstern told Mark that Carol was decerebrating (losing cerebral function), and Mark agreed that it didn't look hopeful. Hemoperfusion (dialysis) was decided upon as the next course of treatment.

Mark was reminded by Morgenstern that he was the one who set the tone in the ER and that he should treat Carol as a friend to whom something terrible had happened.

Dialysis was ineffective after three hours of treatment.

[We know now that Carol survived and returned to the ER after a little over eight weeks of recuperation and extensive psychotherapy.

In the original version of this pilot episode, Carol died, but after screening the episode for a test audience, the ending was changed when the audience reacted very negatively to her death. (As Mark told Morgenstern, "She was . . . *is* very popular.").]

At the end of the show, Carol's fate is left up in the air, she is still undergoing dialysis, and still being monitored carefully.

1.25. The blonde in the waitress uniform

This young woman showed up at the ER with lacerations on her right arm. She was wearing an extremely short, black low-cut waitress's uniform, and Carter was the lucky one who got to treat her.

1.26. Mr. Larkowski

After having attended a party, Mr. Larkowski presented at the ER with abdominal symptoms, including pain and tenderness severe enough to make him believe he had stomach cancer.

Dr. Greene examined him and ordered lab tests, which showed that Mr. Larkowski had a duodenal ulcer with complicating pancreatitis (*mild* pancreatitis from the lab results, Mark assured him).

Mr. Larkowski broke down and sobbed that he *knew* he had cancer, even though Mark told him he did not have a malignancy.

Mark went on to explain that Mr. Larkowski's painful symptoms were from smoking and drinking at the party he had just attended and informed him that he would have to give them both up if he wanted to get well.

Upon hearing this, Mr. Larkowski went from fear to anger and asked Mark if he was crazy—asking him to give up drinking and smoking!

1.27. The abused baby boy

This baby was brought to the ER by his babysitter when he refused to stop crying.

The sitter told Dr. Ross that the baby's mother had said he had fallen out of his crib. Upon examination, Doug saw that the baby had multiple contusions at least twelve-hours old, a skull fracture, and several healed burns on his legs.

Doug confronted the baby's mother when she arrived at the ER and told her that her son had been beaten.

She denied it.

Doug told her she better get an attorney, and she shot back that she *was* an attorney. At this, Doug almost lost it and shouted at her, "He's a little kid!" and asked her how in the world she could do that to a baby.

Children and Family Services was called, and Doug was so upset by this incident that he shouted furiously at his medical student Tracy after he left the examining room.

1.28. Liz

This young woman (who would later also refer to herself as Persephone) appeared at the ER holding her skirt up to her waist and fanning her thighs as she walked down the hall.

A student at Sacred Heart College, she had burned herself as she was pouring hot water into the sink.

Dr. Greene diagnosed first-degree burns and applied a topical ointment and bandaged her thighs, as she expounded on how nice his hands felt on her thighs, and how she had thought about changing her panties because she knew that he'd be seeing them.

R.N. Lydia Woodward was in the examining room "observing" (much to Liz's dismay), and, after the patient was discharged, Mark thanked Lydia for her "help."

1.29. Mr. Harvey

Mr. Harvey, age fifty-seven, presented at the ER with severe pain in the mid-back, peritoneal irritation, and a reduced hematocrit count.

Mr. Harvey had been seen at the hospital eight weeks earlier, and a pulsatile (beating) abdominal mass with aortic calcification had been diagnosed. It was scheduled to be surgically corrected in a month.

Dr. Benton correctly diagnosed that Mr. Harvey now had a ruptured aortic abdominal aneurysm, and that he was bleeding into his abdomen. Peter realized that if Mr. Harvey was not operated on immediately, he'd die.

Unfortunately, as Dr. Susan Lewis put it, "there's no one to do him." Ashley and Jimmy were doing an appendectomy; Gil and Levine were handling the knife wound; Ed and his intern were doing the lady with the small bowel; the whole vascular team was in Minneapolis at a conference; and Baker was in the Bahamas with his family.

Peter decided to do a laparatomy (a surgical incision of the abdomen) and try to buy Mr. Harvey some time until Dr. Morgenstern arrived to repair the aneurysm. As Peter put it, "I'm his only chance."

He ordered the anesthesiologist to have 20 units of blood ready and began the operation at 2:13 A.M. Peter knew that a patient with a ruptured aortic abdominal aneurysm had a 50 percent mortality rate, even *with* the surgery to repair the hole.

Peter made the incision (Mr. Harvey's systolic was holding at 100) and rooted around in an attempt to find the aneurysm. He finally found it and simply plugged it with his finger while waiting for Dr. Morgenstern to arrive. Mr. Harvey's pressure started falling from 100/70, but Peter didn't sweat it.

Dr. Morgenstern finally showed up and took over.

Mr. Harvey's pressure went to 90/65 and he had already gotten 12 units of blood. Dr. Morgenstern ordered dopamine standing by, and the operation was ultimately a success.

At first, Morgenstern lambasted Peter about the ragged abdominal incision he had made, but as he was walking out of the operating room, Morgenstern told Peter that he was lucky as hell, but that he had made the right decision to open Mr. Harvey up, and that he had done good work.

As a now ecstatic Peter walked down the hall after hearing this, he did a lunging karate move [now seen in the opening credits of the series].

Later, Mrs. Harvey sang Morgenstern's praises to Peter, and Peter modestly took no credit for saving her husband's life. Only after he gave Morgenstern the credit did Peter notice the chief of surgery standing in the doorway of the hospital room.

1.30. The comatose diabetic

A uniformed police officer brought this elderly patient into the ER in a comatose state. After smelling his breath (it was fruity from the acetone in his blood), Dr. Greene immediately diagnosed diabetic ketoacidosis and ordered 10 units of regular insulin IV push and normal saline hydration, 10 units per hour. He also ordered a CBC, lytes, potassium, and blood gas tests. The patient was initially treated in the ER, but it is likely that he was later admitted into the hospital.

The police officer who found the man was beaming with pride after Dr. Greene told him that he had probably saved the guy's life. Jerry immediately deflated his joy, though, by sarcastically asking him if he wanted a medal for his actions.

1.31. Mr. Murphy

This intoxicated patient had a laceration on his head that Dr. Carter successfully sutured. (There was no apparent relation between this Mr. Murphy and patient 1.23, the pregnant thirteen-year-old identified as Miss Murphy.)

● ●

Original Broadcast Date:
Monday, September 19, 1994
Written by Michael Crichton;
Directed by Ron Holcomb

"DAY ONE"

"I don't want you to go!"

**—Mr. Franks, to his wife, upon hearing
that her condition was terminal**

In this episode (which takes place eight weeks after Carol Hathaway's suicide attempt), Susan Lewis and attending psychiatrist Dr. Div Cvetic clash over the treatment of a senile old black patient, and we learn that these two are romantically involved. We're also told that Doug has not been to see Carol since she went home from the hospital.

The episode begins with Susan extracting an earring from the throat of an unconscious baby while Haleh asks Connie to give *her* the patient who keeps sticking his hand up the fronts of the nurses' shirts.

John Carter continues his ER rotation, which today involves giving rectal exams to a bunch of sick German tourists and actually saving a cardiac patient's life with the defibrillator.

Mark Greene is thrilled to learn that his wife, Jenn, passed her bar exam (so thrilled that the two of them get caught having sex in an examining room), and Carter gets caught sleeping while sitting on a toilet bowl. Later, Mark and Jenn discuss Mark's commitment to the hospital, and it is clear that their marital problems were not solved by their quickie in the ER.

Mark has to help an elderly man accept his wife's inevitable death, and Peter correctly diagnoses a dangerous blood clot, only to have the patient's private doctor overrule him.

Liz, the doctor groupie, returns and this time sets her sights on Carter; while Mark and Doug discuss Doug's blaming himself for Carol's attempted suicide.

Doug finally visits Carol and brings her flowers, and the episode concludes with Dr. Benton being proved correct about his blood clot patient (see Patient 2.41).

PATIENT HISTORIES

● ●

2.32. The Downey infant

This one-year-old girl was brought to the ER by her parents, Kevin and Sharon Downey, after they found her unresponsive in her crib. She had no spontaneous respiration, was cyanotic, and was in sinus tachycardia with a heart rate of 180.

Dr. Lewis used a laryngoscope to examine the child's throat, and she was intubated and bagged. Then Dr. Lewis removed an earring from the baby's esophagus and thus established a clear airway. After that Dr. Lewis ordered the baby hyperventilated. The baby's blood sugar was 20 (normal is between 80 and 120), so Susan ordered an IV of dextrose and a lumbar puncture using an 18-gauge spinal needle. She also ordered a blood gas, a chest film, a CBC, and a Chem 7.

The child recovered.

2.33. The German tourists

This large group of rather ample German tourists all got food poisoning from something they ate at the buffet at Gerber's Haufbrau House. Carter was assigned to supply emesis basins as needed, as well as Compazine and 5 percent dextrose IVs in normal saline if anyone looked like it was needed.

Carter also got the unpleasant task of doing rectal exams on all the food-poisoning victims in order to get stool samples and rule out something other than food poisoning (also see Patient 2.45).

2.34. Mr. Zambano

Mr. Zambano presented at the ER with chest pain. Since he had previously been diagnosed with angina pectoris, cardiac enzyme tests were ordered. His EKG was normal.

John Carter examined him under the supervision of Dr. Lewis, and Zambano was left to rest while awaiting his test results. (Carter used the PQRST mnemonic device to evaluate the patient's chest pain. See the Glossary.) Carter went in to check on Mr. Zambano a short time later, and, while they were chatting, Mr. Zambano went into full cardiac arrest.

Carter attempted to find help, but everyone else was occupied.

He ran into the hall, located a defibrillator, turned it on, and dragged the entire cart into Mr. Zambano's room, pulling it by the paddles.

Carter shocked Mr. Zambano once (the joules were not mentioned), which immediately restored a normal cardiac rhythm. Help arrived, but by this time Mr. Zambano's vital signs were normal.

This was John Carter's first life-saving act in the ER.

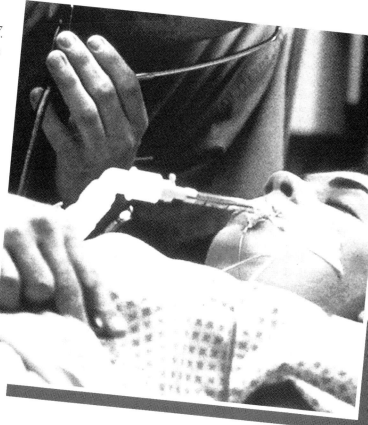

2.35. Mrs. Ring

Mrs. Ring was riding with her husband and daughter when their car was struck by a drunk driver.

She was brought to the ER with head, neck, chest, and hip injuries. Her pressure was 50/30 and her pulse was 120. Mark ordered her blood typed and crossmatched for 6 units of packed cells, a CBC, a Chem 7, and a chest tube tray. X-rays showed that Mrs. Ring had a spinal fracture, massive internal bleeding, and DIC-disseminated intravascular coagulation (her blood wasn't clotting).

She ultimately died, and Dr. Benton got the task of asking her husband about organ donation.

2.36. Miss Ring

Miss Ring was also in the car with her parents when it was hit by a drunk driver. She was brought to the ER with head, chest, and abdominal pain.

Her pressure was 60 palp (see the Glossary), her pulse was 150 and thready, and her GCS (Glasgow coma scale) was 4–5–6. She also had a scalp laceration and a forward right humerus retraction.

Mark ordered her blood typed and crossmatched for 4 units. Her pulse went to 180, her pressure went to 80/50, and she was diagnosed with a ruptured spleen. She was then sent to surgery for an emergency splenectomy and survived the operation.

2.37. Wayne

Wayne was the drunk driver who hit the Ring family, killing the mother, and causing massive injury to the daughter and a leg injury to the father. He was unconscious when he was brought to the ER and handcuffed to his bed.

Doug ordered a tox screen and a CT (computerized axial tomography scan, see the Glossary) of his head. Wayne's blood alcohol came back at 435. When he finally awakened he was informed of what he had done.

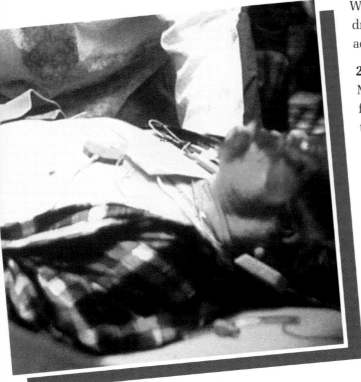

This was the sixth time Wayne had been involved in a drunk-driving motor vehicle accident.

2.38. Mr. Ring

Mr. Ring was the father of the family that was hit by Wayne the drunk driver. Mr. Ring suffered a leg injury.

2.39. Ivan Gregor

Ivan was a liquor store owner, in business for fifteen years, who was shot in the arm by a robber. He had previously been robbed seven times.

Peter ordered a gram of Ancef by IV, a CBC, and chest and shoulder films. He then sent him to surgery to have his arm repaired.

Ivan was so pleased with Dr. Benton's prompt treatment that he offered him cognac and cigars, which Peter respectfully declined.

[Ivan reappeared at the ER later as Patients 3.59, 5.89, and 6.103.]

2.40. Victor

Victor, a senile (and possibly homeless) old man, showed up at the ER with a low-grade fever, a slightly productive cough, postural hypotension, and dehydration. Susan ordered a GGF1, which is shorthand for Grandpa's Got a Fever and consists of a battery of tests, including a CBC, Chem 7, chest X-ray, U/A (urinalysis), and blood cultures times two.

Victor was agitated, and Susan ordered 300 ccs of 5 percent dextrose in normal saline IV and a noncontrast head CAT scan. The CAT (computerized axial tomography) scan showed diffuse atrophy, and Susan wanted Victor admitted to the psych ward. Div Cvetic, the attending psychiatrist, refused to accept Victor into his service and told Susan that Victor had an upper respiratory infection, and to give him 2.5 Haldol (a psychotropic drug used to treat schizophrenia and other mental disorders) and release him.

Susan went over Div's head and tried to convince Dr. Wurtz to sign Victor in, but to no avail. Victor (who was quite upset about his two dogs) was released but was soon found walking naked down Halstead, and was returned to the ER. Susan ended up signing Victor in to Div's service herself, an act for which she was lambasted by Div later that night when the two of them were in bed. (Susan tried to defend herself by asking Div why they were there if not to help people like Victor, but it didn't do any good.)

2.41. Mr. Thunhurst

Mr. Thunhurst, sixty-five, presented at the ER with abdominal pain, and Dr. Benton gave Carter the job of doing the workup and coming up with a prognosis. Benton ordered Carter to do a focused H and P (history and physical exam, see the Glossary), and Carter reported the following:

> Sixty-five-year-old male with severe peripheral vascular disease manifested by claudication of the left calf. He's ten days post-op from Mercy General after having an aorta bifemoral bypass. Normal postoperative course until about six hours ago when he began to experience the gradual onset of lower left quadrant pain with no palliative or provoking factor . . . other than a large Mexican dinner.

Benton asked Carter what meds Mr. Thunhurst was on, and Carter replied, "300 cc milk of magnesia, constipation." (Benton also asked Carter what Thunhurst's mother's maiden name was, and, as Carter furiously searched his notes, Haleh told him Benton was only kidding.)

Dr. Benton proceeded with the examination of Mr. Thunhurst and noted that his leg was warm, his capillary refill was normal, there was no rebound or guarding present, and his CAT scan was normal. He then asked Carter what he would do, and Carter told him he'd order a CBC, Chem 7, U/A amylase, and K.U.B. (kidney, ureter, and bladder) tests and, if all were normal, he'd discharge the patient and advise him to follow up with his regular physician. Peter then calmly told Carter that he would have just cost the hospital a $2 million malpractice settlement.

Benton diagnosed a thrombosis (blood clot) at the graft site with potential extension into the renal or mesenteric arteries and ordered an arteriogram.

Later, Mr. Thunhurst's cardiologist, Dr. Joe Arnott, arrived and completely overruled Peter's diagnosis and recommendations. Arnott said that Thunhurst had a urinary infection from a Foley catheter that was inserted during his surgery and that he could go home. He accused Benton of showing off in front of his medical student by ordering unnecessary and expensive tests.

Carter privately told Benton that he believed his order for an arteriogram was correct, and Peter sarcastically replied that he would notify the *New England Journal of Medicine* that Carter concurred.

And that seemed to be the end of that.

A few hours later, however, Dr. Benton's judgment was validated when the EMTs brought in Mr. Thunhurst with a suspected ruptured bowel. His pulse was 140 and his blood pressure was 60/40. The EMTs had given him 1500 ccs of fluid, and his abdomen was rigid and extremely tender.

Benton ordered Thunhurst's blood typed and crossmatched for 6 units, a CBC, and an NG tube. He also ordered chest and abdominal X-rays (with the portable X-ray machine) and instructed that Thunhurst be prepped for exploratory surgery.

It would be nice if we could assume that the patient survived and that Dr. Arnott apologized to Peter, but we don't know the outcome of this patient's case.

2.42. The Lobster Man

This gentleman fell asleep in the sun and showed up at the ER with the front of his body completely sunburned.

The poor soul happened to arrive, however, at the same time as Dr. Greene's wife, Jenn. She had wonderful news for Mark: She had passed her bar exam! Mark was ecstatic. So ecstatic, in fact, that he ordered Malik to take some vitals on Lobster Man, and he and Jenn retired to an empty examination room where they proceeded to make love.

During their passion, Mark hit the emergency call button and most of the ER staff burst in on them as they were in the throes of what looked like oral sex. (Jenn was on her knees in front of Mark, who was standing naked before her, so oral sex is a likely guess.)

The laughter could be heard throughout the ER, and Mark never lived it down.

Later Susan Lewis remarked that, by what she could see, she could tell that Mark was "excited" by Jenn's passing the bar, so it is assumed that Susan, at least, was one of those who saw Mark in flagrante delicto.

Lobster Man probably received some topical ointment and some Benadryl for the burning (and possibly a narcotic analgesic for pain) and was sent home.

2.43. Liz

This is the same Liz who previously visited the ER as Patient 1.28 (and who would return again as Patients 3.58, and 5.94). This time Liz presented with a rash on her buttocks and asked to see Dr. Carter. Carter began to examine her without a woman present (which was against hospital policy), and when Dr. Lewis heard that Liz was back, she went in to "observe."

Susan found Liz bent over an examining table with her skirt up and her panties off and Carter seated behind her, innocently examining the poison ivy on her butt. (He had no clue that Liz had already come on to Dr. Greene.) Susan stayed with Carter until he completed his examination and treatment of Liz.

Carter "ran into" Liz again when she broke into his 4-wheel drive and invited him back to her place. Carter went, a decision that eventually resulted in his becoming ER Patient 5.86.

2.44. Mrs. Franks

Eighty-six-year-old Mrs. Franks (who had thirteen grandchildren) was brought to the ER by her husband in a comatose state and in severe respiratory distress. Her blood pressure was 70/50, her pulse was 120, her respirations were 32, her temperature was 102.5°, and her arterial oxygen tension (oxygenation level) was only 85 percent.

Her husband brought with him a bag containing her current medications. Mrs. Franks was taking the following: Lasix, a diuretic; digitalis, for congestive heart failure; Kay Ciel, a potassium supplement; Isordil, an antianginal; nitroglycerine, another antianginal; Captotril, an antihypertensive and ACE (angiotensin converting enzyme) inhibitor; Antivert, for nausea and dizziness; Darvocet, a painkiller; and Timoptic (for high blood pressure and to reduce the possibility of another heart attack).

Mark ordered a chest film, EKG, CBC, Chem 7, digitalis level, U/A, blood cultures times 2, and blood gases. He also ordered that Mrs. Franks be hydrated with a 300 cc bolus of normal saline. Mark was convinced, however, that Mrs. Franks was on the verge of impending complete respiratory failure.

Her blood gases came back bad, and Mark informed her husband that she was terminal. He told Mr. Franks they could put her on a respirator that would maintain her in a vegetative state, or they could let nature run its course. The husband furiously demanded that they put her on the machine and not let her die. Mark ordered nebulizer treatments and decided to postpone any big decisions for a while.

Mrs. Franks eventually woke up thanks to the hydration treatments, and Mark asked her directly if she wanted to be put on a respirator. She said no. Her husband began weeping and telling her that he didn't want her to go.

Shortly thereafter, Mrs. Franks died. Mr. Franks sang "That Old Black Magic" to her, kissed her, and left the hospital.

2.45. The vomiting bride

This newlywed's wedding reception was at Gerber's Haufbrau House, and she unwisely ate the potato salad.

She arrived at the ER puking her brains out, and Susan ordered 10 milligrams of Compazine IM, a CBC, and a Chem 7. Sixty more wedding guests (all of whom must have liked potato salad) were also on their way to the ER.

It is assumed they all survived.

● ●

Original Broadcast Date:
Thursday, September 22, 1994
Written by John Wells;
Directed by Mimi Leder

"GOING HOME"

ER 3

"I'm here to unload that new shipment of barbiturates."

—Carol Hathaway, to Susan and Jerry, upon arriving at work the first day back after her overdose suicide attempt

This episode takes place on Carol Hathaway's first day back at the ER after her suicide attempt more than eight weeks earlier. It opens with her laying out her uniform, stethoscope, and name badge on the bed and looking at them thoughtfully (and with perhaps a little bit of fear?).

Carol marshals her strength, and shows up at the hospital. She is funny and charming to all her friends and coworkers, but periodically she is haunted by visions of herself being brought in on a gurney.

Carol tells Mark that her shrink wanted her to consider working in a doctor's office instead of the ER, but she decided to come back to the ER.

In the meantime, Susan treats a heart attack patient with drugs instead of angioplasty and, because of her decision, has to defend herself before a review board.

An Alzheimer's patient known as Madame X sings her way around the ER;

while Mark makes a point of assuring Carol that none of them have any doubts about her being back. Mark also tries to deal with an obviously abused wife who is reluctant to defy her violent husband.

Susan and Div Cvetic talk baseball, Susan tries to decide on a new 4-wheel-drive vehicle, and Carter tries to comfort Madame X.

Doug asks Carol to lunch, but she refuses and tells him that she's dating John Taglieri. He was there for her before the suicide attempt, she explains, and he's been there for her through her recovery, and for that she's grateful. Doug doesn't get the message.

We learn that Mark's wife, Jenn, went on an important job interview with a prestigious law firm; and that Carter is unwisely pursuing a lusty relationship with Liz.

Even though she has already turned him down, Doug once again confronts Carol about rekindling their relationship. She sees right through him, though, and tells him that he just feels guilty because he blames himself for her suicide attempt. She explains that there were far more depressing events in her life than her relationship with him and refuses his plea for a second chance.

Back in the ER, Susan summons Carol with an urgent "Mark's hurt!" They rush to the locker room, where the entire ER staff has put together a surprise party welcoming Carol back. Mark gives Carol an orthopedic brace with "Welcome Home" written on it, and the emotional Carol makes a heartfelt speech telling them all that she feels lucky.

PATIENT HISTORIES
● ●

3.46. Mr. Resnick
We don't know precisely what brought Mr. Resnick to the ER, but it was probably some kind of fecal impaction or constipation problem because when Mark looked in on him, Mr. Resnik was having an enema. (Mr. Resnick was less than thrilled with this development, by the way.)

3.47. Grace Yakamoto
This four-year-old girl, was brought to the ER by her mother with a lingering cough and a runny nose. Dr. Doug Ross's diagnosis was that Grace had a cold.

3.48. Huey
Infant Huey was brought to the ER by his extremely nervous father because the little boy was lethargic and had a persistent fever. Dr. Ross ordered a CBC, blood culture, chest X-ray, urine sample, and blood swab.

Huey's tests came back normal, so Doug decided that he needed to do a lumbar puncture (a spinal tap) to rule out meningitis. Upon hearing this news, Huey's father became a "crasher" and fainted.

The lumbar puncture (which was performed by Doug) was negative, and there were no other signs of infection, so Doug sent Huey home with his now-conscious father.

3.49. Arthur Smith

We don't know what brought Arthur to the ER except that Mark did refer to him as "a patient" for Carol. (It was her first patient on her first day back after her suicide attempt.)

Carol, who was obviously familiar with the homeless, alcoholic Arthur, found him sleeping on a chair in the ER waiting room. She woke him by whacking him on the arm and yelling at him. (Arthur reappeared as Patient 6.101, when we learned his last name was Smith from his blood/alcohol toxicology report.)

3.50. Mary Cavanaugh (a.k.a. Madame X)

The first time we met Madame X was when she opened the door to the room where Dr. Peter Benton was sleeping and sang "Nice and Easy" to him.

After no one on the ER staff claimed Mary (played by legendary singer, and George Clooney's aunt, Rosemary Clooney) as their patient, Carter examined her and Dr. Div Cvetic was called in for a psychiatric consult. He asked her a series of questions designed to gauge her mental state and determined that she was suffering from Alzheimer's disease. Carter had suggested hypothyroidism, Cushing's disease, hepato-lenticular degeneration, and Scholz's disease, but Div told him, "When you hear hooves, think horses, not zebras."

Mary's moods swung from exhilaration to tearful depression, and Carter tried to

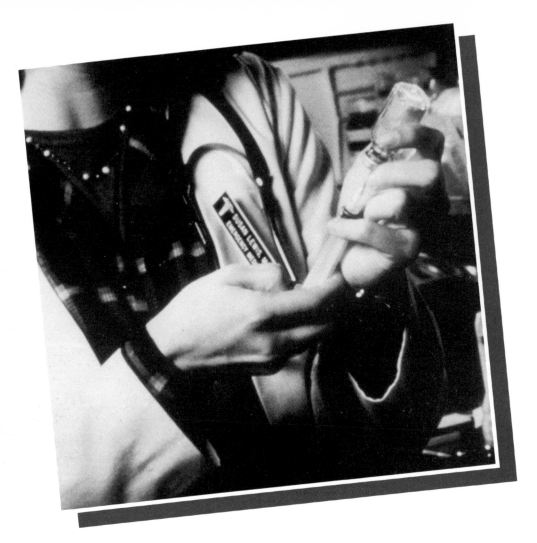

comfort her and spend time with her, talking about music whenever he could.

Mary's real identity was revealed when Mrs. Packer, a leukemia patient in the ER for a hand laceration and a transfusion, told Susan and Carol that she recognized Madame X as the great singer Mary Cavanaugh. Mr. and Mrs. Packer had seen Cavanaugh when they were on their honeymoon in San Francisco in 1948.

Once they knew who she was, it was a simple matter to find her family and ask her granddaughter to come and get her. (Her granddaughter Ellen apologized to Carter, telling him that Mary usually didn't wander so far.) As she was leaving, Mary hugged Carter and told him she loved him, and he returned the sentiment. Mary and Ellen sang "Nice and Easy" as the elevator door closed.

3.51. The GSW (gunshot wound) to the chest

This young man was brought to the ER with a gunshot wound in his chest. He was in shock, and Dr. Mark Greene ordered his blood typed and crossmatched for 6 units and a CBC. He ordered the boy intubated and told his staff to keep his IVs wide open.

The boy had no breath sounds and was hyporesonant on the left side. Mark ordered a 7 1/2 chest tube and an X-ray. The boy's pressure was 50/30, his respirations were 36, and his pulse was 140. He went into cardiac fibrillation and Mark shocked him twice with the defibrillator.

The boy did not survive.

3.52. Mr. Flannigan

Mr. Flannigan had experienced the sudden onset of crushing substernal chest pains radiating down this left arm with accompanying diuresis (increased production of urine), and an ambulance was called. On the way to the hospital he was given nitro spray times 2 and 5 milligrams of morphine, but with no relief.

When Flannigan arrived at the ER his blood pressure was 90/50, his respirations were 24, and he was in normal sinus rhythm. He began to exhibit more severe symptoms as the ambulance pulled up to the ER door.

Dr. Susan Lewis ordered an EKG, chest X-ray, CBC, Chem 7, and an enzyme and coag panel. Flannigan's pulse was now racing at 180.

Susan decided not to shock him with the defibrillator and instead ordered a 6 milligrams adenosine IV push. His blood pressure had dropped to 50 palp, and Susan ordered the external pacemaker. She also ordered an initial dose of atropine.

Flannigan's blood gases were bad, so Susan ordered another 1 milligram of atropine as well as doses of Pavulon and Versed. She now had to decide between referring him for angioplasty or trying a dose of tPA to break up any clots in his arteries.

Flannigan was confirmed as having had an acute inferior wall myocardial infarction, and Susan ordered 5,000 units of heparin and another EKG. She also ordered 10 milligrams of tPA per 60 milligrams over one hour. His blood pressure went to 90/60.

Shortly thereafter, Mr. Flannigan's cardiologist, Dr. Kayson, arrived. Kayson was livid that Susan had started tPA therapy. He preferred angioplasty. Flannigan's pressure was now 110/70, his pulse was 90, and the external pacemaker had captured. Another 1 milligram of atropine was ordered, and the nurses were told to keep bagging him.

Later, Susan had to present her case for review. Present were Dr. Kayson, Dr. Morgenstern, Dr. Benton, Dr. Langworthy, and later, Dr. Greene. Kayson complained that because of Susan's decision to start tPA, his angioplasty was a mess. When the doctors were surveyed, Benton, Langworthy, and Greene all said they would have done angioplasty instead of trying tPA therapy, even though, in the end, Susan's treatment worked.

Susan was very upset with Mark for not backing her up regarding her decision.

Mr. Flannigan recovered.

3.53. Mrs. Cheung

Mrs. Cheung came to the ER with her son Frank, a teenager who acted as her interpreter. Her eye and cheek were badly swollen, she had facial lacerations, and she had bruised ribs.

When Mark questioned her (through Frank), she told him that she had fallen down the stairs and injured herself. Mark pursued this line of questioning by quizzing them about their address, which was 311 West McArthur, Apartment A.

Apartment A was on the fourth floor, right? Mark asked Frank, who sheepishly admitted that, no, their apartment was on the *first* floor.

Mark told Malik to take Frank and show him how to get free stuff out of the candy machine. He then ordered left orbit, chest, and rib X-rays for Mrs. Cheung, giving instructions to look for healed fractures.

Mark left Mrs. Cheung and went out to talk to Frank, who was using the new skill Malik had taught him to steal candy from the machine. Mark asked Frank if his parents ever argued, and, after some initial reluctance to admit the truth, Frank told Mark that his father often hit his mother. Mark then instructed Haleh to find a shelter for Mrs. Cheung and Frank.

While they were trying to persuade Mrs. Cheung to go to the shelter, Mr. Cheung arrived, determined to take his wife and son home. At this point, Mrs. Cheung denied that her husband hit her, and when Frank was asked about the abuse in front of his father, he, too, was so frightened of his father that he said that nothing had happened.

Since Mrs. Cheung and Frank had to *want* to go to the shelter in order for the hospital to help them, Mr. Cheung ended up leaving the hospital with his wife and son, thanking Dr. Greene for his concern before he left.

3.54. Mr. Cornell

Mr. Cornell was in the ER for unknown reasons. The only time he appeared was when Dr. Benton opened the door to his room and scolded Carter for spending time talking to Cornell instead of seeing other patients. (When Dr. Benton left, Mr. Cornell asked Carter, "Who was that asshole?")

3.55. The teenager in a boating accident

This young lady, age sixteen was in a serious boating accident and was brought to the ER by helicopter.

She had been under the water for three minutes and had multiple trauma, hypotension, tachycardia, scalp lacerations, and head trauma. Upon arrival at the ER, her GCS was 3–4–3, and she had multiple extremity fractures, but her neurological and vascular systems were intact. Her pressure was 60/40, and her pulse was 140 and thready. CPR (Cardiopulmonary resuscitation) had been performed on her in the helicopter.

Dr. Benton ordered a cross-table cervical spine X-ray, Chem 7, and CBC; and ordered her blood typed and crossmatched for 8 units of packed cells.

This teenager's ultimate fate was not revealed.

3.56. Huey's father

This patient was the father of Patient 3.48. He fainted when he was told that his infant son, Huey, had to undergo a spinal tap so as to definitively rule out meningitis.

Huey's father eventually woke up and recovered fully with no apparent permanent ill effects.

3.57. Mrs. Packer

The elderly Mrs. Packer came to the ER because she fainted in her kitchen and cut her hand. Through blood tests, Dr. Susan Lewis discovered that Mrs. Packer had aplastic leukemia and that her white cells and platelet count were very low. Susan told Mrs. Packer that her low blood counts were the real reason she fainted and that she desperately needed a blood transfusion, which Mrs. Packer refused. She only wanted her hand stitched.

Susan reluctantly agreed and had Carter stitch Mrs. Packer's hand laceration.

As Mrs. Packer was leaving the ER, she collapsed, and this convinced her to let Susan give her the blood transfusion. But she couldn't stay long: Her granddaughter was being christened that evening at eight o'clock, and she planned on attending.

Susan ended up giving Mrs. Packer part of the transfusion and allowing her to leave, with the promise that she'd return the next day for the remainder of her transfusion.

3.58. Liz

Liz [This is the Liz who was also Patients 1.28 and 2.43.] showed up at the ER complaining that her breasts hurt the day after her rendezvous with Carter (they did it in the car, in the kitchen, and on the stairs).

She asked for Dr. Carter, and the two of them stole away to the radiology lab where they were caught in the act by Dr. Steve Flint, the radiologist.

Carol Hathaway and Steve later teased Carter about his dalliance with Liz, and Steve told him he once knew a girl like Liz when he was in his freshman year at college. Her middle name was "Penicillin."

3.59. Ivan Gregor

Ivan (also Patient 2.39, as well as 5.89 and 6.103) was back at the ER because he had once again been shot during a holdup.

Dr. Benton ordered an X-ray of Ivan's left fibula.

● ●

Original Broadcast Date:
Thursday, September 29, 1994
Written by Lydia Woodward;
Directed by Mark Tinker

"HIT AND RUN"

"Anything more than three hours and

I'm sluggish all day."

—Peter Benton, responding to Carter when
Carter asked him if he ever got used to
just three hours of sleep a night

"We lose them all the time, Carter."

—R.N. Haleh, after Carter witnessed a
seventeen-year-old accident victim's death

This episode opens with Benton angrily waking up Carter, who had unwisely fallen asleep without putting his beeper on his pillow and, thus, slept through Benton's page.

Mark and Doug talk about Mark's wife, Jenn, leaving town for a job interview, and it's obvious that the Greene situation is deteriorating.

Doug lies to a little boy about being able to stay with his mentally ill mother, and Carol holds him accountable for it, telling him it's typical cowardly behavior for him.

We learn that both Peter and Sarah Langworthy have put in for next year's Starzl

Fellowship, even though Peter is only second year and Sarah is third.

Carter gets the horrible task of putting a name on a dead teenager using a high school yearbook and begins to identify with the boy and get involved emotionally. And *then* Carter calls the wrong parents.

Mark treats a Spanish woman who stinks up the ER, and Susan tries to find the patience to deal with a "type A" salesman who can't seem to be bothered listening to Susan's diagnosis.

Peter's brother-in-law Walt delivers Peter's car, which needed a new transmission. Walt confirms that Peter will sit with his mother that evening. Walt and Peter's sister Jackie are celebrating their tenth wedding anniversary by going out to dinner at Oprah Winfrey's Chicago restaurant and can't leave Mrs. Benton alone. Peter agrees to be home by eight-thirty.

Carol takes care of the little boy Doug lied to, and again rips Doug for lying to him. Doug finally finds the strength to tell Ozzie the truth, and Carol watches thoughtfully as he embraces the sobbing child.

Carter eventually correctly identifies the dead teenager and decides to take the responsibility of informing the parents of their son's death.

Peter is given the opportunity to assist on a Whipple procedure and grabs it—completely forgetting that he promised to be home to watch his mother. Hours later Walt confronts him in the waiting room and accuses him of putting everything before his family.

Carter confides in Jerry that he's not sure he's cut out for the ER and then has an amazing life-affirming experience. Doug makes a huge error in judgment and shows up drunk at Carol's door at midnight. Tag answers the door, Doug makes some kind of lame excuse for being there, and Carol chases him to the train station where she screams at him, "What were you thinking? I will not let you do this to me again!"

The episode ends with Doug kicking a trash can and walking home alone.

PATIENT HISTORIES

4.60. Scruffy

Scruffy was described by Dr. Benton as an "unwashed and undomiciled male with laceration to forehead." Scruffy was in room 2, and Benton ordered Carter to clean and stitch the wound and under no circumstances to remove Scruffy's shoes and socks: "God knows what you'll find there."

4.61. Ozzie Sheff

Little Ozzie was brought to the ER by his mother, Mrs. Sheff, who was concerned that Ozzie couldn't hear right. Dr. Ross determined that Ozzie didn't have an ear infection, and when he tested the boy's hearing by whispering, Ozzie heard him fine.

Doug then questioned Mrs. Sheff about what specifically Ozzie couldn't hear.

She told him Ozzie couldn't hear her mother's voice, her ex-husband, the ice-cream man, and Princess Diana.

When Doug learned that Mrs. Sheff's mother was dead, he ordered Carol to call Psych Services for a consult and get Social Services in there for Ozzie, who, of course, had nothing wrong with him.

4.62. Mrs. Sheff

Mrs. Sheff came to the ER because she claimed her son Ozzie couldn't hear. The truth was that it was *Mrs. Sheff* who was sick, not Ozzie.

After Mrs. Sheff complained that Ozzie couldn't hear his dead grandmother's or Princess Diana's voice (both of which *she* could hear), Doug Ross called in Div Cvetic for a psych consult. Div learned that Mrs. Sheff had been on Prolixin and Ativan but had stopped taking them, and that she was now "floridly" schizophrenic. He diagnosed her as delusional and determined that she needed to be admitted to the hospital.

As she was being escorted to the fifth floor (the Psych Ward) she became violent and needed restraining by Malik. During Div's struggles with her, she bit him on the hand. He shouted an order for 5 milligrams Haldol IM, and she was taken away. Her son Ozzie was unfortunately a witness to this dramatic scene and ran away as his mother was being carried out.

4.63. The little old lady with leg pain

This elderly woman presented at the ER with leg pain. Her left calf was 4 centimeters larger than her right and she also had colon cancer. Carter noted two elements of varicose triad: trauma, and hypercoagubility; and after his initial examination, his differential diagnosis was cellulitis, an injury, a Baker's cyst, or deep vein thrombosis.

Carter suggested a CBC, Chem 7, coag study, and duplex scan of the leg, which Dr. Benton approved. Carter also suggested a renogram because of the varicose triad symptoms, and Dr. Benton also okayed that test.

4.64. Mr. Mattson

This unseen patient was being treated by Dr. Greene for an unspecified gastrointestinal ailment. Mark ordered a GI cocktail (see the Glossary) for Mr. Mattson, and that was the last we ever heard of him.

4.65. Velma Zevallo

Elderly Mrs. Zevallo was brought to the ER by her husband. Mrs. Zevallo had had two previous heart attacks and had an internal cardiac defibrillator. She was complaining of severe chest pains and breathing difficulty.

Mark ordered a 12 lead EKG, a CBC, a Chem 7, cardiac enzymes, and a coag profile. Velma's blood pressure was 150/105, her respirations were 28, and her pulse was 120. Mark ordered .4 nitro sublingual, and her respirations went to 32. Mark then ordered morphine, because she was beginning to panic from the pain, but as they were preparing the injection Mrs. Zevallo sat up and let out a belch that was loud, long, and smelly.

She belched several more times, which created quite a stink (the belches were so bad that R.N. Lydia Wright put on a surgical mask), and immediately relaxed, obviously feeling much better.

Shortly thereafter, Velma's lab results came back. They were fine, and her heart rhythm had returned to normal. Mark gave her a prescription for some antigas medicine and told her to lay off the kielbasa for breakfast. It was at this point that Velma's defibrillator went off, shocking Mark, and causing her arm to fly up.

Mark was fairly sure that her defibrillator was malfunctioning and decided to take her to Cardiology and have it looked at. As Mark was waiting for her chart at the front desk, Harry Stopeck's (Patient 4.67) cellular phone rang, and Velma's arm started flying around, and an electric wheelchair started spinning around on its own. Mark deduced that Velma's electrical problems were being caused by Stopeck's phone, and when Harry turned the phone off everything stopped.

Stopeck left the ER and Mark discharged Mrs. Zevallo.

4.66. David Fisher

This seventeen-year-old, was brought to the ER in full cardiac arrest, his pupils blown, and with negative vital signs.

Dr. Sarah Langworthy ordered 5 units of O-negative blood and a cross-lateral cervical spine X-ray. She also ordered IV administration of epinephrine, an endotracheal tube, and then began external heart massage.

Fisher's left side was full of blood, however, and he had no heart sounds. His X-rays showed a skull fracture, a C5 (fifth cervical vertebrae) neck fracture, a ruptured diaphragm, and a hemopneumothorax (a massive sucking chest wound). Dr. Benton knew the situation was hopeless, and after thirty-one minutes of external massage, Langworthy finally concurred and declared the time of death at 10:06.

Carter was given the task of identifying Fisher (which he did with a copy of Fisher's high school yearbook) and notifying the boy's family. Carter erred in his identification, however, and called the family of Steven Tierny. Carter was present when Dr. Benton told the Tierny's their son had died. He was also present when Mr. and Mrs. Tierny viewed the body and told them that the boy was not their son.

Carter redeemed himself by finding the dead boy's correct name and informing his parents without having anyone else present to back him up.

4.67. Harry Stopeck

Harry Stopeck, an office equipment salesman, came to the ER complaining of stomach pain and constipation. He also told Dr. Lewis that occasionally there was blood in the toilet bowl after a bowel movement.

After walking out of his room once because he took a sales call when she wanted to speak to him, Susan determined that Mr. Stopeck needed to see a specialist to rule out ulcerative colitis, although she felt that he actually just had irritable bowel syndrome. Mr. Stopeck said he'd be happy to see a specialist, if any of them had hours evenings or Sundays.

Susan told him then to at least increase his bran intake and reduce the stress in his life. Mr. Stopeck told Susan that each year, as a bonus, his company sent the salesmen who sold more than $10 million worth of equipment to Palm Springs. Harry said he had *never* missed the trip to Palm Springs.

Dr. Lewis resigned herself to the fact that Mr. Stopeck was not going to change and discharged him. As he was leaving the hospital, Harry's cell phone triggered Mrs. Zevallo's defibrillator and an electric wheelchair.

4.68. Dr. Div Cvetic

Div became an ER patient when Mrs. Sheff bit him on the hand during a violent schizophrenic outburst. Dr. Susan Lewis cleaned, sutured, and bandaged his hand. While bring treated, Div angrily told Susan that all potentially violent patients should be in four-point restraints and a muzzle.

4.69. Blair

This teenager came to the ER with a hand injury, which Dr. Ross treated. Doug ordered an X-ray and pain medication, but Blair said she didn't need anything for pain.

4.70. Steven Tierny

For a very brief time, teenager Steven Tierny was logged as a dead patient in the ER. Tierny was the boy Carter mistakenly confused with the real deceased boy, David Fisher. Carter even went so far as to have Dr. Benton tell Tierny's mother and father that their son had died.

4.71. Neal Shearer

Mr. Shearer, age sixty-five, was brought to the ER with substernal chest pain and a suspected myocardial infarction. At the time of his arrival, Mr. Shearer was unconscious, was wearing leather pants, and was handcuffed to a naked blonde named Priscilla. (Mark considerately pulled up the sheet that had dropped and exposed her buttocks as she walked down the hallway next to the gurney.)

Shearer's cardiac rhythm was off, and he was having multifocal PVCs (premature ventricular contractions).

Mark ordered a drip started and a 100 lidocaine IV push. He also told Malik to get the bolt cutters.

During monitoring, Shearer's PVCs stabilized to normal but he still had ST (sinus tachycardia) elevations in the anterior leads of his EKG.

It was at this point that Mrs. Shearer arrived. Mr. Shearer, who had briefly awakened, passed out again when he saw his wife. Dr. Greene told her that her husband had had a small heart attack and then asked her to leave the examining room. She refused, and found, first, his leather pants, and then, the naked Priscilla, whom we find out was Mrs. Shearer's secretary. As everyone stood around in embarrassed silence Mrs. Shearer said, "I suppose you all think this is very very funny, don't you?" and then left the hospital.

We can assume Mr. Shearer survived. We can be less certain, however, about the survival of his marriage or Priscilla's job.

4.72. Priscilla

Priscilla was not technically a patient, although an ER staff member did (sort of) treat her: Malik cut off the handcuffs with which she was attached to the heart attack patient Mr. Shearer (Patient 4.71). It is assumed that Malik or one of the nurses also found her something to wear, since she was naked when she arrived at the ER shackled to the unconscious Mr. Shearer.

4.73. Harriet

Elderly Harriet came to the ER with abdominal pain and was first examined by Dr. Lewis, who ordered a series of abdominal X-rays, an ultrasound, a CBC, a Chem 7, a U/A, and a serum amylase enzyme test. Every test came back negative or normal. Harriet's sed (erythrocyte sedimentation, see Glossary) rate, however, was 50.

Susan called in Peter Benton for a surgical consult because Harriet was still in pain, and Susan suspected gall bladder or appendix trouble, or possibly a mesenteric infection.

Dr. Benton, who Susan called away from his first hernia surgery, was not pleased with Susan's request for a consult. Peter diagnosed arthritis of the back and explained away Harriet's elevated sed rate as due to chronic inflammation. He said that because she had no GI (gastrointestinal) symptoms, no rectal mass, and her stool test was negative for occult blood, she was not a surgical candidate.

He then went back to his hernia.

Not long after Peter left, however, Harriet's white count shot to 20,000, and Susan urgently told Haleh to call Dr. Morgenstern. Harriet's retrocecal (behind the cecum) appendix had burst, and she needed immediate emergency surgery, which is always much riskier than carefully planned and scheduled surgery.

Dr. Morgenstern blasted Susan for not calling for a surgical consult for a patient presenting with stabbing lower back pain, and Susan did not respond. Peter then spoke up and admitted that Susan had called *him* but that he had dismissed Harriet's symptoms as arthritis. Morgenstern then asked Dr. Sarah Langworthy to assist on the appendectomy, even though Peter had offered to assist first.

Harriet recovered.

Dr. Morgenstern took Peter aside later and told him the most important thing a doctor could do is listen to the patient.

4.74. Joey Scarneccia

Joey was a pediatrics car accident case Doug had treated three months earlier. Nothing else is known about the never-seen Joey except that three months after his accident his insurance company was still looking for information and documents from the hospital.

4.75. Bob Brickley

Bob Brickley was a strapping bear of a guy Mark Greene had treated on August 25, 1994. According to Bob, Mark had saved his life, and, therefore, every August 25 was going to be "Dr. Greene Day."

Bob came into the ER with a case of Texas T-bone steaks for Mark and then picked him up and hugged him.

Mark did not remember Bob, but thanked him for the steaks.

4.76. The drug addict

This unnamed man went through withdrawal in the ER. He moaned rhythmically and Mark and Susan hummed along in harmony.

4.77. Dr. Morgenstern's Whipple procedure

This unnamed sixty-two-year-old gentleman, was a patient of Dr. Morgenstern's. He had pancreatic cancer and Dr. Morgenstern scheduled him for a Whipple procedure (see the Glossary). Morgenstern asked Benton to assist, and when they got into the OR, he actually let Peter perform the operation.

4.78. Carter's first delivery

This woman was brought to the ER in a station wagon in the final stages of labor. Carter delivered her daughter in the car with Haleh talking him through the delivery. This was the patient who convinced Carter that he *did* want to stay in the ER. The David Fisher incident (Patient 4.66) had so shaken him that he wasn't sure he belonged there. Then this woman showed up, and the episode ended with Carter standing outside the ER covered in blood, ecstatically shouting "Yes!" to whatever gods med students pray to.

• •

Original Broadcast Date:
Thursday, October 6, 1994
Written by Paul Manning;
Directed by Mimi Leder

"INTO THAT GOOD NIGHT"

"We can't fix everything."

**—Mark Greene, responding to little Sarah Gasner
when she asked him why he couldn't fix
her daddy, Sam, who died shortly thereafter**

This heart-wrenching episode gives us the dramatic stories of some very memorable patients, the most poignant tale being that of the gravely ill Sam Gasner, a building supplies salesman who dies before Mark can find him a heart for transplant.

The episode begins with Doug and Carter sleeping in the doctor's lounge. Carol wakes Carter up, telling him, "Med students don't sleep at four in the afternoon."

Jenn calls the ER and asks Mark to meet her. She has news. He refuses at first, but then Doug tells him to go, and he does. While walking by the water, Jenn tells Mark that she's won a clerkship with a federal judge in Milwaukee and that she has to live there. Mark tells her he'll make some calls and see what medical jobs are available in that area.

Back at the ER, Doug has to deal with a premature delivery while Peter (somewhat reluctantly) treats the gang member who hit the mother in labor with a stolen car.

Meanwhile, Carter (thanks to Liz) nervously awaits the result of his VD test; Mark returns for his shift; and Doug has to come up with a way of treating a teenage girl's asthma when her mother cannot afford the medications her daughter desperately needs.

As the hours pass, Mark and Peter work feverishly to keep the aforementioned Mr. Gasner alive while they search for a donor heart.

Carol is on a double shift, Susan is working all night, and Carter watches as Peter practices one-handed knots while listening to a tape. When Carter asks him what he's listening to, he sarcastically replies, Snoop Doggy Dogg. Susan shows Carter the real cassette box: *Trends in Cardiac Surgery, Volume 2.*

Ivan returns with a self-inflicted gunshot wound, and Susan talks to Div about her escalating problems with Dr. Kayson.

Susan then treats a college kid on the verge of death from alcohol poisoning, and Mark learns a lesson about priorities from the dying Sam Gasner.

After a very long shift, during which two patients died, Mark returns home at 7:30 in the morning and tells Jenn he'll go to Milwaukee. She tells him, "You'd hate it," thereby letting him off the hook. Their daughter, Rachel, gets into bed with them, and when she asks her visibly moved father what's wrong, he tells her "nothing," but fiercely hugs them both.

PATIENT HISTORIES

● ●

5.79. The woman in 3
This woman was an ER patient Carol told Doug to see. The woman had a headache that she self-diagnosed as a brain tumor.

5.80. The little kid in 5
This kid had chewing gum in his eye, and Doug treated him.

5.81. The old lady in 4
According to Carol, this woman just wanted her hand held. Doug obliged.

5.82. The abdominal pain in 2
This was another unnamed patient Carol told Doug to treat.

5.83. Sally Niemeyer
Sally Niemeyer was riding in a car that was hit by a gangbanger driving a stolen vehicle.

Sally was seven months pregnant, and when she arrived at the ER her vital signs were stable.

Dr. Doug Ross ordered her blood typed and crossmatched for 4 units and a CBC. He also ordered her hooked up to a fetal monitor. The baby, which Sally told them was a boy, had a steady heartbeat, and Doug told Carol to call Obstetrics for an ultrasound.

While being treated in the ER, Sally went into labor. Dr. Susan Lewis assessed her at 2 centimeters with the cervix 20 percent effaced. Doug estimated the pregnancy at only twenty-eight weeks and felt that it was too soon for Sally to deliver. He believed that the baby would have major lung trouble if it was born so prematurely. Susan, on the other hand, felt that Sally was actually thirty-four weeks into the pregnancy. She deferred to Doug, however, and ordered a bolus of 6 grams of magnesium sulfate in an attempt to stop labor.

Doug ordered a fetal lung profile and shouted, "Where the hell is OB!?"

The magnesium sulfate did not work, and Sally's labor progressed, with her contractions coming two minutes apart. The fetal heart rate dropped from 135, quickly going to 128 with late decelerations. Susan identified fetal distress and determined that the baby might have been acidotic (having an abnormally high level of acidity in the body fluids and tissues).

Then Sally's water broke.

Doug decided there was no choice but to deliver the baby and ordered Carol to call OB (Obstetrics) and Neonatal and tell them to expect a preemie.

Sally ended up delivering right out of the elevator, and, as Doug expected, the baby's lungs were bad. Sally pulled through fine, though.

5.84. Arabella Suarez

Arabella Suarez was the Hispanic gangbanger who stole a car and crashed into the pregnant Sally Niemeyer (Patient 5.83).

When Dr. Benton began treatment, her blood pressure was 170/100 and her pulse was 120. Peter ordered a CBC, tox screen, and a chest film. Suarez was conscious and answered no when Peter asked her if she had taken any drugs or done any cocaine or crack.

Suspecting an aortic rupture, Peter sent her to the O.R. (Operating Room) for emergency surgery. The rupture was ultimately confirmed and repaired, but while Peter was practicing one-handed sutures in the doctor's lounge after her operation, Suarez died in recovery.

5.85. The Niemeyer infant

This infant son of Sally and Randy Niemeyer was born prematurely when his mother want into labor after being injured in a car accident. His lungs were bad, and the last we heard of him, he was in the Neonatal Intensive Care Unit (NICU).

5.86. "Dr." John Carter

Carter became an ER patient when he did a culture and a gram stain on himself after

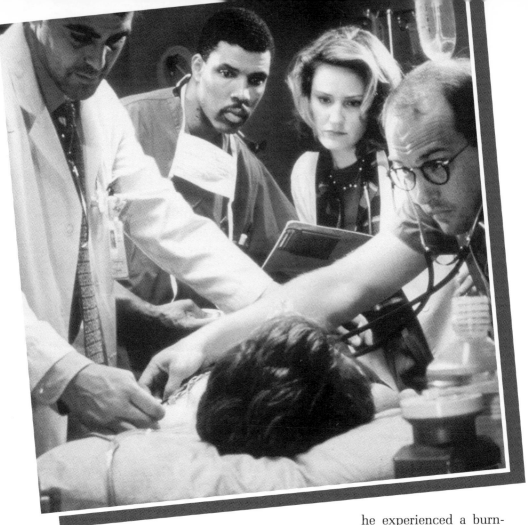

he experienced a burn-
ing sensation when urinating. The results showed a venere-
al disease (given to him by the wildly promiscuous Liz), and Jerry thoughtfully posted
shis lab results on the ER bulletin board.

5.87. Sam Gasner

When builder Sam Gasner, forty-three, collapsed at a convention, he was originally
called into the ER as a Code 3 (full arrest), but as the EMTs on Rescue 63 put it, after
they "fried his chest hairs" in the ambulance, he converted really fast and came out of
arrest. The EMTs also gave him 100 milligrams of lidocaine in the ambulance.

When Mr. Gasner arrived at the ER he was conscious, and Dr. Mark Greene
ordered a CBC, Chem 7, blood gas, and coag panel.

While being attended to, however, Mr. Gasner passed out, and when he awakened, he told them that he was awaiting a heart transplant. He had severe cardiac
myopathy and had suffered an inferior wall myocardial infarction.

Gasner was in town for the aforementioned builders' convention, and he told the
ER staff that his cardiologist was Mike Ditky ("great guy") at St. Luke's Hospital in
Cleveland.

Once again, Gasner went into arrest with no pulse, and Mark ordered the patient bagged and an ampule of epinephrine administered. As Mr. Gasner so succinctly put it when he came to yet again, "I just pass out." Mark ordered a dopamine drip, 400 milligrams in 250 of D5W (5 percent dextrose in water) at 10 drops a minute.

While being observed, Sam *again* went into fibrillation and needed to be shocked at 200 joules. Mark ordered another 50 milligrams of lidocaine and instructed his team to start a drip, 2 grams at 500.

Mark and Peter consulted on Mr. Gasner and determined that he was in cardiogenic shock. Peter ordered an echocardiogram, and Mark ordered calls made to the transplant coordinator and Mr. Gasner's wife in Clevelend. Lydia told Mark she was trying the Clevelend number every ten minutes.

Gasner's pressure went to 80/60 and continued to drop. Mark ordered a dobutamine drip at 250 and 250 at 4 ccs a minute. Dr. Kayson looked at Gasner's echo and identified the problem as being in the left ventricle. The facts were unavoidable and inevitable: If Mr. Gasner did not get a heart transplant, he wouldn't last the night.

Gasner had type A blood and a negative T-cell crossmatch, a difficult donor match. Kayson reevaluated Gasner and diagnosed advanced dilated cardiomyopathy with severe mitral regurgitation and an ejection fraction of less than 10 percent. Dr. Susan Lewis suggested putting him on heart/lung bypass, but it was agreed that the stress on his heart would be too much and that it would kill him.

Gasner wasn't putting out fluids, so Mark ordered 160 milligrams of Lasix and told him honestly that if he didn't get a transplant, he wouldn't last the night. Gasner said, "It's two in the morning, I'm dying, please call me Sam. This is not the time to be formal."

Gasner's wife and nine-year-old daughter, Sarah, arrived from Cleveland and Mark told Mrs. Gasner the sad facts.

At four in the morning, Mark was still trying to find a heart, but to no avail. Gasner's blood-oxygen saturation was down to 80 percent, so Mark ordered 2 liters of oxygen.

Sarah visited her father one last time and then asked Mark if her daddy was going to die. He told her yes and explained that doctors can't fix everything when she asked him why couldn't he fix him.

Shortly thereafter, Gasner's cardiac monitor alarm went off, and he went into fibrillation—for the last time. Mark performed external heart massage, but it was useless. Mr. Gasner's last words were to his wife, about his daughter. He said, "Remind her I love her."

5.88. Sandy Rochon

This thirteen-year-old was brought to the ER by her mother because she couldn't breathe. Dr. Doug Ross ordered blood gases, and when they came back, they were 27, which was not good.

Doug diagnosed asthma and told her mother that Sandy had had a severe attack and needed treatment and tests. He ordered therapy with a handheld nebulizer, plus albuterol 2.5 milligrams, a Solu-Medrol IV of 50 milligrams, and he told Haleh to keep the flow going pre- and post-.

Eventually, Sandy's peak flow went from 190 to 300, and, with the treatment, her blood gases were better. Doug told Sandy's mother that the girl needed to take prednisone and have an inhaler with her at all times. He wrote the prescription and sent her home.

Later that same day, Doug was told that Sandy was back at the ER because she had had another asthma attack. Her mother had not bought the drugs because she didn't have the money. They cost thirty dollars, and Medicaid did not come through for another week.

Doug rustled up some Prednisone samples (with Carol's help) and told Mrs. Rochon to take Sandy to the free clinic every day for inhaler treatments. (He had also wanted to give her some Proventil samples and an inhaler, but the ER did not have any in stock.)

Later that day, Doug borrowed forty dollars from Mark and went and bought Sandy an inhaler. He then walked through the ghetto where the Rochons lived and delivered it to Sandy's mother, who realized that Doug had paid for the drugs himself (with Mark's help, of course). The mother promised to get Sandy to the clinic on a regular basis and thanked Doug.

5.89. Ivan Gregor
Ivan Gregor came to the ER with a gunshot wound to his foot. This time, however, he had not been shot by a holdup man. Ivan had shot *himself* in the foot with a Glöck pistol defending himself during a stickup.

Dr. Benton ordered a gram of Ancef, 150 milligrams of gentamicin IV, and 10 milligrams of Procardia sublingual, and then treated the wound. Ivan recovered.

[Ivan would fire his gun again, resulting in his return to the ER in episode 6, but this time, his pulling the trigger would have much more dire results than a simple foot injury. (See Patients 2.39, 3.59, and 6.103.)]

5.90. The baby in 4
We don't know why this unnamed infant was in the ER, but whatever it was there for, Doug treated it.

5.91. Mrs. Fadem
Mrs. Fadem, a woman who was easily in her eighties, was brought to the ER because she had fallen. Doug ordered an X-ray, and when he informed her of the need for the test, she warned him to be careful of her baby. She told Dr. Ross that she was six-months pregnant, and the ever-diplomatic and empathic Doug passed along her concerns to Lydia before they went to Radiology.

5.92. The knife-wielding psychotic
This unnamed psycopath was a patient of Dr. Div Cvetic's, and during a conversation

with Susan, Div got beeped that the psychotic had awakened from his nap.

5.93. Daniel Quinn

Teenager Daniel Quinn was brought to the ER by his fraternity brothers in a comatose state from drinking all night. Dan's friend Elliot told Dr. Lewis that they had all been playing a drinking game called Whale's Tails? and that Daniel (whose father was assistant dean at the university) had drunk between fifteen and twenty shots of Tequila followed by beer chasers.

Daniel was hypotensive with blood pressure of 80/70 and cyanotic.

Carter started a second arterial line, and Susan ordered an ampule of D50 (50 percent dextrose in water) and 2 milligrams of Narcan. She also ordered an EKG and his drip speeded up with dopamine added, and she ordered Quinn hyperventilated.

Even with the initial treatment, though, Quinn's blood pressure dropped to 70/40 and continued to fall.

Susan then ordered a CBC, a blood alcohol, a Chem 7, a tox screen, and she had him intubated. Quinn's blood-oxygen saturation was only 80 percent. Susan then ordered a dextrose stick and had him bagged. Quinn's glucose was normal and his blood pressure went to 80/65 and remained steady. Susan then ordered blood gases.

They continued hydrating Quinn like crazy, but his blood pressure did not move. Susan then ordered LFT (a liver function test), BUN (a test for blood urea and nitrogen), and creats (serum creatine). Quinn's blood alcohol came back at 832, and Susan decided he needed immediate dialysis.

The dialysis worked, and Susan spoke to Quinn when he awakened and told him that his kidneys were functioning, his liver was fine, and that he had lost a few million brain cells, but "you can spare them." She then said to him, "Blink if you will never do this again."

Daniel blinked.

5.94. Liz

This is the Liz who had formerly appeared at the ER as Patients 1.28, 2.43, and 3.58. This time she complained to Dr. Kayson that she was nauseous, and he escorted her (a tad too eagerly, if the truth be told) to an examining room. On her way to the room she said hello to John Carter, who had just learned that she had given him a venereal disease.

5.95. The kid throwing up in 3

Jerry gave this patient to Dr. Ross.

● ●

Original Broadcast Date:
Thursday, October 13, 1994
Written by Robert Nathan;
Directed by Charles Haid

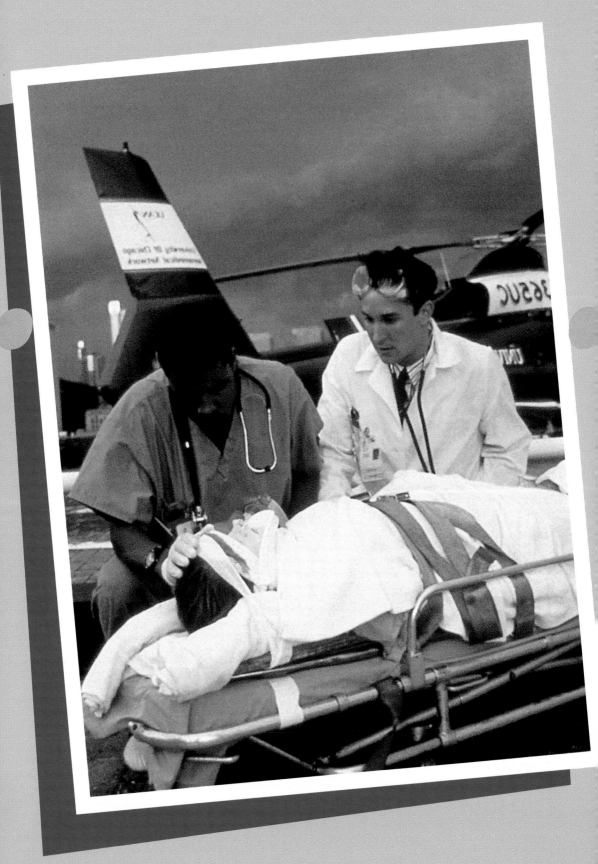

"CHICAGO HEAT"

ER·6

"That's what doctors do."

—Rachel Greene, commenting to little
Kanesha Freeman about Rachel's daddy making Kanesha better

This episode begins with Mark bringing his daughter Rachel to work because the babysitter, Tommy, missed his return flight from his brother's wedding.

Upon arrival at the ER, Mark learns that the air conditioning is out and that it's hot as hell in the hospital. Lydia takes Rachel to the TV room because Doug needs Mark's help with a five-year-old girl.

The day begins with a vengeance shortly thereafter when a pizza delivery guy drives his car through the front door of the ER. Doug passes by the wreckage and says, "Call Security. Someone's in my parking space."

Susan gets the unpleasant news that her troubled and troublesome sister Chloe is in the lounge waiting for her. Chloe tells Susan she lost her apartment and asks if she can stay with her. Against her better judgment, Susan gives her the apartment key.

Mark brings Rachel in to talk to little Kanesha (Patient 6.96) and keep her company, but Rachel inadvertently gets an eyeful as she watches them try to save the life of the stickup kid that Ivan shot.

Doug runs into Carol and apologizes for showing up at her apartment uninvited.

Doug also apologizes to Div.

Linda Farrell, the hotshot rep for Novell Pharmaceuticals, arrives with a pepperoni pizza for Jerry, who declines, since he's a vegetarian. (Carnivore Malik jumps in and claims the pizza for himself.)

Carol and Tag talk about moving in together, but Carol isn't so sure.

Wendy reads to Rachel, and Susan discovers that her locker has been broken into and her credit cards stolen. Div tells her to report them stolen, but she won't because she knows that Chloe would get arrested. Div also refuses to talk to Chloe, even though Susan asks for his help. "Awful idea," he says.

Doug tells Carol that Tag accepted his apology. Doug also tells her that he feels that they should now behave like adults. Carol looks at him incredulously and says, "We!?"

Linda Farrell smoothly wraps a compliant Doug around her little finger—as Carol watches disgustedly (and hits him in the arm as she leaves).

The heat is finally broken by a torrential downpour and the air conditioning comes back on.

Mark takes Rachel home, and she asks him if he'd fix her if she got hurt. He tells her she's the most important thing in his life, and she is comforted.

Susan arrives home to find the cat loose; the door open; and her TV, VCR, and stereo gone. The house is a mess, and Susan burns her hand when she takes a pan off the stove, which Chloe had left on.

Just as Div arrives, Susan breaks down and sobs. He comforts her and promises her he'll try to get Chloe some help.

PATIENT HISTORIES

● ●

6.96. Kanesha Freeman

This five-year-old girl, was brought to the ER in severe respiratory distress with signs of a serious cardiac problem. She was cyanotic, her respirations were 40, her blood pressure was 180/100, and her heart was beating at the tachycardic rate of 180.

Mark learned that Kanesha had a known coarctation of her aorta and a systolic murmur, and he began to worry about congestive heart failure. He ordered blood gases, a chest film, and 20 milligrams of Lasix. He also ordered an angiogram, and his concern grew when her fever went to 102°.

While under observation, Kanesha's heart went into ventricular tachyarrhythmia, and Mark ordered 20 milligrams of lidocaine IV push.

Mark went to talk to Kanesha's father (and her sister Shandra), who told him that Kanesha had had the aortic malformation since she was a baby.

Kanesha's electrolytes came back normal, but she was still hypertensive with a blood pressure of 180/100. With her additional symptoms of agitation and fever, Mark suspected poisoning and ordered a tox screen and a lavage.

The tox screen results indicated that Kanesha had overdosed on cocaine, and

Doug suspected she had gotten it from her father. He then brought the Department of Child and Family Services into the picture and refused to let Mr. Freeman take his daughter home.

After Mr. Freeman reluctantly agreed that he and Shandra would take drug tests, the results came back clean for him, but positive for cocaine for Shandra.

Doug made the necessary referrals, and Kanesha went home with her father.

6.97. The dead guy

This unfortunate (and unnamed) man was brought to the ER DOA from a nursing home by paramedics. The heat had gotten him. While waiting for the city to pick him up, he lay on a gurney, under a sheet, while everyone worked around him. At one point Dr. Greene suggested that they move him to Pathology, but everyone was so busy that by the end of Mark's shift, the dead guy was still there. (Mark got so sick of seeing him that he frustratedly asked Jerry if he was waiting for the guy to get ripe.)

6.98. The seedy man

This gentleman got into a vocal and hostile argument with his wife as they waited in a curtained area. The reason he and his wife (see Patient 6.99) were at the ER was not revealed.

6.99. The Seedy Woman

This was the seedy man's wife. We were not told if the seedy man or the seedy woman was the ER patient. All that was revealed about them was that they were loud.

6.100. Mr. Ettger

Mr. Ettger drove his pizza delivery car through the front door of the ER, screaming that he had been stabbed in the side during a holdup attempt. His blood pressure was 210/120, and Carol asked Dr. Benton if she should prep for a peritoneal lavage.

After examining Ettger, Peter disgustedly told Carol to get some Bactine and a Band-Aid. The "stab wound" was only a scratch. Upon hearing the good news (and seeing the look on Peter's face), Ettger said, "It was a really big knife."

6.101. Arthur Smith

Arthur was one of the homeless alcoholics who showed up at the ER with depressing frequency, always in an alcoholic stupor and usually injured in some manner.

This time, the ER staff set up a betting pool as to what Arthur's blood alcohol (BA) level would be. They each bet five dollars on the following BA levels:

Haleh	300
Malik	350
Jerry	375
Wendy	200
Lydia	465
Susan	550

Arthur's level came back at 473, and because Lydia won the pool she also got the job of cleaning him up. Much later, she brought out a sober, clean-shaven, good-looking guy who, according to Carol, "look[ed] better than [Lydia's] last husband."

The "Arthur" Blooper

At the beginning of episode 6, "Chicago Heat," Jerry makes a remark that the day the episode takes place is the "hottest day in October." (He said this because the hospital's air conditioning system went on the blink.) Later in the same day, Malik and Jerry watch the computer print out Arthur Smith's blood alcohol level and the report reads September 4, 1994.

6.102. The bearded guy with the ice bag

This patient walked through the ER holding an ice bag to his head. He was not seen again.

6.103. Ivan Gregor

Ivan returned to the ER this time with a head injury he had sustained during a holdup in which he shot the stickup boy (see Patient 6.104) in the back. Benton made Carter sew up Ivan's head. [Ivan was also Patients 2.39, 3.59, and 5.89.]

6.104. Ivan's victim

This young boy was shot by Ivan Gregor during a holdup. The boy was unarmed, and Ivan chased him onto the street and shot him in the back.

The boy (whose name we never learn) was brought to the ER with multiple gunshot wounds, a thready pulse of 150, and a blood pressure of 50 palp. The EMTs had started two large bore IVs but the boy's pressure was still crashing.

Peter ordered six units of O-negative blood, but within seconds the boy had no palpable blood pressure, and his capillary refill was bad.

Peter realized the boy was bleeding out and ordered blood in a pressure bag and a bilateral chest tube. The boy had decreased breath sounds bilaterally, and Benton instructed Carter to put a stitch around the chest tube.

Sarah arrived, and Peter told her the boy had a bilateral hemothorax (intrapleural bleeding from penetrating trauma).

As they were working on him, he lost his pulse, and they discovered a bullet in his right ventricle and cardiac tamponade (see the Glossary).

Sarah decided to open his chest, but Peter overruled her, telling her the kid was *his* patient. The boy's heart was racing at a tachycardic rate and Peter did a thoracotomy. The pericardium was full of blood, and Peter plugged the hole with his finger, jumped up on top of the gurney, ordered 10 units of blood, and yelled to tell the OR to prep for a heart/lung bypass.

During surgery, the boy went into asystole (cardiac arrest) and died.

Peter got the job of telling Ivan that his gunshots had killed the boy.

6.105. HIV-positive Monty

Dr. Lewis saw Monty after he had a seizure in the waiting room and hit his head on a metal cabinet. Monty told Susan that he was HIV positive, and she asked him what medications he was on, suggesting AZT (an antiviral agent), Bactrim (an anti-infective), and Dilantin (an anticonvulsant).

He told her that he was on Dilantin and that he had been drinking, and she explained that alcohol and Dilantin should not be mixed. Susan then ordered a CBC, tox screen, Chem 7, Dilantin and blood alcohol levels, and went on to another patient.

Later, as Monty was leaving the hospital, he approached Susan and thanked her for her help, but then asked her for money. When she refused, he got loud, aggressive, and threatening, and Jerry ended up carrying him out. He screamed "Bitch!" at Susan all the way out of the ER.

6.106. Mr. Kenneth

Mr. Kenneth had a water-skiing accident and dislocated his shoulder. Someone in the ER sedated him, and, when he was unconscious, Carol and Tag wrapped him in a sheet and gently pulled his shoulder back into its socket. Tag then ordered an X-ray and a postreduction film.

6.107. The inquistive elderly woman

This woman was in the bed next to Mr. Kenneth and she listened attentively as Carol and Tag discussed their forthcoming wedding. She then asked Carol about "that Doug."

6.108. The kid with a bellyache

Haleh gave this patient to Doug.

6.109. Mr. Freeman

Mr. Freeman wasn't technically ill (his daughter Kanesha was Patient 6.96), but because he had to submit to a drug test that was administered by ER personnel, he is included here as a patient.

● ●

Original Broadcast Date:
Thursday, October 20, 1994
Story by Neal Baer;
Teleplay by John Wells;
Directed by Elodia Keene

"ANOTHER PERFECT DAY"

"See one, do one, teach one."

**—Mark Greene, stating the operating
principle for medical students, to Carter**

This episode begins with Patrick manning the ER desk, and Carter looking for an apartment.

Doug is still stuck on Carol, and Peter is nervously awaiting his Starzl Fellowship interview. (The fellowship allows thirty residents to study with surgical transplant teams for a year.)

Mark calls in late for work thanks to the amorous advances of Jenn, and Susan finally admits to Carol that she's been dating Div Cvetic for the past couple of months. Susan is shocked to learn that Carol knows she is going out with Div that evening for her birthday and even that he has asked her to wear "that black dress." (A very low-cut, very short little frock that Susan looks fabulous in.)

The ER staff gives Susan a little surprise birthday party, and Tag and Carol sneak away to the roof for a little midday romance. Tag once again brings up the subject of them moving in together, and, once again, Carol refuses.

Mark finally shows up for work (he says he had car trouble) and Doug asks, "How *is* Jennifer?"

Officer Grabarsky shows Lydia his dog pictures, and Div gives Susan a massage.

Susan is mad at Div because he told Doug ("Dr. Intercom") about their date. Div explodes when Malik asks him to look at a patient, foreshadowing big problems to come.

Doug and Carol indulge in an illicit spontaneous kiss, and later Patrick does a card trick for Carol.

As Peter is changing clothes for the Starzl interview, Haleh confronts him about not treating her friend Mookie. Sarah Langworthy also interviews for the fellowship. After the interview Peter feels like he made a fool of himself in front of Morgenstern. (He reasons, perhaps justifiably, that it was premature for him to even apply, since he is only second year.)

Mark meets Jenn for coffee, and she tells him Judge Franklin did not like her zoning appeal and that she has to work that evening to repair it. Their evening together is called off.

Linda Farrell breaks a date with Doug so she can attend a seminar on advances in cardiomyopathy. (He and Mark joke that they were both stood up for the evening.)

Susan's sister Chloe shows up at the ER drunk, and with a creep named Billy. She makes an excruciatingly embarrassing scene that culminates in Susan breaking her date with Div because she's so upset about Chloe's behavior.

Carol makes a decision and tells Doug that she's moving in with Tag. Doug cooly thanks her for letting him know.

Susan retreats to the roof where she is joined by Carter, who offers her a drink from his "lumbar puncture" bottle of champagne. They drink to her birthday, and he assures her she is not the only one with a crazy family. Based on their new closeness, Susan tries to call him John, but it doesn't work. "Okay," he responds. "Call me Carter."

The episode ends with Susan proferring her mug for another drink of champagne.

PATIENT HISTORIES

7.110. Retarded Patrick

Patrick was a big, loveable retarded man who visited the ER because of an injured elbow sustained when he fell off a stool. Patrick always wore a football helmet and had a large repertoire of Knock Knock jokes. Susan ordered an X-ray of Patrick's elbow and told him he could keep it when he excitedly asked for it. On his way out he told Carol a Knock Knock joke, which went as follows:

Patrick:	Knock, knock.
Carol:	Who's there?
Patrick:	Patrick.
Carol:	Patrick who?
Patrick:	Me! Patrick!

Patrick returned in episodes 10 and 11.

7.111. The woman in the suture room

This woman needed stitches in her face, and Benton told Carter to go in and "bat cleanup" for the plastic surgery guys, who were already in there.

Benton also told Carter to give her a really big scar, but when he saw the horrified look on Carter's face, he told him he was only kidding.

7.112. The stabbing victim

This unnamed twenty-year-old was brought to the ER with stab wounds to the neck.

His pulse was 150 and thready and his blood pressure was 50 palp. His blood oxygen was 70, and he was cyanotic. Peter tried a 7.5 intubation tube but could not establish an airway. (Because of his injuries he couldn't be intubated.)

The patient's pressure went to 60/40, and his pulse shot to 160. Peter decided to "crike" him: do a surgical airway known as a cricothyrotomy. The crike was a success, and Peter declared, "We have a breather." He ordered him hyperventilated and sent him to the O.R.

After the patient was stabilized, Dr. Morgenstern arrived, and Peter filled him in: "Stab wound to the neck, unable to intubate due to bleeding, performed a cricothyrotomy, airway established, good bilateral breath sounds, and patient is stable."

Morgenstern was impressed. He told Peter he did excellent work, used "sound judgment," and performed "a solid execution."

After Morgenstern left, Carter turned to Benton and said, "Pretty cool."

Peter just gave him a disgusted look and left.

7.113. The guy who crumped

When Carter told Jerry he was looking for an apartment, Jerry told him he had found his place about six months ago thanks to this eighty-five-year-old cardiac patient.

The guy didn't make it out of the hospital, and, as Jerry so sensitively put it, "He crumped and I jumped." Jerry finagled a way to rent the deceased's apartment and recommended the same approach to Carter (see Patient 7.115).

7.114. Mookie James (a.k.a. Slice)

Haleh had known Mookie James since he was four years old, and when he was brought to the ER in handcuffs for an injury he sustained putting his foot through a window while breaking and entering, she asked Dr. Benton to treat him. She hoped that Mookie would see a strong, successful black man and look to him as an example.

Mookie had a foot laceration, and Peter agreed to treat him just to placate Haleh. As soon as she left, however, Peter gave the chart to Carter and told him to do it.

Mookie was handcuffed to the bed, and as Carter examined him, he took Carter's EKG caliper and tried to pick the handcuff lock.

Carter managed to stitch up Mookie, and when Haleh found out that Benton had blown her off, she burst into the men's locker room and confronted Peter. He told her he couldn't be the resident Big Brother and turn every gang kid into Nelson Mandela.

Haleh later got her way when she hired Mookie to work in the ER as part of the

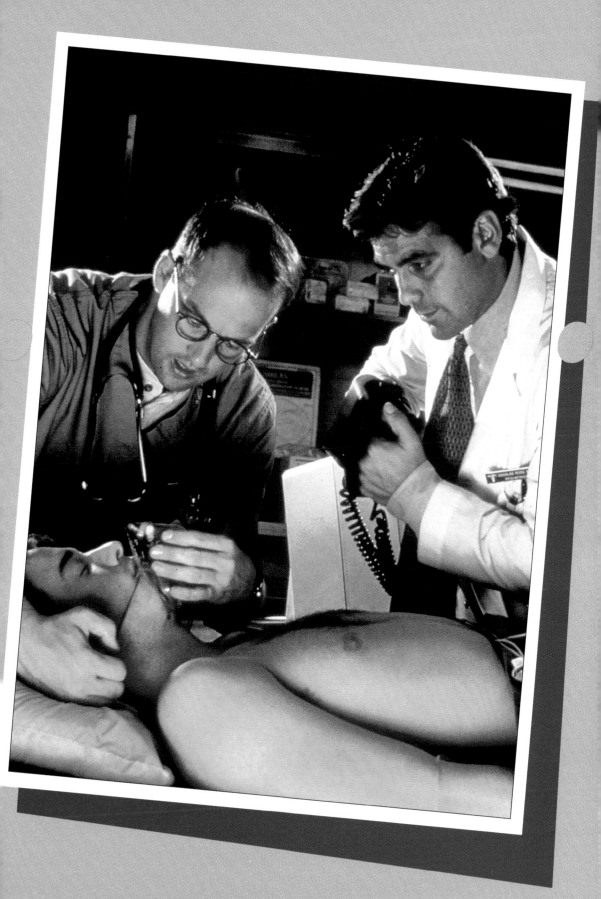

City Kid's Intern Program (she got him a suspended sentence) and made Peter his supervisor.

7.115. The ninety-six-year-old stroke victim in curtain area 3
This guy lived at 1680 North Lake Shore Drive, and Jerry suggested that Carter make a move for his apartment if the poor soul didn't make it.

7.116. The lady in 5
This patient's blood samples were taken to the lab by Mailk. That's all we know about her.

7.117. The motorcycle-versus-semi victim
This "patient" didn't exist. They made this guy up to get Susan to the back door of the ER where the ambulances arrive. When she reached the ambulance, the

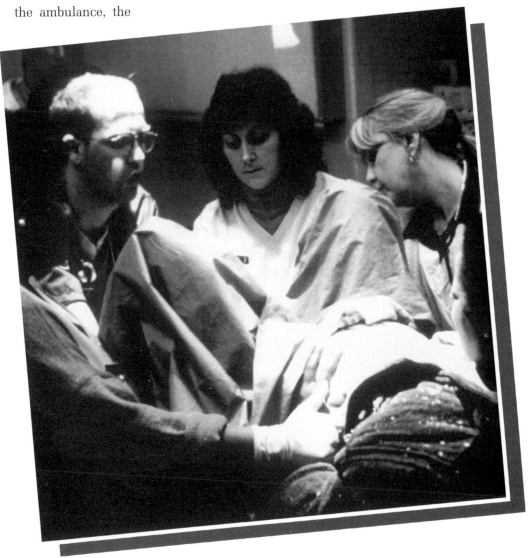

rear doors flew open, and everyone jumped out and sang Happy Birthday to her. The ever-subtle Doug gave her a jar of Vaseline.

7.118. Malik's psych patient

This was a patient that Malik wanted Div to look at, and when he asked him to do so for the third time, Div exploded and told him his patient would have to wait for the afternoon shift. (See Patients 7.119 through 7.123).

7.119. Div's attempted suicide No. 1

This was one of the five psych patients Div had admitted in one morning and was why he refused to see Malik's psych patient (7.118).

7.120. Div's attempted suicide No. 2

Another one of Div's five psychiatric admissions in one morning.

7.121. Div's bipolar No. 1

And another.

7.122. Div's bipolar No. 2

And another.

7.123. Div's living dead guy

This forty-year-old was the last of Div's psychiatric admissions the morning Malik asked him to look at one more patient. This guy walked in off the street claiming to be dead, but suffering from a headache. [Even though we did not see him in this episode, it seems as though he returned in episode 15, "Feb. 5th, '95," played by Bobcat Goldthwaite.]

7.124. The boating accident victim

This twelve-year-old boy was found unconscious in the water after a boating accident and when he was brought to the ER his blood pressure was 70 palp, his pulse was 140, and his GCS was 2–1–4 (see the Glossary).

Carol, Susan, and Doug were part of the treating team, and they started an IV and intubated him with a 6.5 endotracheal tube.

They administered lidocaine, and because his heart rate was only 32, they also gave him atropine and epinephrine. Carol also ordered O-negative blood.

Doug determined that the boy's peripheral vein had collapsed and that he needed an external jugular vein catheterization.

Doug did the catheterization with Carol's assistance, and it went perfectly.

By this time the O.R. was prepped and it was decided they would do a c-spine (cervical spine) X-ray upstairs. As they were preparing to move him, the boy went into fibrillation and Carol shocked him twice, once at 200 joules and once at 300 joules, but to no avail. Doug then took the paddles and shocked him at 360 joules and he converted to normal sinus rhythm.

Peter arrived, and Doug told him that the patient was now stabilized. Peter

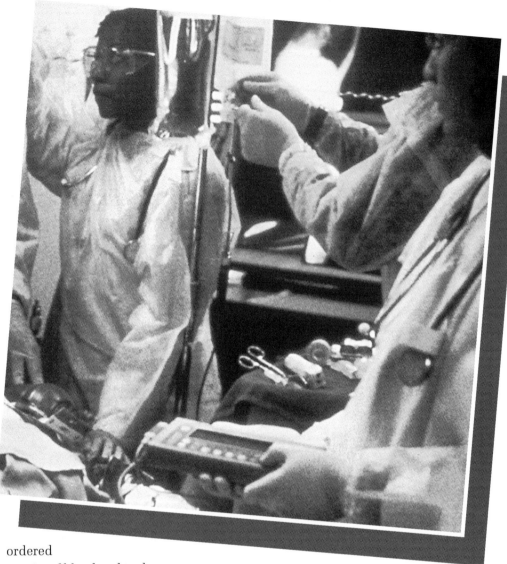

ordered
6 units of blood and took over.

After the boy was on his way to the O.R., Doug and Carol were still pumped about the way things had gone ("seven minutes door to door!") and they ended up embracing and then kissing.

Doug apologized, and Carol said, "You didn't do it alone."

7.125. The fever in 2
Lydia gave this three-year-old patient to Doug.

7.126. The kid in 4 not keeping anything down
Lydia gave this six-month-old patient to Doug at the same time she gave him Patient 7.125.

7.127. Michael Carson
This patient, age thirty-five, was the victim of a five-mile-per-hour car accident that

left him without a scratch, but in an unexplained coma from which he could not be awakened.

Peter and Mark initially consulted on Carson and determined that the result of his CT was normal, and that there was no improvement from glucose (an amp of D50) or Narcan therapy.

Peter decided that the patient was not a surgical candidate and left it for Mark to resolve the always-puzzling "differential diagnosis of coma."

Carter suggested hypoglycemia or diabetic ketoacidosis, but Mark said the blood tests ruled those out. There was no cardiac arrhythmia, he had not had an MI (myocardial infarction), and his CAT scan ruled out mass lesion and trauma.

While under observation, Carson's white count went up to 14,500, and his pulse dropped to 50. His blood pressure also began to drop, and Mark ordered his IVs speeded up and a 300 cc bolus of saline. Carter suggested atropine, and Mark agreed, ordering .5 IV push.

Carter suggested that Carson might have had a seizure, and Mark ordered Connie to get a temperature. It was 101.5°. Carter noticed a slight abrasion on the tongue, which is seen in seizures, and Mark found that the patient had partially palpitated metabolic acidosis, which is also found in seizures.

Carter opined meningitis, Mark agreed it was a possibility, and decided Carson needed a lumbar puncture, which he ordered Carter to do.

Carter performed his first spinal tap perfectly (See "champagne tap" in the Glossary), and it was determined that the patient did indeed have meningitis.

7.128. Doug's patient Murdoch
Doug spent an entire morning looking for the Murdoch chart. He finally found it.

7.129. Dr. Lewis's sister Chloe
Chloe became an ER patient when she smashed her hand through a window during an emotional and violent drunken outburst. Peter sewed her up and Div talked to her about her problems.

● ●

Original Broadcast Date:
Thursday, November 3, 1994
Story by Lance A. Gentile;
Teleplay by Lydia Woodward;
Directed by Vern Gillum

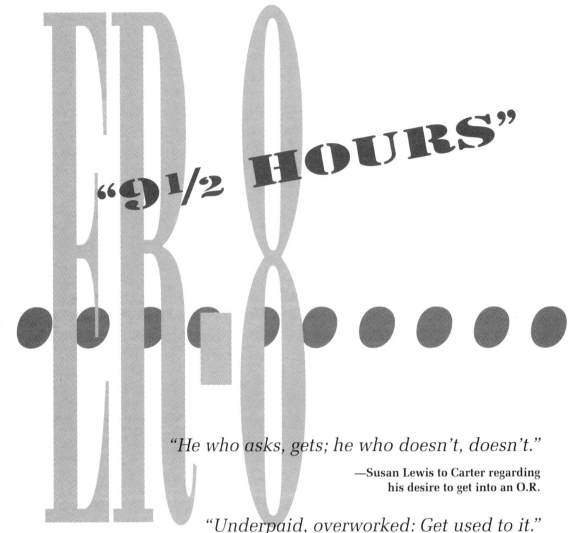

"9 1/2 HOURS"

"He who asks, gets; he who doesn't, doesn't."

—Susan Lewis to Carter regarding
his desire to get into an O.R.

"Underpaid, overworked: Get used to it."

—R.N. Haleh, to Mookie James

This episode opens in the doctor's lounge with Peter complaining that the refrigerator is disgusting and that someone stole his salad. Susan's ignition is shot (Chloe burnt it out), and we learn that Susan knows how to hot-wire a car. She learned it from one of Chloe's boyfriends, now in Joliet serving time for grand theft auto.

Div continues to exhibit worrisome behavior, and Doug is temporarily in charge of the ER because Mark has called in "sick." (He's really home having sex with Jenn.) When Doug asks how Mark handles all the paperwork that goes with being chief ER resident, Jerry tells him that Mark puts in four hours after every shift just working on reports.

The Starzl Fellowship announcements are due today and Peter is anxious. In the meantime, Carter offers to pay for Susan's ignition if she'll help get him into an O.R.

Mookie James is late for his first day in the ER, and Haleh scolds him for it.

Even though Mark is feeling guilty about leaving Doug on his own at the ER, he and Jenn find other ways (and places) to make love. Jenn tells Mark that Judge Franklin loved her zoning rewrite and admits that she now understands why Mark loves to go to work.

Peter calls about the Starzl and gives Mookie his first ER assignment: Clean the refrigerator.

Peter's mother, Mrs. Benton, invites Carter to Thanksgiving dinner, and Peter finally learns that Sarah Langworthy won the Starzl Fellowship.

While taking a bath together, Mark assures Jenn that he and Susan Lewis are just good friends and we know he's telling the truth.

Sarah confronts Peter about his ignoring her and accuses him of wanting her to lose the Starzl. She tells him she could help him be a better surgeon and suggests that he hates losing to a woman. She tells him he wants to sleep with her because then he wouldn't be so threatened by her. He responds that not only does he not want to sleep with her, he never even fantasized about it . . . but obviously she has. She laughs and says, "Yeah, right."

Doug confronts Peter about overstepping his authority with a patient (8.137) and assures him that all he lost today was a Starzl, not a patient. Doug then tells Peter that Peter saved two lives in five minutes today: "Not a bad day."

Back home, Jenn takes a call from her colleague Craig and talks animatedly with him about her zoning opinion, after she earlier refused to let Mark talk to Doug when *he* called. Mark has a sudden realization about the future of their marriage.

Back at the ER, Miss Bighdonovichski, the new Polish ER aide, arrives to start work, and because no one can pronounce her name, Doug christens her Bob.

After his shift, Peter stops by his brother-in-law Walt's garage, and Walt tells him he "never lets anyone in"—just like his dad used to be.

The episode concludes with Carol finding rape victim Jamie alone on the street in tears and convincing her to come back into the hospital.

PATIENT HISTORIES

● ●

8.130. The Rollerblader with the bashed head

Lydia gave this patient to Peter.

8.131. The patient without a chart

Div shouted at Jerry (loudly and publicly) about this patient.

Apparently Jerry had turfed (referred) this patient to Div's psychiatric service, but without a chart. (It had been temporarily misplaced.)

Susan told Jerry to ignore Div's hostility and then blasted Div for his unnecessary overreaction (and also for snapping at a cashier at Starbuck's that morning). This episode was just one more sign of trouble to come with Div.

8.132. The diverted severe head trauma

Doug ordered this patient diverted to St. Luke's because all of Cook County's neuro-surgeons were unavailable. Doug was acting chief resident because Mark had called in "sick with the flu."

8.133. Jamie Hendricks

Jamie was brought to the ER because she had been gang-raped by two friends of her boyfriend.

Carol, a certified psychiatric counselor, did the rape kit and tried to convince Jamie that she needed to testify against her assailants.

Jamie walked out of the hospital, and later Carol found her outside leaning against a fence. She had no place to go: Her boyfriend wouldn't let her come home because he didn't believe she had been raped.

Carol told Jamie she needed to take care of these personal demons or they would come back. "They always do," she told her. "I know."

Jamie agreed to let Carol help her, and the two wounded women went back into the hospital.

8.134. The wrestler

This seventeen-year-old wrestler was brought to the ER because he had passed out. He was a student at St. Robert's, and when he got to the hospital his vitals were stable. After a quick examination, Dr. Benton determined he was not a surgical candidate and told Susan, "I need a pill-pusher."

While waiting for a consult, Peter did a dextrose stick and told Carter to start a second line. He also ordered a CBC, lytes, and a tox screen.

The patient was hypotensive with pressure of 70/60 and falling. He was exhibiting PVCs (premature ventricular contractions), and Susan wondered if he was showing normal cardiac rhythm but with a block. While they were discussing the possibilities, the boy's heart began having extra beats, and he went into arrhythmia.

His pressure continued to fall to 60/45. The tox screen showed no drugs in his system but his electrolytes were screwed up. His potassium was 200 (which was extremely low), and Susan ordered piggyback 20 millequivalents of potassium and told them to keep on eye on his EKG.

Carter suggested hyperaldosteronism or Barter's syndrome, and Peter yelled at him to put down the damn medical book he was looking things up in and come and help.

The patient's heart rate began racing at 240 beats per minute and continued to climb. He was given a rapid bolus of 6 milligrams of adenosine, but it did not bring down his rate. Peter decided to shock him. At 100, his pulse was faint; at 200, he had no pulse; and, after no results at 360, Peter decided to "overdrive" him.

Peter could not wait for a fluoroscope, however, and actually floated a catheter into the boy's heart "blind," without an X-ray to guide his hand. He achieved a capture, ordered the pacemaker set to 300, and brought down the heart rate very slowly

until the boy achieved normal sinus rhythm.

The patient was admitted, and Carter was the first one to see him after he woke up.

When Carter walked in he found the boy doing strenuous exercises. Carter told him that he had just experienced a major coronary event and should take it easy. The boy explained that he was a wrestler on the junior varsity squad at Penn. Carter told him that his blood tests showed that he was not eating and then tried to impress upon him that he had almost died that morning.

Carter, who used to wrestle when he was younger, told the boy that he knew he was cycling his weight up and down between matches, and that it was a form of anorexia that would eventually kill him. The boy told Carter that he had a match against Western coming up and that he *had* to wrestle.

Carter knew his words were falling on deaf ears and left the boy to make his own decisions, as foolhardy and dangerous as they obviously were.

8.135. The three-hundred-pound diabetic in 2
Haleh briefed Doug on this patient, who was suffering from diabetic ketoacidosis. Doug told Haleh to see if there was an endocrinologist upstairs.

8.136. The cop with the superficial gunshot wound
Haleh called Peter for this patient.

8.137. Ben McCabe
This little boy was brought to the ER by his mother because he wasn't eating. Doug and Haleh examined him and discovered he had a fever of 100.2° and a sore throat.

Doug ordered an X-ray and told Haleh to have an intubation tray standing by in case his throat got worse.

While Doug was dealing with an irate internist (see Patient 8.138), Haleh interrupted and told him that Ben had stopped breathing. Doug told her to get an ENT (ear, nose, and throat) surgeon and told her the boy was hypoxic. Doug recognized the condition as epiglottitis (closure of the glottis, the space between the vocal cords at the top of the larynx: an almost complete airway obstruction).

Doug began intubation but could not accomplish the procedure successfully because of the closure. Peter came in and asked how long the boy had been without oxygen. When he was told two minutes, he suggested Doug immediately do a needle cricothyroidotomy (create a surgical airway), but Doug said, "not yet."

Peter grabbed a needle, waited a few more seconds, and then performed the needle cricothyroidotomy himself. He ordered a 3.0 endotracheal tube hooked to a catheter and ordered the child bagged and hyperventilated. The boy's blood oxygen saturation immediately went to 95 percent and his pulse went to 120.

Peter then ordered 750 milligrams of ceftriaxone (a cephalosporin antibiotic) IV q 12 (every twelve hours).

Peter then left the room. Doug called him a sonofabitch as he left.

Doug later confronted Peter about overstepping his bounds, and Peter admitted that the needle cricothyroidotomy was a judgment call that he should have let Doug make.

8.138. The irate internist's patient

Doug assigned one of this doctor's patients to a resident on call and the doctor was a tad upset about it. Doug stood his ground and defended his decision as acting chief ER resident.

8.139. Mrs. Benton, Dr. Benton's mother

Mrs. Benton was brought to the ER with a sprained ankle. She was a bit disoriented and asked Peter when he had grown his moustache, even though he had had it for three years. When she learned that Carter's father had family in Tennessee, she mused that she thought Carter's people had once owned her people. (Peter *loved* hearing that.)

Peter ordered Carter to take care of his mother's ankle, and then sent him to take care of Patient 8.141, all to prevent Carter from joining him in the O.R., something he knew Carter wanted to do.

8.140. The shunt

Morgenstern asked Peter to join him in the O.R. for this surgery.

8.141. The patient with lacerations in 2

Dr. Benton made Carter clean and stitch up this patient after he took care of Mrs. Benton's sprained ankle.

8.142. Mr. Randall

Mr. Randall was brought to the ER by the police. He was drunk, disorderly, and had a head laceration.

Susan had Div Cvetic called in for a suicide-depression assessment, and during his exam, Div and Susan learned that Mr. Randall had been in a car accident in which his wife had been smashed against a streetlight and his son's head had been cut off.

When Div tried to talk to him, Mr. Randall lunged at him, and Div ordered him committed for seventy-two hours. Susan was astonished and outraged.

Later, Susan went up to the psych ward and signed Mr. Randall out, without Div's approval or knowledge.

8.143. Mr. Kelman

The EMTs brought this fifteen-year-old patient to the ER cyanotic with diminished breath sounds on the right, and also hyporesonant. Peter identified a tracheal shift, a collapsed lung, and a tension pneumothorax and ordered a 14 gauge needle. After Mr. Kelman was stabilized, Peter left to assist Doug with Patient 8.137.

● ●

Original Broadcast Date:
Thursday, November 10, 1994
Written by Robert Nathan;
Directed by James Hayman

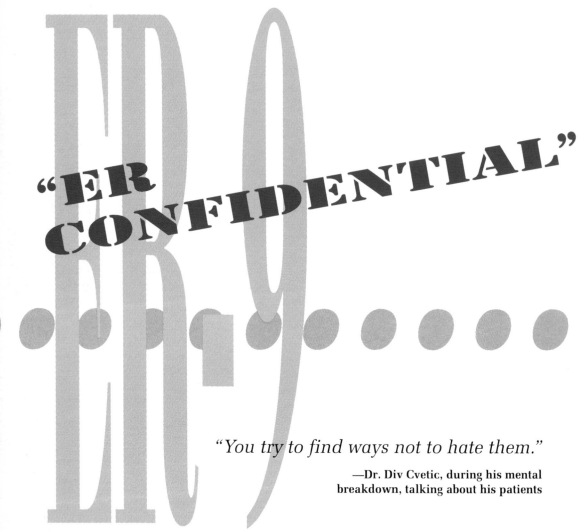

"ER CONFIDENTIAL"

"You try to find ways not to hate them."

**—Dr. Div Cvetic, during his mental
breakdown, talking about his patients**

This episode begins at 3:55 in the morning in Susan Lewis's apartment. Susan awakens and realizes that Div is not in bed with her. She finds him in the livingroom ostensibly dictating patient notes, but really talking about his hatred for his patients and how "every drop of pleasure has drained from [his] life."

Doug wakes up in Linda's apartment, and we learn that they are going to Nassau together for three days. Linda is not only paying Doug's way, she has also been buying him clothes and telling him how to dress.

At the ER, Bob puts up Halloween and Easter decorations for the Thanksgiving holiday and Carter practices doing sutures on a pig's foot. (He's got a half dozen of them in his refrigerator at home.)

Mark tells Carol that Jenn, Rachel, and Jenn's parents are coming to Chicago for Thanksgiving, and Carter tells Benton that he's planning on honoring Mrs. Benton's invitation by having Thanksgiving dinner with the Benton family. Peter is not pleased to hear this. (Carter's parents are in Switzerland visiting his sister.)

When discussing the car accident that brought the two patients Andy and Larry

to the ER, Doug reveals that he used to pin the speedometer on a pal's TR7 at 120 miles per hour; Carol admits she used to climb three-hundred-foot TV antennas with her friends; and Jerry confesses that he and a friend used to steal boxes of dynamite and play chicken with them. Mark is stunned by their revelations and admits that the worst thing he and Howie Dolan used to do was Chinese fire drills at the Velvet Freeze.

Over coffee, Susan confides in Mark that Div is exhibiting signs of a serious depression. Later we learn that Tag used to pluck turkeys as a kid. (This skill comes in handy when Patient 9.152 shows up at the ER.)

Susan has to deal with an obnoxious, critically ill patient, and Doug and Mark discuss the fact that Mark is a little boring and that he's never done anything irresponsible in his life.

Susan later visits Div in his office, where she finds him asleep. He awakens and admits to her that he's been difficult to get along with and pretty depressed lately, but promises Susan that he's coming for Thanksgiving dinner that evening.

While being wheeled to the O.R., a patient (Andy Bohlmeyer) confides to Carol that he was driving the car during the accident that killed two people, and later Carol tries to convince him to tell his mother and the police the truth.

The ER staff has a potluck dinner for Thanksgiving, and Haleh tells Peter it's a buffet and to get his own yams. While waiting for Doug, Linda gets annoyed when she realizes that hers and Doug's plane tickets are, OmiGod!, coach! (Not for long, however.)

Carol tells Tag that she slept with Doug Ross during the time she and Tag have been together and that two weeks ago he kissed her and she let him. Tag tells her to go to hell, but she tells him that she wants him, but just felt that she had to tell him about what happened.

Sarah tells Peter he did a great job on the emergency pericardial centesis and that she's leaving the next day for her Starzl Fellowship. Peter then talks to Carter about the upsetting suicide of Carter's patient Henry Carlton and insists that Carter come home with him for Thanksgiving dinner.

Back at her apartment, Susan repeatedly calls Div, but there's no answer. Chloe cooked the turkey, but only for a couple of hours. It's still raw, and when her "friend" Ronnie starts complaining and arguing with Chloe, Susan blasts both of them for acting like two children.

The episode ends with Div Cvetic standing in the middle of traffic in the pouring rain, challenging oncoming cars and talking to himself.

PATIENT HISTORIES

● ●

9.144. The wheezer in 3
Mark asked Carol what was holding up the blood gases on this patient.

9.145. The kid with the croup in 3

Lydia gave this patient to Doug.

9.146. Mr. Luck

This patient was an obnoxious, insulting creep (played by *Saturday Night Live*'s Garrett Morris) who had no kidneys and who came to the ER because he was in end-stage renal failure.

He was uremic and had a blood alcohol level of 250. The clinic where he usually went for dialysis had banned him because of his disruptive behavior and offensive remarks, and thus it was up to Susan to get him dialysed and save his life. When told he was about to be saved, Mr. Luck replied, "You know, the more I see of people, the more I like pigs."

Mr. Luck (who didn't believe in God and who also felt that the space shuttle program was a waste of money) underwent dialysis successfully, and Susan later contacted the clinic and persuaded them to take him back. Luck thanked Susan by saying, "Shove it, you little pinhead puke."

Susan got even with Mr. Luck in the end (pun intended), however. She told him he needed to have his temperature taken—rectally—and instead of a thermometer, she stuck a big sunflower in his butt and pulled open the curtain so that everyone in the ER could see him lying there with a flower growing out of his anus.

9.147. Henry Carlton (a.k.a. Miss Carlton)

Henry Carlton was an emotionally devastating experience for John Carter, since he was the first patient Carter ever lost.

Carlton, forty-two, was brought by ambulance to the ER after losing control of his car and hitting a bridge abutment. He was initially identified as a forty-two-year-old female because he was dressed and made-up completely as a woman.

Henry was alert and oriented, his vitals were normal, and Peter and Carter did the initial examination. While examining Carlton's head Carter found a deep laceration (about 10 centimeters), but no blood in his ear canals.

Peter identified a penetrating laceration on Henry's right side; a few scratches on his upper back; a contusion to his left scapula; abrasions along T3, 4, and 5 (3, 4, and 5 Thoracic vertebrae); and superficial bruises along the coccyx.

It was at this point that Carter called Peter's attention to Carlton's genitalia, which were obviously male. Henry then told them he preferred to be called "Miss" Carlton.

Carter sewed up Henry's scalp laceration with 40 absorbable subcutaneous thread. Mark checked the sutures and said he did a good job.

During the stitching, Henry confided in Carter that it took him three hours to put on his makeup every morning, and still people noticed. Carter, clearly uncomfortable with Henry's blatant honesty, remained guarded and cooly professional.

Later, Jerry came running to tell Carter there was a jumper on the roof. The jumper was Henry, and Carter tried to convince him to come down. "I can't pass for a

woman anymore," he told him. "That's all I've ever wanted to be." At this point Div showed up, but before he could do or say much of anything, Henry jumped and landed on a parked car.

Carter was emotionally destroyed by the suicide, and later Peter tried to convince him that it wasn't his fault and that he, as the more experienced resident, should have recognized Henry's car accident as a suicide attempt.

9.148. Larry Parks

Teenaged Larry was brought to the ER in full cardiac arrest with massive head injuries and no vital signs. He also had no heart sounds, and there was a lot of gray matter visible from his head injury.

Sarah and Doug worked on Larry for over a half hour, using external heart massage and other trauma protocols, but there was no hope.

Finally, Sarah declared Larry dead at 9:33.

9.149. Andy Bohlmeyer

Teenager Andy Bohlmeyer was actually driving Larry Parks's car when the accident that killed Larry Parks and a twenty-two-year-old pedestrian occurred.

Andy was conscious when he was brought to the ER by ambulance. His pressure was 90/60, his pulse was 110, and he had a broken right femur.

He was in a lot of pain, so Mark gave him 50 milligrams of Demerol and did a peritoneal lavage to see if he was bleeding internally. He was, and he was then brought to the O.R. where his spleen was removed successfully.

9.150. The decapitated girl

This twenty-two-year-old woman was killed when she was hit by Larry Parks's car, which was being driven by Andy Bohlmeyer. Andy hit her when he ran a red light at high speed and decapitated her. She was left at the scene by the EMTs to be picked up by the coroner.

9.151. The kid with the swollen elbow

This was a patient Doug wanted Tag to look at, but Tag had to kiss Carol first.

9.152. Francis the animal rights activist

Francis was attacked by a wild Narragansett tom turkey when he tried to steal the bird from a display that he believed was exploiting animals.

Doug treated Francis for multiple facial lacerations, and then Francis remained at the ER to eat the turkey whose neck he had broken when it attacked him. (Tag did the plucking.)

9.153. Dr. Div Cvetic

Div technically became a patient in Susan's eyes when she discussed him with Mark. She confided in Mark that Div was experiencing signs of major depression.

9.154. The old lady in the bed next to Andy Bohlmeyer

Carol poured a drink for this woman as she listened to Andy lie and tell his mother that it was Larry Parks who was driving the car.

9.155. The woman with lupus

This forty-year-old woman presented at the ER with chest pain. Mark and Haleh initially saw her, and Mark ordered an EKG, a cardiac enzyme test, and a chest film and told Haleh to call for a cardiac consult.

Mark learned that the patient had a history of lupus, which was in remission, and that she had been treated with prednisone.

Her heart rate was 112 and her pulse was paradoxus. Her EKG showed ST elevation (S and T waves) and Mark confirmed an effusion. There was also a silhouette sign on her X-ray. While being monitored, her blood pressure began to drop and she slipped into unconsciousness. Sarah determined the woman needed a pericardial centesis and told Peter to get an 18 gauge needle and an alligator clip. In the meantime, Mark went to explain to the patient's husband that his wife's pericardium was filling with fluid, and that they needed to go in and drain it.

Peter asked Sarah if he could do the procedure, and she willingly agreed. He ran into difficulty, however, because the fluid was infected and too thick for the needle. The patient began to fibrillate and Mark had to shock her.

Sarah instructed Peter to do a window in the patient's chest of about 8 centimeters and suction the fluid out of the pericardium.

Peter successfully performed the emergency operation, and the patient's heart began to beat normally after the infected fluid was removed.

The woman recovered and was fine.

● ●

Original Broadcast Date:
Thursday, November 17, 1994
Written by Paul Manning;
Directed by Daniel Sackheim

ER-10 "BLIZZARD"

"County General on full open status."

—Carol Hathaway, to Dispatch before
the multivehicle accident

"Never say 'dead' to a charge nurse."

—Carol Hathaway, to Mark after he tells
her the ER has been dead

"Implement Disaster Protocol."

—Dispatch, to Carol *after* the
multivehicle accident

*"My brother in faith, I entrust you to God who
created you. May you return to the one who formed
you from the dust of this earth."*

—A nun, praying over Mr. Ramos

This incredible episode starts off quietly.

Jerry walks through the snow on his way to work, singing "Jingle Bells," and it is a full fifteen minutes into the episode before the ER staff sees their first patient.

With seventeen shopping days left until Christmas, a record-breaking monster snowstorm (the biggest since January 1967) has dumped seven inches on the ground before dawn, and much more is expected.

The ER is so slow that the staff has turned to snowball fights, pranks (see Patient 10.156), and games of desk-chair hockey. Even the perpetually busy Haleh finds time to do a crossword puzzle, and Malik takes over the P.A. for an impromptu rap with Mookie.

We learn that Mark's wife, Jenn, left for Milwaukee early; and Carol shows off her engagement ring and announces that she and Tag are getting married. Doug is crushed but puts up a good front, congratulating Carol in front of the others.

Linda Farrell's Lexus gets snowplowed in, and when she notices Carol's ring she does an on-the-spot appraisal—Marquise cut, two carat, F color, SI-1 (slightly imperfect), platinum setting—and then tells Carol that she's wearing a twelve-thousand-dollar ring. Carol is stunned, to say the least.

And then all hell breaks loose.

Dispatch calls the ER and tells them to implement Disaster Protocol. There has been a multivehicle pileup on the Kennedy Expressway with fifty to one hundred casualties, all of whom are on their way to Dr. Greene and company.

The patients start streaming in, and the ER staff triages them at the door: green for Walking Wounded; yellow for Urgent; red for Critical; and black for DOA.

Dr. Morgenstern finally arrives, and Mark runs the situation down for him: There was a forty-car pileup and they were the major receiver. They logged in eighteen red tags, ten of which went up for surgery; nineteen yellow tags; and thirty-three green tags. They had three DOAs and four black tags that didn't make it. Six O.R.s are operational and the fire department is out bringing in fresh doctors.

In the midst of the chaos, Dr. Angela Hicks, the new attending ER physician, shows up for her first day of work, and Doug unknowingly gives her bedpan duty. When she tells him who she is, he says, "Oops."

Linda Farrell pitches in by answering the phone and ordering thirty large pizzas delivered to the ER, while Patrick plays peekaboo with a lost little girl. Patrick also plays Christmas tapes over the P.A. and fixes the decorations for Bob.

Ultimately, close to one hundred patients are seen and treated at the ER. The flow of injured finally stops and thirty pizzas arrive.

Patrick dims the lights and puts on a Nat King Cole Christmas tape as the staff takes a breather and eats pizza.

Mark chooses to leave instead of hanging around with the others, and, as he's walking out, Mr. and Mrs. Blinker arrive with their new baby. "God bless you, Dr.

Greene," Mr. Blinker exclaims as he embraces Mark. The Blinkers go into the hospital, and the episode ends with Mark walking off through the snow to go home alone to an empty house. Merry Christmas, indeed.

PATIENT HISTORIES

10.156. John Carter

Carter became an unwilling patient at the ER when Mark and Susan put a full leg cast on his right leg as he slept in an examination room. Mark decided to put a cast on him because he felt that putting Carter's hand in a bucket of warm water would be juvenile.

Carter's cast was removed by a motorcyclist named Ace (Patient 10.184) who knew how to wield a power saw.

10.157. Dr. Doug Ross

Doug was not actually treated at the ER for his groin pull, but his vacation injury *was* mentioned by Linda Farrell in front of the ER staff when she and Doug returned from the Bahamas.

10.158. Mrs. Blinker

Mrs. Blinker's husband called the ER because his wife was in labor. Mark took the call and, after hearing how far apart her contractions were, told Mr. Blinker, "Call 911 now."

Mr. Blinker called later to tell Mark that his wife had locked herself in the bedroom and wouldn't let him in because she wanted to deliver the baby at home while watching the snow fall. Mark told him to break down the door.

Mr. Blinker called one last time, while Mark was in surgery working on Dexter's reamputation (Patient 10.173), and Mark talked him through delivering his own son.

Mark met Mr. and Mrs. Blinker when they arrived at the ER as he was leaving for the day.

10.159. Infant

A firefighter was seen bringing this crying infant into the ER.

10.160. The burn victim

This patient was trapped in a cab, and when he was first brought to the ER he was hypotensive. Comacho, the EMT, reported second- and third-degree burns over an estimated 25 percent of his body surface. He was red-tagged to Trauma 2.

Peter treated this man and removed 500 cc of fluid from his right chest. He determined the patient had 18 percent second-degree burns and 9 percent third degree-burns over his leg, abdomen, and right shoulder and then turned the patient over to Dr. Bradley.

10.161. The head wound

This patient had a bleeding head wound and Doug green-tagged him and sent him to the waiting room.

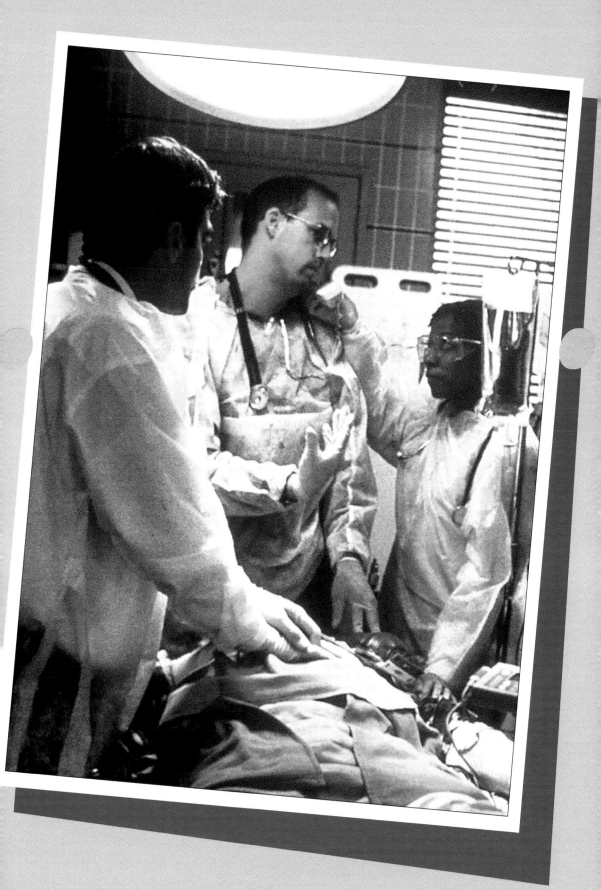

10.162. The truck roll

This twenty-five-year-old man was in a truck roll without a seatbelt and was in full arrest when he arrived at the ER. Malik performed CPR and external heart massage.

Mark took charge and gave this patient to an ER doctor, telling him, "Do what you can and move on." It isn't known for certain whether or not the patient pulled through, although it seems unlikely, since Mark later told Dr. Morgenstern that four black tags had not made it. This patient was probably one of the four black tags Mark was talking about.

10.163. The spinal shock

This patient was brought in with a suspected spinal-cord injury. His legs were flaccid, and Susan ordered a call for a neurosurgical backup consult. The patient's blood pressure was 90/60 and his pulse was 60. Mark ordered his blood typed and crossmatched for two units and a CBC.

The patient exhibited flaccid paralysis and areflexia, and they decided to cancel the cervical-spine films and instead do a spinal X-ray and a CT.

Mark told Susan to consider spinal shock and then moved on to his next patient.

10.164. The neck injury

This patient was lying on a gurney in the hall when Carter walked by and noticed that he was trying to take off his neck collar. The patient told Carter that he "had to take a leak" and that his neck injury was no big deal. It was only whiplash, he said.

Carter told him that if he was wrong and it was really a spinal fracture then he could end up a quadriplegic if he did any more damage by walking around.

The guy stayed put.

10.165. The hand wound

This rather nervous Spanish gentleman presented with nothing more than a small puncture wound in his hand. ("Poquito," Carol told him.) He fainted anyway.

10.166. The right-hip trauma

This elderly woman was in a car accident in the blizzard and had neck, chest, and right-hip trauma. Peter ordered "rings and relief": Ringers solution (see the Glossary) and 5 milligrams of morphine IV push. He also ordered a cross-table c-spine X-ray as well as X-rays of her right hip and pelvis. He then told Conni to round up a bone crusher.

10.167. The eye injury

This elderly woman had an eye injury, and Doug ordered her eye double-patched and told Carol to green-tag her and send her to the waiting room.

Doug was less than thrilled that the patient wanted to talk to Carol about the huge engagement ring Tag had given her.

10.168. Edward Kaplan

Mr. Kaplan ("Call me Eddie") had neck, back, and abdominal pain, a falling blood pressure of 70/40, and a pulse of 120. His skin was cool and dry.

When Susan asked him how he was feeling, he replied, "Haven't been tied up this tight since last Saturday night." Susan responded, "Thank you for sharing, Mr. Kaplan."

As part of his treatment, Mr. Kaplan had a Foley catheter inserted, something he was not too thrilled about.

10.169. The firefighter with smoke inhalation

This patient was in serious enough condition from smoke inhalation that Doug ordered him yellow-tagged and sent to curtain area 2.

10.170. The thumb amputation

This teenager walked into the ER with his hand wrapped in a cloth. When Doug unwrapped the hand he saw that the boy's thumb was missing. When he asked him where his thumb was, the boy handed him a plastic bag with the finger inside.

Doug ordered him red-tagged and sent immediately to surgery.

10.171. Mrs. Twee

Mrs. Twee, who did not speak English, came to the ER to pick up her husband, (Patient 10.184). Mr. Twee had been in a car accident, had been treated, and was ready to go home.

The fact that Mrs. Twee was not a patient was not something Carter was aware of, and he sedated her and told her husband she was resting comfortably when he came looking for her.

Oops.

10.172. Ashley

This little girl was found in the snow after the pileup and was kept at the ER until her parents tracked her down. She was not hurt. Haleh sang to her and Patrick played peekaboo with her.

10.173. Dexter

Dex lost his leg in the big accident and was brought to the ER with the limb still not found and presumed to be at the site of the crash. While EMTs searched for the leg, Dex was put in Trauma 1, and Peter ordered his blood typed and crossmatched and a CBC.

There was a tourniquet on the remainder of Dex's leg, and Peter yelled at Mookie to put pressure on the bleed, telling him he'd make a surgeon out of him yet. Mookie, a street kid who had been in and out of trouble all his life, was stunned by this possibility, and it was obvious that Peter's remark was a moment of epiphany for him.

Dexter was panicked, agitated, and hysterical and his blood oxygen saturation was only 62. Peter ordered a rapid-sequence intubation and had Dex injected with Pavulon (a paralyzing drug), Versed (a powerful benzodiazepine sedative), and 2 milligrams of succinylcholine (a short-acting muscle relaxant). Dex had recognized Peter from their old neighborhood, and Peter wanted to do all he could for him.

Dr. Hicks arrived and asked for the bullet (a rapid briefing on the patient's situation). Peter told her they had a left below-the-knee amputation with estimated blood loss at 30 to 40 percent. The patient had a bilateral hemothorax and 750 cc of fluid had been removed from a right thoracostomy. A rapid sequence intubation had been performed and succinylcholine and Pavulon administered. A Foley had been inserted and ringers and six units of O negative administered. The cervical spine was cleared and his vitals were stablized.

After this rapid-fire delivery, Dr. Hicks asked if he was Peter Benton. When Peter said he was, she said she'd heard about him.

At this point Dex went into ventricular fibrillation. He was shocked at 200 joules, and his heart quickly converted to normal rhythm.

Dex remained stable and in a "holding pattern for vascular" with a blood pressure of 110/70 and a strong pulse of 112. His oxygen saturation was at 95 percent, and he was given a total of 8 units of packed cells and 4 liters of Ringer's.

It was then that an EMT brought in Dex's amputated leg.

Because the vascular team was still occupied, Dr. Hicks decided to begin the reamputation in the ER, with Peter, Mark, and Doug all taking part in the surgery.

Surgery went well (although Dex had to be given .5 milligrams of atropine because he was cyanotic as hell) and Dr. Hicks confirmed blood flow and finally announced that Peter's friend Dex had his tibial artery back.

Peter then knew that Dex would walk again.

10.174. The woman in labor
Malik was seen wheeling this patient through the ER.

10.175. The DOA
This patient was trapped in a car during the big accident and was dead on arrival when he or she arrived at the ER. Doug pronounced this unnamed patient DOA and pulled the sheet up over his or her head.

10.176. Mr. Ramos
Mr. Ramos was wearing his seatbelt when he was in the blizzard pileup and when he presented at the ER his vitals were normal. Doug determined that all he had were multiple contusions and abrasions. He was green-tagged and sent to wait in the doctors' lounge.

Shortly thereafter, Jerry came to Doug and asked him if Mr. Ramos was supposed to be dead. While waiting for treatment Mr. Ramos had experienced chest pains and had then gone into full cardiac arrest.

Doug worked valiantly to resuscitate him by performing CPR and external heart massage, but to no avail. Mr. Ramos's EKG showed a flat line, and Doug then ordered an external pacemaker, which, unfortunately, did not capture.

After thirty minutes, Mr. Ramos's pupils were fixed and dilated, and Doug finally called time of death. "I green-tagged him by mistake," he told Mark. "I missed it."

Mark reminded Doug that he had triaged over seventy patients and that he was

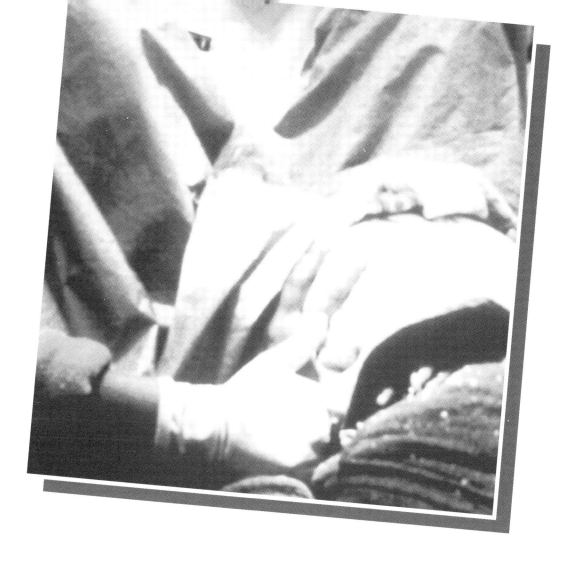

human, but it did not console Doug. Doug personally informed Mr. Ramos's wife and family of his death.

10.177. The firefighter in full arrest
This patient was in full arrest when he arrived at the ER, and CPR was performed. It isn't known if he pulled through.

10.178. Regina
Even though we had never seen her before, the ER staff was apparently very familiar with this female psychotic.

Regina showed up while the ER staff members were all trying to deal with the victims of the multivehicle accident She complained that aliens had implanted something in her nose. Doug told Carol to page Cvetic (whom we know from last episode was nowhere to be found) and to give Regina a quiet room and "five of Vitamin H." Doug was actually ordering 5 milligrams of Haldol and Regina knew it: As Carol led her away she shouted that the things in her nose could detect abbreviations.

10.179. The guy with the cigarette lighter embedded in his chest

This guy had chest pain, and for good reason: His car's cigarette lighter was embedded in his chest. (He had gotten hit from behind while trying to light a cigarette.) When Mark opened his shirt and saw the lighter sticking out of his chest, he said, "Ouch."

10.180. The impatient skier

This yuppie-ish guy injured his left wrist, although it wasn't said if he, too, was in the big accident or if he had done it skiing.

He was impatient and arrogant, and Jerry promised him an ice bag for his wrist, but basically blew him off.

A short while passed, and this guy then interrupted Susan to ask how long he would have to wait.

10.181. The head laceration

Dr. Steve Flint, the radiologist, sutured this patient's head laceration, even though he had not done sutures in years. During the sewing, Carter asked Flint to review an X-ray for him, and Flint confirmed that Carter's patient did indeed have a trimalleoli fracture and that Carter should call Ortho.

Carter noticed Flint's suturing technique and told him that if he threw a deep dermal in there and trimmed the edge, the suture would line up a lot better.

10.182. The patient with a fracture

Carter asked Dr. Flint to look at this patient's X-ray to confirm a trimalleoli fracture.

10.183. Morris Bozinsky

Elderly Mr. Bozinsky was in the big blizzard accident, and was brought to the ER with no apparent injuries. His blood pressure was okay, but his pulse was a little high at 120. His capillary refill was questionable, and Susan decided to do a set of postural vitals. She also ordered Malik to run in a 300 cc fluid challenge.

Throughout Susan's evaluation and treatment of Mr. Bozinsky, his wife Myra questioned every decision and insisted that her husband's *real* doctor, Dr. Harvey Stern, be called.

Before long, Morris's blood pressure dropped to 60 palp and his trouble began: Morris registered no femoral pulse, and Susan diagnosed an aortic aneurysm ready to burst.

Since there were twenty-two surgeries in progress, and no surgeons available, Susan decided to do the surgery (cross-clamping the aorta) in the ER. She ran to get Hicks or Benton to do the actual procedure, and when she was gone, Morris coded.

Lydia and Wendy opened his IVs wide and gave him an amp of epinephrine and a gram of atropine, but it was obvious he was bleeding out.

Just when it looked like he was going to bleed to death and no one would be able to save him, Bob, the Polish desk clerk, pulled on a pair of rubber gloves, grabbed a scalpel, and performed the surgery, as Lydia and Wendy watched in stunned disbelief.

Bob saved Morris's life and, when he registered a pulse, ran out of the ER in tears.

Later, Dr. Morgenstern, who had no idea what had happened, congratulated Susan on a job well done.

As Carter was leaving for the day he found Bob sitting on the curb crying. She told him what had happened, and he learned that in Poland she was a vascular surgeon and that now, after illegally operating on someone, she was afraid that she'd never be allowed to become a surgeon in America. Carter assured her they'd be grateful she had saved a patient's life and promised to help her with her English for the board exams.

10.184. Mr. Twee

Mr. Twee was treated at the ER for a head injury he sustained in the accident. (See Patient 10.171.)

10.185. The patient in trauma 1

Mookie summoned Dr. Lewis to treat this patient, whose injury or illness was not specified.

10.186. Ace

Ace was a biker who got a big kick out of Carol when she told him that at the ER they called motorcycles "donorcycles."

Carol wheeled him into an examination room where Carter was trying to scratch inside his cast. Ace sympathized and told Carter that he had once had eight casts in six months.

Ace then cut off Carter's cast with an electric saw. He scared the hell out of our Dr. Carter when he came at him like Leatherface in the *Texas Chainsaw Massacre* movies!

● ●

Original Broadcast Date:
Thursday, December 8, 1994
Story by Neal Baer and Paul Manning;
Teleplay by Lance Gentile;
Directed by Mimi Leder

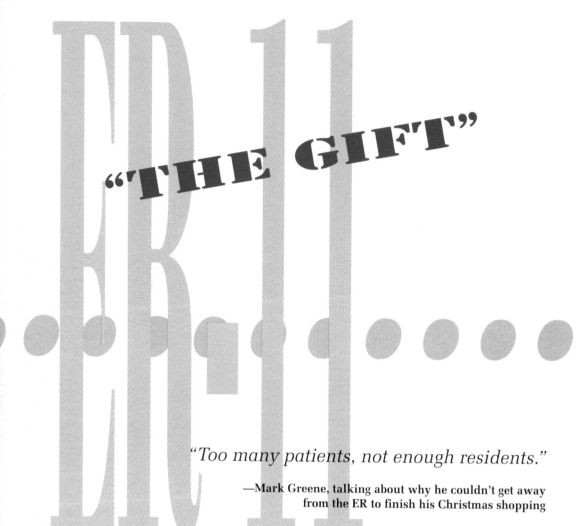

"THE GIFT"

ER-11

"Too many patients, not enough residents."

—Mark Greene, talking about why he couldn't get away
from the ER to finish his Christmas shopping

"You gotta know when to jump."

—Doug Ross, to Carter, after Carter was vomited
on by a little kid who ate part of a poinsettia plant

"Stay out of my life."

—Carol Hathaway, to Doug, after Doug
made a scene at her engagement party

This powerful and moving Christmas episode, which takes place on Christmas Eve, begins with Santa Claus and ends with a life-saving gift flying off into the sky early on Christmas morning.

Mark is in a quandary: He has already bought skates for Rachel, but he hasn't been able to get anything yet for Jenn. He gets increasingly worried and frustrated (last year he got her a Dustbuster and look at where *that* got him!) as he continually tries to

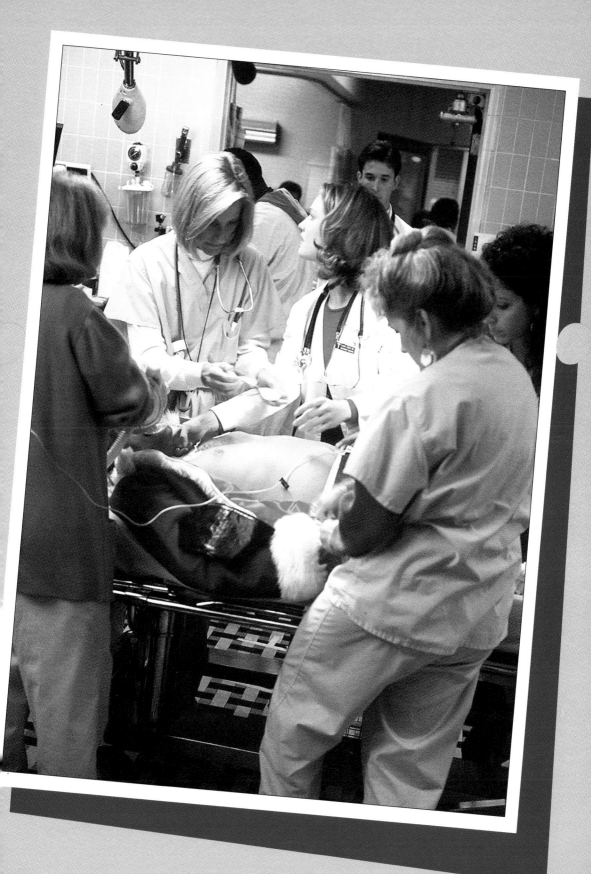

sign out and go shopping, but never seems to be able to get out the door.

This evening is Carol and Tag's engagement party. Mark asks Doug if he's going, and Doug tells him he wasn't invited. He's going to Winnetka to eat goose in a tux with Linda Farrell's parents.

Lydia kisses Mark after tricking him into standing under mistletoe, and Linda comes in looking for Doug. She hears of Mark's predicament and offers to get him something for Jenn. ("I'm a killer shopper.") Carter puts on the bow tie and suspenders that he received from his Secret Santa Haleh, and Jerry mans the ER desk in a red elf suit. Peter jeopardizes his career when he calls in a transplant *before* obtaining permission to harvest a brain-dead patient's organs from the patient's next-of-kin.

Susan, who has not been able to reach Div all day, learns from Timmy that Div has quit and asks Carter for a ride to Div's apartment. When they arrive, Susan is stunned to find the place torn apart and almost empty. Div moved out and didn't even tell her.

When Carter takes Susan to her own apartment, he reveals that he's her Secret Santa and gives her a music box. She kisses him on the cheek, and Carter tries to kiss her back, this time on the lips. Susan almost gives in, but stops at the last minute. Instead she gives him Div's gift (a bathrobe), and he gets caught by Susan's neighbors modeling it in the hall.

In the doctor's lounge Doug admits to Mark that he thinks about Carol all the time, and Mark tells him, "She's not married yet."

Doug goes to meet Linda, but at the last minute changes his mind and instead goes to the restaurant where Carol's engagement party is taking place. He goes in and confronts Carol and tells her he loves her. She tells him she does *not* love him, and, when Tag comes out, Doug demands that she admit she thinks about him when she's with Tag. Tag decks him with one punch, and Carol tells Doug to stay out of her life.

Back at Susan's, Chloe wakes up and tells Susan that she's pregnant and that she's naming the baby after her. Susan is stunned by this news and is clearly overwhelmed by the turn of events of this evening that began with learning about Div's disappearance.

Back at the ER, Haleh puts a red bow on the container holding a heart for transplant, and the episode ends with Mary Cavanaugh singing "Have Yourself a Merry Little Christmas" as Peter's gift of life flies off to Cincinnati.

PATIENT HISTORIES

11.187. Santa Claus

This patient made his first appearance sitting in full Santa Claus costume in a wheelchair in the ER waiting room. He was asleep, and Carter woke him up. It turned out that Santa came to the hospital because he felt dizzy, which he attributed to working double shifts. When he saw that it was ten o'clock, he insisted on leaving the ER without even letting Carter check his blood pressure. Kids would be lined up waiting for him, and he did not want to disappoint them. Carter reluctantly let him leave.

Later that day, Santa was brought back to the ER not breathing. Susan called a code (signaled a patient is in arrest), and Carter explained to her that Saint Nick had left that morning AMA (Against Medical Advice).

Santa had no pulse, and blood gases were ordered, along with an amp of epinephrine and 1 milligram of atropine in an IV.

Even though they used all their resources, Santa (who had no ID on him) died at 19:22. Carter was devastated and kept saying, "I killed Santa."

11.188. Raymond
We don't know anything about this patient except that Haleh told Susan that he or she was waiting to be discharged, along with Zinberg and Wu.

11.189. Zinberg
This was one of the three patients (along with Raymond and Wu) that Haleh told Mark were waiting to be discharged.

11.190. Wu
This was one of the three patients (along with Raymond and Zinberg) that Haleh told Mark were waiting to be discharged.

11.191. Regina
This patient (who was also Patient 10.178) was busy hallucinating in an examination room and Mark, Haleh, and Lydia treated her by comforting her and singing "It's My Party" with her. (For some reason she was convinced that the Grinch had spiked her eggnog.) Mark also ordered her given 5 milligrams of Haldol.

11.192. Mr. O'Neill
Mr. O'Neill opened up his hand as he was opening up a can of mixed nuts. Peter began suturing him and then turned him over to Susan when Teddy Powell (Patient 11.197) was brought in on the chopper.

11.193. Mr. Kaminski
Mr. Kaminski was a Christmas lights buff (fanatic is more like it) and every year strung so many bulbs on his house (86,239 to be precise) that he used enough wattage to light ten city blocks.

He came to the ER after receiving severe electrical burns on both arms when he tried to tap into the main power box after the electric company told him he couldn't use any more electricity.

Susan ordered a CBC, lytes, and a CPK (creatine phospholcinase) test to make sure there was no muscular damage and kept him on the EKG to make sure the power surge did not hurt his heart. She prescribed a topical antibiotic for the burns and finally told him that the EKG showed no permanent damage.

"How can that machine tell about a broken heart?" Kaminski asked her.

As Mr. Kaminski was leaving, Susan gave him a bag of Christmas lights, antique twinklers that she had swiped off the main desk. He said they would go perfectly with next year's "An Olde Fashioned Christmas" theme. (This year it had been "An Alpine Christmas.")

11.194. The weak and dizzy all over in 2
Lydia gave this patient to Susan.

11.195. The torn cartilage in 3
Lydia also gave this patient to Susan.

11.196. Murray Valerio
Near-drowning victim Murray was brought to the ER by his father, Dante, after the boy was submerged under water in a lake for around five minutes. (They were ice fishing and the ice broke.) Murray was cyanotic and not breathing, and Mark and Doug began treatment in Trauma 1.

The boy's blood pressure was 30 palp with a weak pulse, and his heart rate was bradycardic at 32. His body temperature was 80°. They started pulmonary suction, and Mark ordered a 5.5 ET tube for laryngyscopic examination. Mark also ordered blood studies, a coag panel, and a chest film.

They treated Murray with heated humidified oxygen, and Doug suggested pleural lavage to warm up his heart, to which Mark agreed. Mark asked Lydia to get two 36 gauge French thoracostomy tubes and told the team that they might have to do a cardiopulmonary bypass.

During treatment Murray went into asystole (see the Glossary) and Doug suggested atropine, which Mark vetoed because the boy's body temperature was too low.

They eventually got Murray's heart restarted and continued the warm peritoneal lavage. His clotting factors looked normal, and they also continued the warm IVs. Murray's temperature rose to 86° and his blood pressure remained steady. Murray eventually opened his eyes spontaneously but he manifested no signs of recognition or vocal responses to Doug's telling him "Merry Christmas."

They continued to monitor and treat Murray, but he still didn't make a sound, and they all worried about permanent brain damage. (He didn't even respond to Mrs. Cavanaugh and Patrick singing "We Three Kings" to him!)

Finally, right around midnight on Christmas Eve, Murray's EEG (electroencephalogram) showed a normal reading and he recognized his father.

Dante Valerio's greatest Christmas gift was getting his son back.

11.197. Teddy Powell

Teddy Powell, twenty-five, was not wearing a helmet when he crashed his snowmobile on a golf course. When he was brought to the ER, his pulse was 110, his blood pressure was 140/90, his respirations were 12 and agonal, his GCS was 4, he was hypoxic, and his right pupil was blown. (See Glossary for *agonal*, *GCS*, and *hypoxic*.)

The EMTs had tubed him in the field and suctioned CO_2 out of a right hemothorax. On their way to a trauma room, Dr. Benton asked John Carter for a diagnosis. Carter told him the patient had a hematoma on the right side, the same side as the blown pupil, and that his prognosis was poor.

Peter ordered Powell hyperventilated. His blood pressure was 130/90, and Peter ordered Mark to rapid bolus him with 75 grams of mannitol. Powell manifested a positive Babinski's reflex but had cerebrospinal fluid draining from his ear. Peter ordered a head CT and a nuclear scan and told Haleh to track down his next of kin. He told Carter to ascertain Powell's blood type.

Dr. Hicks told Peter that he would have to keep Powell as his patient. The patient had a big right-side bleed with a midline shift that was herniated, and there was no optic activity in his brain stem. When Carter asked Benton if there was anything they could do for Powell, Benton gruffly told him that Powell was brain dead.

They decided to keep his heart beating until the next of kin okayed harvesting his organs (even though his driver's license identified him as an organ donor). They put him on a ventilator, and Peter explained to Carter that the machine would keep Powell's blood hyperoxygenated and his heart, liver, and kidneys profused until he was ready for harvesting.

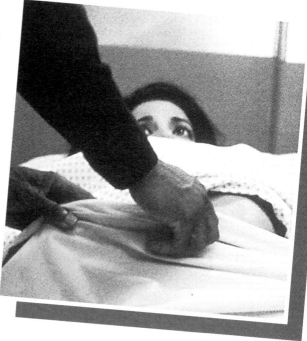

Connie told Peter that Powell might be going into DIC (disseminated intravascular coagulation; see the Glossary) and Peter ordered 10 packs of platelets and 2 units of fresh frozen plasma. As this point, Powell went into ventricular fibrillation. Peter shocked him at 100 joules and Powell converted to normal sinus rhythm. ("I just resuscitated a dead man," Peter mused.)

Mrs. Powell finally arrived, but would not consent to signing the release form allowing them to harvest her husband's organs. Against all hope, she wanted a second opinion. Peter, however, had already called in the transplant team and notified the recipients, and he asked Mark to speak to Mrs. Powell as a last resort.

Time was running out, and Powell began developing neurogenic pulmonary edema. Peter ordered renal range dopamine, 40 milligrams of Lasix, and Powell's vent pressure increased to ten. Even with this, it would only be an hour or so before they began losing organs.

Mark talked to Mrs. Powell and learned that she and Teddy had been separated for five months and that she had turned him down when he had asked her to spend Christmas with him the day before.

Later, back in Powell's room, Peter (who was losing all hope of seeing the transplants completed) told Mrs. Powell that they were running out of time. "So what?" she arrogantly replied . . . and then, miraculously, asked for the form to sign.

Peter and Hicks did the harvesting, stopping Powell's heart with an aorta cross clamp at 20:48. Peter sewed up Powell's chest himself and personally carried the heart (which was only good for three hours) up to the chopper pad on the roof.

The chopper took off, and the episode ended with Peter standing on the roof and smiling as he watched it fly off into the early Christmas morning.

11.198. Patrick

Patrick returned to the ER [he was last a patient in episode 7] with a head laceration sustained when he fell down while not wearing his football helmet.

Mark sutured him, and Patrick asked Carol (his favorite) if he could have some chocolate milk. He then told them the following riddle:

Q: Why did the cat walk on sand?
A: To get "sandy claws!"

Later, Malik brought Carol a leather helmet from the Neurology Department and Carol convinced Patrick to put it on.

Patrick had been left with neighbors when his family went away for Christmas and had wandered down to the ER by himself.

Patrick and Mrs. Cavanaugh (Patient 11.205) later serenaded Murray Valerio (Patient 11.196) with "We Three Kings."

11.199. The stabbing victim

Camacho the EMT brought in this sixty-year-old man with a penetrating stab wound to the mid-abdomen. He had been mugged in a parking lot.

On the way to the ER the patient's blood pressure crashed at 60, but they got him up to 130 with a 1,000 cc IV of normal saline. The patient lost 200 ccs of blood, but his bleeding was contained by the time he arrived at the hospital.

Mark ordered 6 units of O negative and ordered the O.R. notified to prep for a possible laparotomy.

It was finally determined that the patient had a mesenteric rupture, which was successfully repaired surgically. Later Peter congratulated Mark for his quick and decisive diagnosis and referral to surgery.

11.200. The guy in Cincinnati needing a heart transplant

This patient was the recipient of Teddy Powell's (Patient 11.197) heart.

11.201. The woman in Altoona needing a liver

This patient was the recipient of Teddy Powell's (Patient 11.197) liver.

11.202. Mrs. Goldberg

Mrs. Goldberg presented at the ER with abdominal pain. Susan performed an ultrasound, which showed no gallstones, but which did reveal a twelve-week-old baby with a steady heartbeat.

Mrs. Goldberg was ecstatic and told Susan that she and her husband Aaron had been trying for years, but without success.

Susan notified Obstetrics.

11.203. Kirby Bower

Kirby was a fat little kid who ate some poinsettia leaves and threw up on Carter when he tried to get him to open his mouth so he could look down his throat.

11.204. Mrs. Abernathy

Mrs. Abernathy came to the ER because she had not been sleeping and was depressed. Doug examined her and prescribed an antidepressant and gave her the name of a therapist.

As she was leaving, Mrs. Abernathy told Doug the story of how she had turned down a marriage proposal forty years earlier because the boy had been Jewish, and that when she had tried to reestablish contact last year, she learned that he had died three years earlier.

Doug realized that this was what she had been talking about when she said she had made some horrible mistakes in her life. Thinking about this was apparently what prompted Doug to crash Carol's engagement party and make a scene.

11.205. Mary Cavanaugh

Mrs. Cavanaugh showed up at the ER after being left with cousins for the Christmas holidays. Her Alzheimer's had gotten a lot worse and she wandered the halls singing Christmas carols, including a poignant "Have Yourself a Merry Little Christmas."

11.206. The bunch of choir kids

Carol told Mark these kids were coming in and that they had all been in a minor fender bender that resulted in nothing but cuts and scrapes.

● ●

Original Broadcast Date:
Thursday, December 15, 1994
Written by Neal Baer;
Directed by Felix Enriquez Alcalá

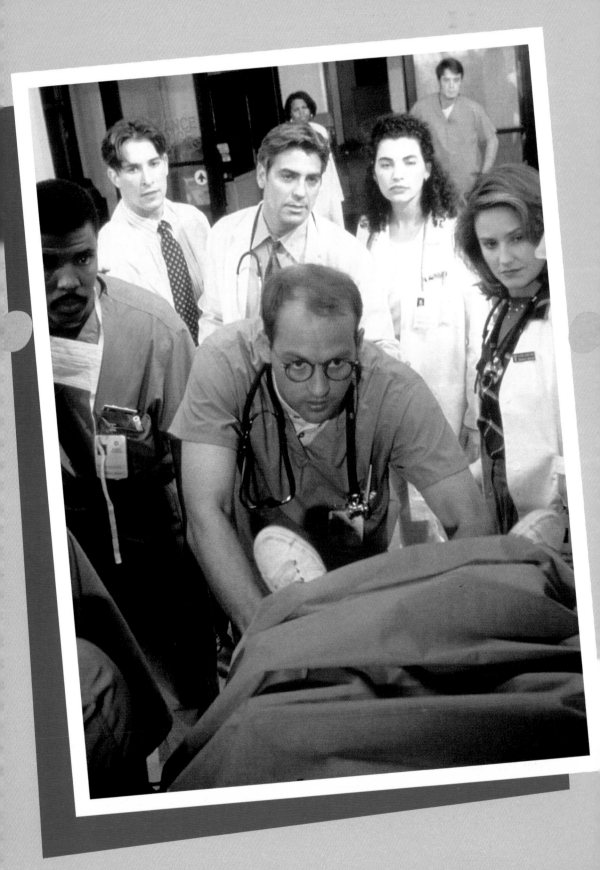

"HAPPY NEW YEAR"

ER 12

"I love my sister, Mark, but she can't even part her hair. So do I think she should bring a child into this world? No, I do not."

—Susan Lewis, to Mark, talking about Chloe's decision to have a baby

This episode starts with Carter doing his first successful intubation and ends with Susan being accused of having caused a patient's death.

Chloe comes to the hospital to tell Susan that she's moving to Texas, where her boyfriend Ronni has an uncle who works in a refinery. Susan doesn't want Chloe to have the baby, and Chloe tells her she doesn't want to stay with people who always think she's doing the wrong thing. Susan gives Chloe her winter coat and watches through the diner window as she walks away.

Peter and his sister Jackie meet for coffee to discuss their mother. Jackie tells Peter that she has a new job with the Parks Department and makes it clear that she can't do for Momma the way she used to now that she's working full time again. She says she absolutely refuses to impose that kind of responsibility on her own children and tells Peter that they have to put Momma in a convalescent home. Peter angrily resists, but Jackie tells him that after six years of caring for their mother in her own home, it's her and her husband, Walt's, decision, not Peter's.

Back at the ER, Carter is upset by Dr. Benton's unwillingness to give him any real duties or responsibilities and talks to Mark about his feelings. Get used to it, Mark tells him. Later, though, Carter gets his chance to scrub in for a surgery and scores points with Morgenstern. (He also hears for the first time about the mysterious piano showroom on the Eisenhower Expressway.)

As a New Year's resolution, Lydia tries to quit smoking and ends up chewing packs of nicotine gum instead, while Carol comforts a young firefighter traumatized by seeing one of his fellow firemen get seriously burned.

Doug and Linda share Doug's bed, and Linda admits to him that she assumes they won't last as a couple. According to her, most men are afraid of responsibility, aging, death, and diminished sexual capacity. Doug doesn't argue with her because he knows deep down that she's right. (And we all think we know who he *really* wants anyway, don't we?)

Mark and Susan have eggs together in the doctor's lounge and bicker over Tabasco sauce. Mark tells Susan she should not let Kayson ride her so much and also that she should not try to push Chloe into having an abortion. At this point Susan gets beeped by Dr. Kayson, who tells her that her patient Mr. Vennerbeck has died.

"Happy New Year" ends with Susan standing stunned after a truly ugly scene with Kayson, while Connie repeatedly calls her to come and care for a woman arriving at the ER in respiratory arrest.

PATIENT HISTORIES

● ●

12.207. The gangbanger with multiple gunshot wounds

This patient ended up in the ER thanks to John Carter, who ran to get Mark and the others after he found the kid hanging on a car, bleeding from several bullet wounds.

Mark ordered 8 units of O-negative blood and had him bagged. He also told Carter to call Security (extension 432) because the kid was obviously a "gangbanger," and there was a risk of violent retaliation in the ER from other gang members.

The boy had gunshot wounds to his abdomen, chest, neck, and legs, and his pulse was 160 and thready. He had decreased breath sounds and was hyporesonant on the right side. Mark decided to decompress and ordered a 14 gauge needle. The boy also needed to be intubated, and Mark gave Carter the assignment, which he performed perfectly.

After the intubation, Benton arrived and Carter gave him the bullet: multiple gunshot wounds, intubated, tension pneumothorax on the right, needs a thoracotomy and a laparotomy. Carter then asked Benton if he could scrub in for the surgery. Benton said no.

The patient died during surgery.

12.208. The dead shovel
This patient, a fat man who had a heart attack while shoveling snow, was in room 2.

12.209. The newspaper attack victim
According to Haleh, this patient claimed his newspaper jumped up and attacked him. He was in the suture room waiting for a psych consult.

12.210. Mrs. Davies
Mrs. Davies came to the ER because of a fractured femur, but she also had heart palpitations from a mitral valve prolapse with resolved SVT (supraventricular tachycardia).

Susan increased her Verapamil and her heart rate normalized. Ortho was called in for her fractured femur.

Mrs. Davies had to stay at the ER longer than necessary because Dr. Kayson kept resisting Susan's efforts to have him hear the case history and sign the release.

When Susan finally persuaded Kayson to sign the release, he scolded her to try a little harder next time.

12.211. Mrs. Davies's daughter with the mumps
This child was not seen or treated at the ER, but Mrs. Davies told Dr. Hicks that her seven-year-old daughter was at home with the mumps and that she wanted to get home to her as soon as possible. Dr. Hicks replied that she, too, had a 7-year-old at home with the mumps.

12.212. Dr. Hicks's child with the mumps
Dr. Hicks revealed during a conversation with Mrs. Davies (Patient 12.211) that she had a seven-year-old home with the mumps.

12.213. Stewie Bimley
Stewie and his brother Binkey (Patient 12.214) were both brought to the ER because they got paint in their eyes from playing with paint guns. Doug treated and released them both, as their mother yelled at him for making them wait so long.

12.214. Binkey Bimley
Stewie Bimley's brother. (See Patient 12.213.)

12.215. Gilbert McCabe, the Bumsicle
Gilbert was a curmudgeonly homeless person who was found by Officer Grabarski with his legs frozen to the sidewalk.

The first words out of Gilbert's mouth when he saw Dr. Hicks in the ER were, "I don't want some colored woman working on me," which won him a slap in the head from his municipal custodian.

McCabe had severe frostbite in both feet and could not feel pin pricks. Hicks ordered a morphine drip, a gram of Ancef, and a tetanus booster. Mark also ordered 5,000 units of Heparin. They then sent him to a whirlpool to defrost his frozen feet.

12.216. The bowel disimpaction in 1

Dr. Benton gave this patient to Carter, reaffirming Carter's suspicion that all he was there at the ER for was to do Benton's scut work. ("Glove up and dig in," Benton told him.)

12.217. The burned firefighter

This firefighter was brought to the ER with full thickness burns to both legs, third-degree burns on his scalp and face, and minor burns on his chest and abdomen. Over 60 percent of his body was burned.

They X-rayed him, and Mark, Lydia, and Carol began stabilizing him for transfer to the O.R. for debridement.

Mark ordered a liter of Ringer's solution the first hour and a 16 line and told Lydia to start a Foley catheter.

The patient's blood pressure was 70/40 and his respirations were shallow at 28. Mark ordered more sterile solution and told Lydia to call Plastics.

The firefighter's blood-oxygen saturation was only 85 percent, and Mark ordered a flow sheet started. The burn unit was notified, and he was given 10 milligrams of morphine.

Mark went out and spoke to the patient's fellow firefighters, who were standing vigil, and told them that the news was not great. He then sent the patient to the O.R. for debridement and then to the Burn Unit.

12.218. The runny nose in 1

This was one of the four patients (also 12.219, 12.220, and 12.221) that Timmy offered to Doug.

12.219. The cough and sore throat in 4

This was another one of the patients Timmy offered to Doug.

12.220. The baby having a baby, No. 1

This was another one of the patients Timmy offered to Doug. Doug accepted this patient and Patient 12.221.

12.221. The baby having a baby, No. 2

This was another one of the patients Timmy offered to Doug. Doug accepted this patient and Patient 12.220.

12.222. Mr. Vennerbeck

Mr. Vennerbeck, thirty-eight, presented at the ER with chest pains. Susan ordered an EKG, chest X-rays, cardiac enzyme tests, and a battery of blood tests, all of which were normal.

She diagnosed that his chest pain was probably muscular, and he then told her that he had been at the ER two months earlier for a pulled back and had then been prescribed Feldene.

Susan went to Dr. Kayson for authorization to release Vennerbeck. She reported that the case was that of a thirty-eight-year-old male at the ER for a "rule out MI." He was admitted with nonradiating left chest pain reproducible with movement, and there was tenderness at the left sternal border that resolved without treatment.

Kayson then asked Susan if the patient's EKG, enzymes, and Chest X-ray were normal, to which Susan replied yes. He asked if Vennerbeck was dizzy or had palpitations, to which Susan replied no. Kayson continued his inquiry, asking if the patient was diaphoretic (sweating), if blood tests showed hyperlipidemia (excessive fat in the blood), or if he had a history of chest pain or any known risk factors. Susan replied no to everything except noting that Vennerbeck had slightly elevated blood pressure.

Dr. Kayson told Susan that it didn't sound cardiac and that the patient could be released, but that he should see his own doctor for a stress test.

Susan went back to give an angry Vennerbeck the news and ended up apologizing for keeping him waiting so long, for which she was berated by Dr. Hicks, who told her there is no need to apologize to a patient for how long it takes to be treated and released.

A few hours later, though, a doctor's worst fear materialized for Susan when Mr. Vennerbeck was returned to the ER (a "bounceback") in the midst of a serious cardiac crisis.

He had severe pain radiating down his left arm, and he had been given nitro spray by the EMTs twice, but without relief. At the ER, Vennerbeck was given 5 milligrams of morphine and a 7.5 endogastric tube was inserted. Susan identified a new holosystolic murmur with a thrill and ordered 500 cc of 5 percent dextrose.

At this point Dr. Kayson stormed in, and Susan reported to him that the patient was hypotensive with a possible ventricular septal rupture. Kayson ordered a 40 milligram IV push of Lasix and sent Vennerbeck upstairs.

A shaken Susan continued with her treatment of patients until later on in the day when she was paged by Kayson. "Vennerbeck is dead," he told her, and furiously explained to her that Vennerbeck's previous back pain had probably been atypical angina and *he* should have been told about it. Susan defended herself by saying he didn't ask about previous admissions and, in any case, she could barely get him to stop and listen to her summation.

Kayson told her that he had informed Dr. Morgenstern about her mishandling of Vennerbeck and had requested a full case review.

12.223. Mrs. Becker

Mark was doing a pelvic exam on Mrs. Becker when Carol suddenly walked into the room and a startled Mrs. Becker tried to squeeze her legs closed. Mark told her not to worry and explained that Carol was a nurse.

12.224. The MVA (motor vehicle accident)

This twenty-five-year-old patient was brought to the ER by the medical chopper. He had sustained a blunt abdominal trauma and his blood pressure was 50 palp. His pulse was thready and his capillary refill was slow. His heart rate was in sinus tachy-

cardia at 150, and Carter intubated him with a 7.5 tube. Benton ordered a cervical spine and an abdominal series of X-rays with the portable X-ray machine.

O-negative blood was on the way, and the patient was given 2 more liters of fluids which, added to the 2 liters he received in the field, made for a total of 4 liters.

At this point Dr. Morgenstern took over, and Carter gave him the bullet: MVA, twenty-five-years-old, pale and diaphoretic, pulse 150, BP 50 palp, resps 25, blunt abdominal trauma, probable ruptured spleen.

The patient was then brought upstairs for surgery, and Benton, who had been impressed with Carter's performance and proficiency, told his eager med student to scrub in by seven-thirty for an eight o'clock gall bladder operation.

12.225. The eight o'clock gall bladder

This patient was Carter's first surgical scrub-in. He blew it initially when he contaminated himself by touching Benton's shoulder so he could see the surgical field. He scrubbed once again and was told by Dr. Morgenstern to hold a retractor after he correctly identified Calot's Triangle as being the cystic duct, the common duct, and the liver.

12.226. Tarita

Nineteen-year-old Tarita came to the ER pregnant and complaining of abdominal pains. Mark ordered a CBC, Chem 7, and FHTs (fetal heart tones) with Doppler, and he ordered Obstetrics called.

Susan took over, and it was determined that Tarita needed Narcan and an amp of glucose. Her blood pressure was 70/30 and her respirations were shallow at 8. Cocaine and other drug abuse (possibly a drug overdose) was suspected and a tox screen was ordered.

Tarita's cervix was fully dilated, she was 100 percent effaced, and her placental membranes had ruptured. Before they could get her to Obsterics, her baby's foot came out, and it was blue. Tarita was brought back to the ER, where it was determined she was having a cocaine-toxic footling breech presentation with a prolapsed umbilical cord. Susan ordered a fetal monitor and Mark took over to finish the delivery (see Patient 12.229).

12.227 and 12.228. Mr. and Mrs. Babcock

This elderly couple was brought to the ER comatose and with cherry red skin under their fingernails.

Doug, Carter, and Carol took charge of the couple, and a sodium hydroxide test was ordered. Respiratory was called, and the Babcocks' neighbor told them that the couple had been using a kerosene heater. Doug ordered administration of 15 liters of oxygen.

The tests showed carboxyhemoglobin present in both their blood samples, which confirmed carbon monoxide poisoning.

The couple was admitted and, even though they remained comatose, after a few hours their blood gases normalized and their PO_2 levels (see Glossary) came down.

It is assumed they recovered.

12.229. Tarita's baby

This was Patient 12.226's baby, who was born blue because of her mother's cocaine abuse. When the baby was born, its blood sugar was 25, and Doug ordered 6 milligrams of 10 percent DW (dextrose in water) over three minutes. Dr. Hicks determined that the baby would be okay.

12.230. Mrs. Maryanski

Mark got the (usually pleasant) task of telling a patient that she was pregnant, but instead of tears of joy, Mrs. Maryanski shed tears of frustration and distress. Why? Mr. Maryanski, her husband, was infertile. Uh-oh.

12.231. The woman in respiratory arrest

This woman was brought to the ER in respiratory arrest, and Susan had to treat her after having been raked over the coals by Dr. Kayson for her role in Mr. Vennerbeck's death.

● ●

Original Broadcast Date:
Thursday, January 5, 1995
Written by Lydia Woodward;
Directed by Charles Haid

"LUCK OF THE DRAW"

ER 13

"That's what I like about you, Peter:

naked ambition tempered by arrogance."

—Dr. Morgenstern, after Peter told him
he was planning on being chief surgical resident

"Confidence, composure under pressure, assertiveness:

These are the requisite qualities of a good ER specialist."

—Dr. Morgenstern, to Susan, on her unwillingness to
go head-to-head with strong-willed men like Kayson and Benton

"Don't tempt the fates."

—Carol Hathaway

This episode begins with Susan and Mark pulling into the hospital parking garage at the same time and ends with Susan pulling out of a parking space alone.

As they walk through the garage, Susan tells Mark that she got a call from Morgenstern about Vennerbeck's death, and that he wants to see her in his office.

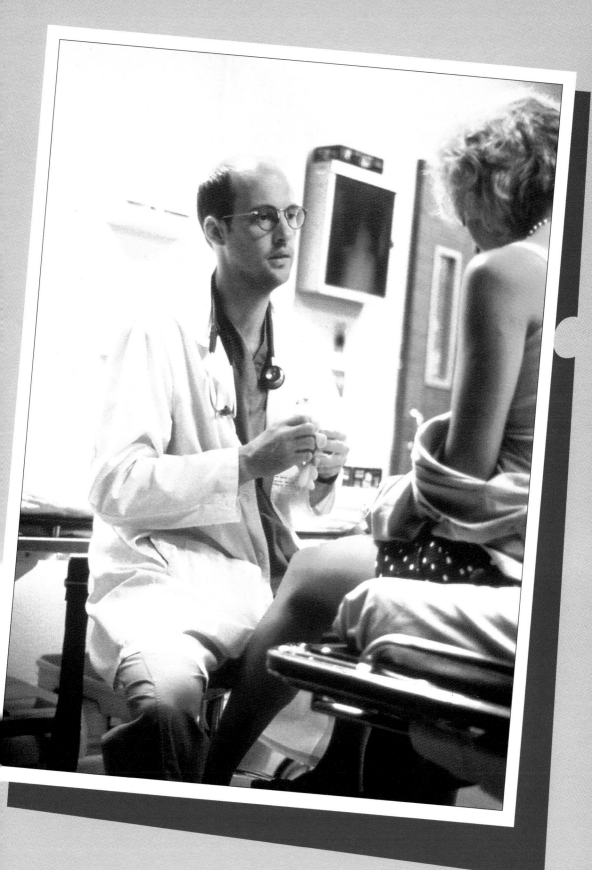

Kayson was playing hardball regarding Susan's role in Vennerbeck's death.

Deb Chen, Benton's new medical student, shows up for her first day, and Peter makes Carter show her the ropes.

Everyone keeps asking Carol if she and Tag have set a date for their wedding yet, and she tells Lydia that she doesn't know if she's ready for the "forever" part.

Doug is obviously working on getting his life in order (see Patient 13.234), and he reveals to Wendy that he's never seen his own son.

Morgenstern tells Susan that she may not be assertive enough to be an ER specialist, and Susan is livid when she learns that Mark knew what he was going to say and didn't tell her. Morgenstern also hit Susan with the fact that she had caved in to Benton regarding her patient with the retrocecal appendix (Harriet, Patient 4.73).

Peter gets an emergency call that his mother is missing and later has a big argument with his brother-in-law Walt about putting her into a nursing home. Peter eventually finds Momma sitting alone on the bleachers at the Little League field where he used to play.

Later, Carol finds Susan crying in the ladies' room after her disastrous performance in a critical situation (see Patient 13.249).

Mark apologizes to Susan about not standing up for her and invites her to Doc Magoo's after work to eat with him and some of the others. Later, everyone shows up at the diner except Susan.

Doug, Mark, Deb, Carter, Malik, Timmy, Wendy, Haleh, Lydia, and Peter are all thrilled to hear Carol announce that she and Tag have set May 18 as their wedding date.

The episode ends with Doug toasting Carol, and Susan sitting outside in her VW watching them all have a good time, then driving off by herself.

PATIENT HISTORIES

13.232. Carter's dead body
Carter was supposed to bring this DB (dead body) to ER room 4 for temporary storage because Pathology was backed up, and then get back to work. Carter used this opportunity, however, to lie on a gurney and pull a sheet up over his own head and grab some sleep. And that is exactly how Benton found him when he came looking for him.

13.233. The suicidal junkie in 4
Susan took this patient from Timmy because after her clash with Kayson she said she needed some cheering up.

13.234. Lucy
This little girl had been bitten on the finger by her pet hamster. Lucy then infected the finger by sucking on it. Doug dressed the finger and prescribed some antibiotics.

Doug also rejected a blatant pass made at him by Lucy's gorgeous aunt, much to Mark's disappointment.

13.235. The HIV-positive kid with a busted tooth in 1
Timmy offered this patient to Mark and Susan, but cautioned them that there was a lot of blood. We weren't told who treated this kid.

13.236. The scissors in the left leg
Mark took this patient from Timmy.

13.237. Evoldo
This guy was a filthy, alcoholic, drug-abusing vagrant who was a regular at the ER. He was brought in drunk and unconscious from a possible seizure, and Carol and Lydia admitted him and went to work on him.

First, they double-gloved. Then Carol sprayed him with Lysol and they began to undress him. While removing his left shoe, Carol was stuck in the right hand by a syringe he had hidden in the shoe. This was the fifth time Carol had been stuck by a needle since she had been working at the ER.

Lydia told her she would try to get Evoldo's consent to test him for HIV and get his T-cell count. By the time the episode ended, Evoldo's T-cell count was still not back from the lab.

13.238. Carol Hathaway
Carol was treated by Lydia after she was stuck with a syringe while removing a drunk patient's shoes (Patient 13.237.) She knew that the odds of getting infected were 1 in 250 if the patient had HIV or AIDS, and Wendy told Carol not to have unprotected sex for six months. [NOTE: The most recent edition of *Current Emergency Diagnosis and Treatment** states: "Exposures as the result of needlestick injuries carry a 1:200 risk of HIV infection."]

13.239. Lydia Wright
While treating Carol for her needle stick, Lydia tried to reassure Carol by telling her that she herself had been stuck nine times in her years at the ER and had never caught even the flu.

13.240. Jorge the body packer
Jorge was picked up at O'Hare Airport on a flight from La Paz by U. S. Customs Agent Serrano. He was a suspected "body packer": a drug courier who swallows condoms filled with cocaine in order to smuggle the drugs into the United States.

Serrano brought Jorge to the ER after eight days in custody because Jorge still had not passed the condoms. (Serrano said Jorge was "retaining evidence.")

Mark checked Jorge over and found no obvious signs of toxicity and told Serrano

---

Current Emergency Diagnosis and Treatment. Saunders, Charles and Mary Ho, eds.; East Norwalk, CT: Appleton and Lange, 1992.

he could not give the suspected courier a laxative or any other medication without his consent.

Mark ordered an X-ray and told Carter to work Jorge up and do a drug screen, a urinalysis, and a rectal. He told Agent Serrano that he hoped nature would take its course before a condom broke.

Carter made Deb do the rectal, and when he heard Jorge screaming, he asked Deb if she had used a lubricant. She had not, and she ended up, ahem, "stuck."

Later on, Jorge's luck ran out when a condom popped and he went into cardiac arhythmia, beginning

We'll work Benton's hours, sleep when he sleeps, which is practically never. We've been on call since yesterday morning and he hasn't even sat down yet. This is one of the four IV carts. Most patients get an IV the second they come through the door. Angiocath, 16 needle, large bore if they're bleeding. You know how to start an IV, right? I thought you were third year.
— John Carter's speech to med student Deb Chen on Deb's first day in the ER

with multifocal PVCs and ending in fibrillation. Mark ordered 150 milligrams of lidocaine IV push and when he asked for the paddles, Deb accidentally hit Carter with them (at 200 joules), causing him to lose consciousness and fall and hit his head. Mark then shocked Jorge at 200 and 300 joules respectively, and the smuggler converted to normal sinus rhythm. He sent Jorge to the O.R. for a laparatomy and had Carter put in an examination room.

A total of 185 cocaine-filled condoms were removed from Jorge during surgery.

13.241. Ben Gather

Little Ben had been brain-damaged two years before when he was struck by a car when an eighty-five-year-old driver waved him across the street and then got confused between the brake and the accelerator.

Ben was brought to the ER in respiratory distress and crashed when they were taking his vitals. He had a temperature of 104°, and his heart rapidly went from bradycardic at 35 to flat line. His blood cultures were sent to the lab, and Doug diagnosed septic shock. He ordered an amp of epinephrine, a milligram of atropine, and 1.5 each of urea and cefotaxime. Ben had no heart sounds, and Doug ordered Lydia and Carol to piggyback an Isopril drip.

Ben's pulse came back, but then he went into v-tach (ventricular tachycardia). Doug told them to hold the Isopril and give him 50 milligrams IV push of lidocaine and get a 12 lead in there because he needed to see what was going on.

Ben's EKG showed peak T waves (cardiac rhythm waves) and an unstable rhythm. Doug guessed his potassium was too high, which was confirmed later by lab results showing a potassium level of 7.5 (hyperkalemia).

Doug ordered Carol to give Ben 15 milliters of calcium gluconate and, when Carol said, "It could kill him," barked at her, "Just do it!"

Ben then went into asystole, and Doug ordered Lydia to repeat the epinephrine and atropine. Ben's pulse was weak and his blood pressure was 35 palp, but his glucose and insulin levels were okay.

Later, while Ben was being monitored, Wendy showed Doug a new DNR (do not resuscitate) order that Ben's father had implemented. Doug confronted Mr. Gather about the order and told him that Ben's blood gases were not good and that if they obeyed the DNR order and did not put the boy on a ventilator, he could die. The father simply asked, "When?"

Ben was eventually moved up to Intensive Care, and Doug told Mr. Gather that the ICU staff was aware of his decision. Gather then told Doug that he had given two years of his life to caring for Ben twenty-four hours a day, and that he needed this to be over. "I need for this to end," he told Doug in tears.

We were not told what ultimately happened to Ben, although it's likely he didn't make it without the ventilator to help him breathe.

13.242. Mark Greene

Mark was probably treated at the ER each of the three times he was stuck by a needle while treating patients.

13.243. Petrarski

Susan wanted this patient's chart.

13.244. Alan the color guy

Alan was a psychiatric patient who lived at the Marymount Home and was brought to the ER with a fever of 101°, and also because he was bringing up sputum. (It was a sulfur color with saffron mixed in, he told Susan.)

Alan brought his "book" with him to the hospital. Alan's book was an obsessively detailed and meticulously complete loose-leaf notebook of his medical history. His medications were on pumpkin-colored pages; his allergies on mauve; his vaccinations on grey; his doctor's names and numbers on plum; and his past medical records were on pages that were shades of red ranging from vermillion to puce. Alan was dressed all in blue because, he explained, it was Monday. Alan was into colors, Carol explained to Susan.

Alan also had a heart murmur, and Susan decided to run some tests and do a chest X-ray, while Alan waited in a yellow examination room. (He refused to even enter the green room. Green was very bad, he explained. He also asked Susan if she had had red hair as a child because he thought he saw a hint of russet in her hair. She told him it was probably the ketchup from lunch.)

When Alan's X-rays were developed, Susan was stunned to see that he had cancer. He had a tumor in his chest that was encasing his heart and infiltrating his lung. He had not said a word about it, and when she confronted him about it and told him she wanted him to see an oncologist, he simply asked if he could be alone.

Later, Carol found Alan standing in the dreaded green examination room. He had almost moved out of the home last year, he told her, but didn't because the bathroom in the new place was green. Now he was thinking, what the hell? Carol smiled and handed him back his medical book.

13.245. Miss Callahan

Dr. Bernardi from Obstetrics called Timmy in the ER to ask what drugs had been given to this patient before she was sent upstairs. Since this was Susan's patient, she took the call and told Bernardi that she had given Callahan a 6 gram bolus of magnesium sulfate. It was while reviewing the Callahan chart that Susan learned that Mark was now cosigning all her charts. When she confronted Mark about it, he told her that Morgenstern had told him to cosign her charts because of Mr. Vennerbeck's (Patient 12.222) unexpected death.

13.246. Mr. Mankins

Susan ordered Wendy to give this patient 350 milligrams a minute of dopamine, when what she should have ordered was *micrograms*. Wendy called her on it, and Mark witnessed the exchange.

13.247. Mr. Desmond

Mr. Desmond was a sociologist at the University of Chicago with a very dangerous job: He was studying violence and went around the city insulting and provoking people until they assaulted him. He would ask two questions to probe for insecurities and then use this information to antagonize the person to the point of violence. This was how he calculated the PVA: the provocation to assault interval.

The day Desmond was brought to the ER he had questioned the EMT about her sexual orientation; made derogatory remarks about a newstand guy's Middle Eastern heritage; made fun of a florist's hair weave; and insinuated that Carol was afraid of commitment and that she probably thought she was too good for Tag.

He was treated for a cracked rib and a variety of cuts and bruises, and Carol got even with him by pouring straight alcohol into an open wound and putting an enraged fighter in the room with him. Within minutes, Mr. Desmond was seen flying through the air into the hall. Mark remarked that someone ought to check on Mr. Desmond.

13.248. John Carter

Carter was accidentally rendered unconscious when Deb inadvertently hit him with the defibrillation paddles and he fell and struck his head.

He was put in an examination room, and, when he woke up, Haleh told him that Deb had taken care of him. His pressure was 90/60, and Haleh also told him that Deb had done a rectal exam and examined his genitalia.

Haleh and Deb admitted it was only a joke, though, and Carter relaxed. Until later, that is, when Benton asked him how his rectal went.

13.249. The drive-by shooting victim
This little girl was shot during a drive-by shooting. Her brother was a gangbanger, and she was an innocent bystander.

When she got to the ER her pressure was 40 palp, and Susan ordered her crits spun, her blood typed and crossmatched, and some O neg. She also told them to call Radiology and a surgeon.

Mark showed up, and Susan told him the little girl had been shot, that she was hyporesonant, and that she had a tracheal shift to the left. Mark said the girl needed a chest tube, and Susan said she'd do it. The little girl started taching and her pressure started crashing, and it was obvious that the bullet had tunneled into her heart. A thoracotomy tray was ordered, and Susan said she'd crack her chest and clamp the artery.

This was when Dr. Kayson entered the room, and Susan immediately lost her confidence. She ordered the O neg wide open and began the thoracotomy. But her incision wasn't deep enough, and Susan could not visualize the lungs or see the pleura. The little girl began bleeding out, and Kayson asked Mark how long he was going to let this go on. Susan finally gave up and let Mark take over. He got in immediately, found the bleeder (it was her pulmonary artery), and successfully clamped it.

The little girl was then brought to the O.R. where it is assumed she survived the surgery and recovered.

13.250. The possible appendectomy in 6
Mark told Peter to take this patient in 6, but Peter blew him off and rushed instead to the O.R. He was too late, though, to scrub in for his scheduled surgery. Morgenstern couldn't wait and had already asked Schneider to scrub in. (Peter had had to leave to look for his mother and was late for the surgery.)

13.251. Mr. Parnell
Parnell, a professional boxer, got knocked out during a fight and was *extremely* angry that he was now in "Chump Cellar." Carol thoughtfully placed him in the same room as Mr. Desmond (Patient 13.250).

Original Broadcast Date:
Thursday, January 12, 1995
Written by Paul Manning;
Directed by Ron Holcomb

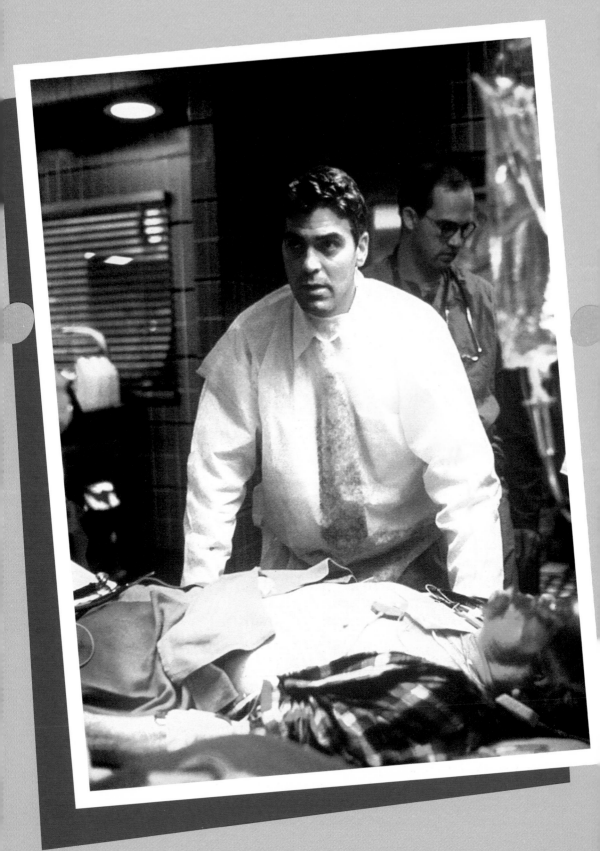

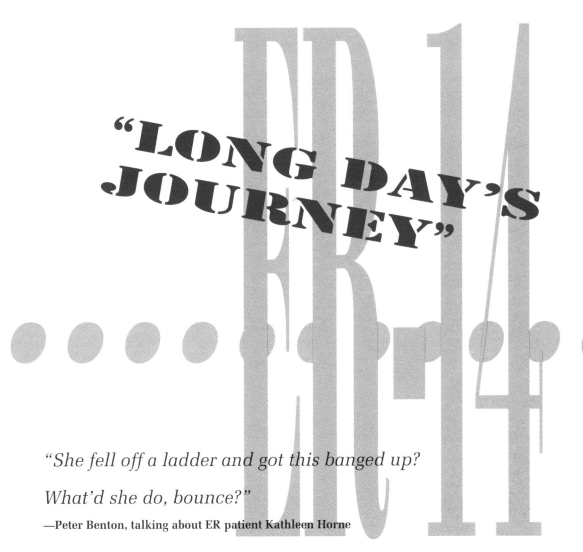

"LONG DAY'S JOURNEY"

ER 14

"She fell off a ladder and got this banged up?

What'd she do, bounce?"

—Peter Benton, talking about ER patient Kathleen Horne

"If you take him out of here, I'll see you at a review

committee, and they will fry your ass so

fast you'll be lucky to keep your license."

—Susan Lewis, to Dr. Steinman when he tried to overrule
her *and* her patient, Dr. Kayson, about doing an angioplasty
on him when he wanted tPA therapy

Carter comes in for work looking exhausted and tells Haleh that he was up all night working on his ER presentation. He is upset to learn that the ambitious Deb has already checked Dr. Benton's patients.

Carol and Tag discuss their planned romantic weekend, and Tag stashes his bag of edible body oils and sex toys under the admitting desk.

A nervous Susan smokes a cigarette while waiting for the review board to convene. When it's all over, the board rules in Susan's favor.

Peter and his sister Jackie argue again about what to do with their ailing mother. Peter insists on hiring someone to take care of her at home and unrealistically says he'll take care of her the other two days when no one is available.

Susan is still mad at Mark for not defending her to Morgenstern.

Peter misses Grand Rounds for the first time in his career, and Doug tells him there are more important things than becoming chief resident. Doug later meets Jake Leeds on the basketball court and learns that his mother, Diane, works for the hospital in Risk Management. Doug's reputation has preceded him, however, and Diane warns him off when he attempts to be charming.

Tag and Carol have their rendezvous and, when it's over, both realize that Tag left their "goodie bag" at the hospital. Tag tells her, "I'll never be able to go to work again."

The episode ends with Mark finding Doug out on the basketball court, lying on the ground, using the ball as a pillow. Doug somberly asks Mark how many patients he'll see this year, and Mark tells him around three thousand.

Mark then asks Doug if he's okay, and Doug says yes and then walks slowly into the ER, dribbling his basketball.

PATIENT HISTORIES

● ●

14.252. Kathleen Horne

This patient was brought to the ER seriously injured from what her daughter said was a fall off a ladder.

Doug and Connie began treatment and noted that her pupils were sluggish and that her blood pressure was 70/50 and her pulse was 45.

At this point, Kathleen went into respiratory arrest. Doug ordered a 7.0 ET tube, and she was intubated and bagged. He also ordered 500 cc of normal saline and had her hyperventilated, rapidly increasing her flow of CO_2.

Peter arrived, and Doug told him that Kathleen had a possible bleed in the brain and that her GCS was 6. She also had hematomas of the left lower quadrant; lacerations of the upper right quadrant and left thigh; and contusions on her back.

She then went into papilledema (edema of the optic disk often indicative of increased intracranial pressure), and Peter ordered abdominal lavage, a chest film, and a KUB. Kathleen Horne was in trouble.

After Kathleen was sent to the O.R., Carol did some digging and found her old charts, which she gave to Doug. Kathleen had been to the ER three times in the last six months. Once she broke her arm "falling down a flight of stairs," but she didn't have any bruises from the fall; and another time she sustained an orbital fracture by "walking into a door."

Kathleen Horne ultimately died. Doug eventually learned that Mrs. Horne had been beaten on a regular basis by her daughter Mandy, who was also at the ER

(Patient 14.253) for hand lacerations she sustained while assaulting her mother.

14.253. Mandy Horne

Mandy came to the ER with her brother David and their injured mother, Kathleen.

Mandy told the doctors and nurses that her mother had fallen off a ladder and that she, Mandy, had cut her hand at the same time.

Doug then asked the children who had been beating their mother, thinking it was a boyfriend or an ex-husband. Neither of them would talk, but as Doug was leaving the room, David blurted out, "It was Mandy!" He told Doug that Mandy used to beat their mother with a baseball bat. Mandy then exploded in a violent rage and screamed at her brother that she was going to kill him, and Doug knew that David was telling the truth.

They restrained Mandy, and David asked Doug, "When can my mom go home?"

14.254. Mrs. Chang

Mrs. Chang was brought to the ER by her husband. She was pregnant and had been throwing up. Her blood pressure was a little elevated, and Mark was concerned that she might have preeclampsia. [See episode 19, "Love's Labor Lost" for details about a patient of Mark's who tragically *did* have preeclampsia.]

Mark ordered a blood workup and refused Mr. Chang's impassioned request that he induce labor. (Mrs. Chang was due in two weeks.)

All of Mrs. Chang's tests came back normal, and Mr. Chang finally admitted that his wife was probably nauseous from the drink an herbalist had given her to induce labor. It seems that on the Chinese calendar the Year of the Pig was coming, and the old folks (especially the Changs' two mothers) believed that children born then would grow up to be lazy. So the Changs were trying to make sure the baby was born in the Year of the Dog instead.

Mark was stunned: "Mr. Chang," he said, "this is an emergency room, not an auto body shop. We don't do procedures just because you want them."

Finally, Dr. Noble the obstetrician arrived and announced that he was checking Mrs. Chang in to induce labor for religious reasons. When Mark told him she wasn't due for ten days, Dr. Noble told Mark that they induce so people can go on vacation and they induce at Christmas so people can get the tax break, so what's the big deal?

Mark just shook his head and wished them all a happy Year of the Dog.

14.255. The GS (gunshot) hunting accident

This was Susan's patient, and she sarcastically told Mark that she was ready to discharge him so would he please sign the release form? Mark got the point and told her to go ahead and discharge him (Mark had been told by Morgenstern to cosign Susan's charts), and then asked her about the review board she had to face that afternoon. It was at three o'clock, she told him, and then asked him to please *not* come to offer support.

14.256. Zach Meeker

Ten-year-old Zach broke his leg when he was thrown by his gym teacher during a wrestling class.

Doug initially didn't want to call in Tag for an orthopedic consult (because of his embarrassment over the incident at Carol's engagement party), but Tag came anyway and blasted Doug for not calling him. "It's not personal, it's professional," Tag told Doug.

Zach had a broken right femur and Tag ordered an X-ray, which revealed a mass in the bone. Tag suspected osteosarcoma and decided to do a biopsy. After the parents couldn't find the strength to tell the boy he might have cancer, Doug told him and stayed with him through the procedure.

Tag did the biopsy with a spring-loaded gun, and Zach told Doug, "Never got shot before." Later, a disheartened Doug confirmed to Benton that Zach did, indeed, have osteosarcoma.

14.257. Mrs. Neely

Peter told Deb to send Mrs. Neely up to the O.R., and Deb told him that Mrs. Neely wanted her surgery explained to her again. Peter responded that he had already explained it twice to her and that that was enough. Deb then offered to do it, because she had been taking a course on patient relations. Peter said "Okay, but don't let it interfere with your work." "He didn't mean that," Deb asked Jerry, "did he?"

14.258. Fran Parris

Fran, age thirty-two, was brought in comatose after a suicide attempt. Her blood pressure was 50 palp and her pulse was 120. An empty bottle of tricyclic antidepressant amitriptyline (known commercially as Elavil) was found by her body.

Mark, Haleh, and Carol immediately went to work on Fran. Mark ordered .8 of Narcan and agreed to Haleh's suggestion of a glucose IV. Carol asked if Mark was planning on dialysis and hemoprofusion, and he said not with tricyclics. He decided to pump her stomach instead.

Mark ordered a tox screen, orotracheal intubation, and gastric lavage. Fran's capillary refill was poor, her blood pressure was falling at 40 palp, and her heart rate was in sinus tachycardia at 140.

Mark ordered 3 liters of saline and lavage until clean.

At this point Fran began having seizures, and Mark ordered a gram of bicarb and 10 milligrams of Valium IV push. He also ordered Dilantin, 1 gram at 50 milligrams a minute. Fran's heart rate went tachycardic with a rate of 241, and Mark ordered an amp of bicarb IV push and said it looked like torsade (torsades de pointes—see the Glossary). He ordered 2 grams of magnesium sulfate and performed external heart massage.

Fran's puls/ox [see Glossary] was 60 and she had no pulse. Mark ordered a high dose of 7 milligrams of epinephrine and another milligram of atropine. Fran was extremely cyanotic, and when she went into asystole, Mark asked out loud why did it have to be tricyclics? Why couldn't she have taken painkillers?

Carol informed Mark that Fran had abnormal doll's eyes and that her pupils were fixed and dilated. Mark realized she had brain-stem shock and that was when he acknowledged that she was gone.

14.259. Mr. Bede

Mr. Bede was a physical therapy patient Jeannie Boulet was treating when Peter first spoke to her about her caring for his mother.

14.260. Willy Kane

Willy, a young man in his twenties, was brought to the ER with a burning pain in his throat sustained when he rushed into a burning building to rescue a trapped fourteen-year-old girl, Nancy Potter (Patient 14.261).

Willy's vitals were normal and his respirations were 30. Upon examination, Mark determined that his throat was fine, and his pupils were normal. Willy's puls/ox was 80 and Mark ordered IV fluids, 15 liters of oxygen by mask, Versed, and a chest film.

Later, Peter and Doug were checking on Willy when his heart went into an S3 and S4 gallop. Doug ordered nitro 50 milligrams. Willy had inhaled toxic chemicals when he was in the fire, and his lungs were badly damaged. "There's more to it than that," Willy told them. He also had cystic fibrosis. Mark told Doug to call for a pulmonary consult, although it was obvious that Willy's condition was essentially hopeless.

Later Mark talked to Willy's father, who told him that Willy's doctor had said that his son had five or six years left. He told Mark that Willy had never had kids. Now his lungs were very bad and he would soon need a respirator to breathe. Conni brought in the results of his blood gases (they were bad) and reported that his PO_2 was 50 and his PCO_2 was only 60.

At this point, Nancy Potter, the young girl Willy rescued was wheeled in to see him. She wanted to thank him for saving her life.

Mark told her that he wasn't sure that Willy would even be able to hear her expression of appreciation. Nancy didn't care: She said it anyway.

14.261. Nancy Potter

Fourteen-year-old Nancy was brought to the ER after she was rescued from a burning building by Willy Kane (Patient 14.260).

Nancy had been hit by a burning beam and had burns on her leg and chest as well as numerous abrasions. Her blood pressure was 90/50 and her pulse was 90. Doug ordered blood gases, a cross-table c-spine X-ray and her blood typed and cross-matched for 4 units. He ordered her given some O negative in the meantime.

Nancy was having trouble breathing, and Doug ordered a gram of Ancef and a call made to the Burn Unit.

At this point Nancy registered no distal pulse and her blood pressure was 70/50 and falling. Doug ordered her IVs opened wide and identified an open green-stick fracture in her leg. He ordered calls made to Vascular and Orthopedic for consults.

Later, after Nancy was stabilized, she visited her rescuer Willy in his room to thank him for rescuing her.

14.262. Uncle Ted

This man was unconscious and unresponsive in a van outside of the hospital and

Jerry called Carter to come and take a look at him.

Carter and Deb checked him out (as the family watched from the sidewalk) and determined that Uncle Ted was dead.

They got him out of the van and onto a gurney, but because rigor had already set in, his legs would not straighten out, and, for the rest of the day, Uncle Ted was wheeled around the ER with his legs sticking up into the air, bent at the knee.

14.263. Mrs. Torledsky

Carter and Deb initially examined this forty-nine-year-old woman when she presented at the ER complaining of sharp, acute stomach pains.

Mrs. Torledsky was already on the medications Norvasc, Allopurinol, Indocin, Zoloft, and Antivert.

Deb asked her what she had eaten that day, and she told them some granola, two poppy-seed bagels, some cheese, and a nice lamb chop. Deb thought it might have been the poppy seeds and said they should call Dr. Benton.

When Benton arrived, Carter gave him the report: The patient's tests showed leukocytosis with a high BUN (blood urea nitrogen) count. Her recent diet included both seeds and nuts. The diagnosis was likely diverticulitis, and Carter told Benton that Mrs. Torledsky was a possible surgical candidate.

Benton then asked Carter what made him ask about her diet, and Carter admitted that it had actually been Deb who asked about it. Benton told Carter that next time, when Deb had an idea, he should let Deb present it to him. Deb then explained to Benton that she had a photographic memory and that during the examination, a page from the *Pocket Manual* had come into her mind. She remembered that stomach pains with seeds could indicate diverticulitis.

Benton told her she was right and then told the patient that she had inflammation of her colon and that if it didn't subside she might need surgery.

14.264. Terry

Terry was a fifteen-year-old street kid who was beaten up in a fight and brought to the ER by his friend, a teenage girl who admitted to Doug that Terry was not yet eighteen.

Doug and Haleh examined Terry and learned that he had a temperature of 102°, his respirations were 24, he had a cough, and his heart rate was tachycardic.

Doug ordered a CBC, lytes, ABG (arterial blood gas reading), and a chest film.

Terry's tests showed that he had pneumocystis pneumonia (PCP). Terry had AIDS, which he had gotten from unprotected homosexual sex with his johns. Terry was a male prostitute, and explained to Doug that his customers refused to use condoms.

Doug wanted to check Terry in and treat him with AZT, but the boy refused and prepared to leave. Before he left, Doug gave Terry some condoms, a prescription for Bactrim, and the phone numbers of a shelter and an AIDS treatment center.

14.265. The guy with the arrow in his head

This patient approached Doug and Susan as they were talking about how well Susan's review had gone and complained that he had been waiting for forty minutes.

Susan told him they were very busy and to please go have a seat in the waiting room.

When the man turned around, they noticed that he had an arrow sticking out of his skull. The neighbor kids had been playing Cowboys and Indians, he explained. He also told them that he had taken the bus to the hospital with the arrow protruding from his head.

Susan immediately took him into her service and escorted him to an examination room.

14.266. Dr. Jack Kayson

After the review committee took Susan's side over Dr. Kayson's, the good doctor, age fifty-three, went to Shaw's Crab House and proceeded to get floridly drunk. While there, he had the misfortune to experience a major heart attack and ended up being brought to the ER by Rescue 61.

Kayson had mid-sternal chest pain and had vomited twice in the ambulance. He was diaphoretic, and the EMTs had already given him 2 milligrams of morphine and some sublingual nitroglycerin.

Susan took charge and asked Kayson if he could chew an aspirin, which he did. His blood pressure was 150/100, and Susan ordered 15 liters of oxygen and a 12 lead monitor.

She then asked Dr. Kayson what he wanted her to do: Angioplasty or tPA. At that point Kayson's heart went into tachycardia with a rate of 120 and his resps went to 24. Susan identified an S and T wave elevation in the inferior leads, and suddenly his blood pressure started crashing and his heart went into bradycardia.

Susan recognized cardiogenic shock and intubated Kayson with a 7.0 endotracheal tube. She said to call Respiratory and open up his IVs. She ordered a bolus of 1 milligram atropine IV, a dopamine drip, and said to bag him. At this point Kayson's blood pressure was 60/35, and Susan said to call Cardiology.

Cardiologist Dr. Steinman then arrived and told Susan he was going to do angioplasty on Kayson. Kayson whispered to Susan that he wanted tPA, but Steinman imperiously tried to overrule both Kayson and Susan. It was at this point that Susan gave her dramatic "fry your ass" speech excerpted above (see the epigraph to this chapter) and ordered tPA therapy.

Dr. Kayson survived.

14.267. The baby with the croup

Mark called Doug in off the basketball court to see this patient.

● ●

Original Broadcast Date:
Thursday, January 19, 1995
Written by Robert Nathan;
Directed by Anita Addison

"FEB. 5, '95"

ER 15

> "Stress, late nights, hard work,
>
> no pay . . . hard to beat."
>
> —**Mark Greene, talking to Carter about emergency medicine**

> "Life goes on. And then sometimes it doesn't."
>
> —**Old hospice joke**

This episode begins with Carter having his new camel-hair coat ruined when gasoline drips on it as he's treating a patient trapped in a car.

Mark asks Carter if he has decided on a specialty, and Carter answers that even though his parents want him to go into cardiology, he thinks emergency medicine is pretty exciting.

Back at the hospital, Benton is in a foul mood because he's spending all his free time watching his mother. Thus, he is less than thrilled when Deb asks him for a half hour off to work on her ER presentation. Unlike the med students, Haleh does not have to put up with Peter's surliness, and after he bites her head off for an imagined slight, she boycotts procedural shortcuts and makes him do everything by the book.

Carol is thrilled to show off her two new crash carts—self-contained cardiac arrest "rescue carts"; (they took "six months and a couple thousand requisition forms" to get) and is livid when they're stolen by Cardiology within hours after their unveiling.

Morgenstern is impressed with Mark's judgment, skill, and teaching abilities and offers him a job as an attending physician for the next year. Mark impulsively accepts without consulting Jenn and ends up sleeping on the sofa. It's obvious the Greene's marriage is getting rockier by the minute.

Deb puts on an ER case presentation that impresses Benton with its use of 3D computer graphics and prepared outlines for everyone, and Carter feels like an idiot for his own, rather unsubstantial eighty-five-word performance.

Doug pays a visit to Diane Leeds in Risk Management, and she admits that she might find him just a *little* charming. He then takes her son Jake out to shoot hoops.

Mark turns to Susan (who's still mad at him) for advice about helping a terminal patient die, and Carter finds out that Deb's mother is chief of surgery at St. Bart's Hospital.

Carol, Doug, Lydia, Carter, Bob, and Conni go on an expedition to Cardiology to steal back Carol's new crash carts, and Lydia decides she's got to start dating again after she hears that Doug and Carol did it on the kitchen floor on their first date.

Peter demands that Carol reschedule Haleh because of the problems he's having with her, but Carol refuses and uses the opportunity to blast the arrogant surgeon: "If you would ever hop off that pedestal you've put yourself on, you might see that the *nurses* make this place work, not you."

Jeannie puts in her first day caring for Peter's mother, and Peter relieves her two hours late. Jeannie is angry and sets the ground rules immediately: She tells him that if he says he's going to be there at eight, he had better be there at eight. Peter is a little taken aback by her demands, but agrees, and the episode ends with an exhausted and frustrated Peter starting to wash the dishes.

PATIENT HISTORIES

● ●

15.268. The woman hit by a plane

This pregnant woman was seriously injured and trapped in a car when a pilot missed the runway and crashed into her on an access road by the airport. (The guy who slammed her ended up "toast.") Mark and Carter had to be taken to the scene by ambulance to intubate and stabilize her before the rescue personnel could safely extricate her from the car.

When Mark and Carter arrived, her blood pressure was 70/30 and two large bore IVs had been started. An EMT told Mark her Golden Hour (see Glossary) was almost over and that she had head trauma. They had been bagging her but she'd been biting down and gagging and they had not been able to intubate her.

Mark decided to do a rapid-sequence intubation and ordered Carter to get the O neg going. He then injected the woman with Pavulon and sedated her with Versed. Mark instructed Carter to apply cricoid pressure (to protect her airway from aspiration) and injected her with succinylcholine. Once the tube was in, Carter released the cricoid pressure and the patient was able to be safely moved.

Both of her femurs were broken, she had a possible spinal-cord injury, and her pressure was 80. Mark flew back to the hospital with the patient and continued bagging her during the flight.

15.269. Bill McClintock

Bill, forty-eight, was an MVA with a fractured right femur. His pressure was 60/40 and his abdomen was rigid. Peter ordered the O neg wide open, which Haleh had already done. Carter suggested peritoneal lavage, but Peter explained that the patient was bleeding out and needed to go to surgery immediately.

Bill McClintock was Deb Chen's first Foley catheter insertion. Haleh explained it to her: "Clean it with Betadine, put K-Y on the catheter, and thread it in."

15.270. The head trauma in 1

Rolando gave this patient to Peter.

15.271. Jonathan Weiss

This forty-two-year-old patient collapsed while playing handball. When he arrived at the ER, his pressure was crashing at 40 palp, his heart rate was tachycardic at 110, and his respirations were 30. He had been given 2 liters of normal saline and 15 liters of oxygen. He had no previous history of cardiac trouble.

Lydia ordered a CBC, Chem 7, enzymes, a coag panel, and a chest film. Weiss was pale, and Mark determined that he was not oxygenating. Susan suggested a possible MI, but Mark suspected it was a pulmonary embolism.

Weiss had had no recent surgery, he had not been in a car accident, he had not experienced a recent trauma, and he did not sit all day. His EKG showed T-wave inversions and Susan again suggested it was Weiss's heart. Mark was not convinced, however, and ordered a V/Q (ventilation/perfusion) scan (see the Glossary), which would confirm an embolism. Susan simultaneously ordered an echocardiogram, which Mark allowed, saying it couldn't hurt.

Weiss's blood gases came back and showed his CO_2 was low. His puls/ox was 71, and Mark confirmed his pulmonary artery was plugged. Susan conceded that Mark had been right and immediately ordered 1.5 million units of streptokinase. Mark countermanded that order and instructed that Weiss instead be brought to a trauma room with a fluoroscope. He also ordered Dr. Morgenstern paged. Mr. Weiss needed an immediate embolectomy.

Morgenstern talked Mark through the procedure. During the catheterization, Weiss's resps were 45 and his puls/ox was 63. Mark successfully aspirated the embolus into the catheter cup, and Mr. Weiss was immediately able to breathe. His resps

While attempting a Rollerblading maneu-
ver, this twelve-year-old male fell on his
outstretched right hand resulting in a
Salter-Harris Type 2 epiphyseal fracture of
the proximal humerus. To avoid damage
to the growth plate, the humeral head,
which is in various angulation and exter-
nal rotation, must be reduced by abduc-
tion and externally rotating the arm and
then slowly bringing the arm down. If the
reduction is not accomplished, the arm
must be maintained in a cast in the Statue
of Liberty position.

—The complete text of John Carter's ER case presentation

came down and his puls/ox went up to 85. "Just like snakin' a drain," Morgenstern said, and left for his "date with a bile duct."

Later Morgenstern told Mark that Pathology had found a polyp in Weiss and that if he hadn't thrown the clot, who knows what that growth would have done to him later.

15.272. Mr. Connolly

Mr. Connolly (played from under a sheet by Bobcat Goldthwaite) came to the ER because he had been suffering from headaches and because, he explained to Carol, he had been dead for two days. Carol asked him what precipitated these headaches and he responded, "Death!"

He then began to shake and twitch, and when Carol asked him what was going on, he explained, "A nervous tic. I've had it for years."

Carol checked on Mr. Connolly later, and he told her he was still dead but that his head felt better.

15.273. Sabidowicz in 4
Haleh told Peter that she had started an IV and ordered a CBC, Chem 7, and blood gases for this patient.

15.274. Luchesi in 6
This was the patient that caused the rift between Haleh and Peter Benton.

Haleh told Peter that the patient was complaining of abdominal pain and was vomiting blood and that she had ordered NPO (nothing by mouth) and an NG (naso-gastric) tube. She also wrote gastric lavage on the chart, which enraged Peter. He said, "*You* ordered a gastric lavage?" to which she replied, "No, I wrote it down. You still have to sign it." He then shouted at her that he would write his own orders, and from that point on Haleh insisted on Peter writing everything down, *without* abbreviations.

15.275. The "Nurse?" guy
This gentleman kept saying "Nurse? Nurse?" to Haleh as she argued with Peter in the hall. When Peter left, she finally turned to the patient and shouted, "What?!"

15.276. Harold
Harold was a young man who liked snakes. He came to the ER after he was bitten by his pet yellow eyelash pit viper. Doug treated Harold's bite and instructed Carol to call Poison Control. Harold then informed Doug that he had the snake with him. When he looked into the bag, however, the snake was gone. The viper was later found by John Carter in a cabinet in an examination room.

15.277. Grace Holsten
Thirty-six-year-old Grace was brought to the ER from the Dignity House Hospice.

Grace had breast cancer that had first spread to her lymph nodes and then metastasized to her pelvis and spine. She had already had a modified radical mastectomy and been treated with tamoxifen, a chemotherapy drug.

Grace was brought to the ER by her hospice nurse, Anita Risberg, because she was in intractable pain and the hospice did not want to increase her morphine without medical supervision. (She was already on 120 milligrams of morphine just to sleep.)

Mark added fentanyl to her morphine but could not increase the dosage of morphine because it would depress her respiration even more and possibly kill her.

Grace begged Mark to help her die. Mark told her they had three choices. The first was to insert a catheter into her spinal cord to deliver the morphine directly. The second was to surgically cut the spinal tracks that carried the pain to her legs and back (a cordotomy). And the third choice was to increase her morphine, but that was likely to kill her.

Grace refused the first two surgical options and again begged Mark to let her die.

Conni told Mark that Grace's respirations were down to 14, and Mark knew that even a little more morphine would probably stop her breathing.

When Grace's resps hit 12, Mark solicited Susan's advice, but she couldn't help him. Ultimately, Mark had to make the decision on his own. And even though we don't actually see him do it, he finally did what he felt he had to do: He increased Grace's morphine and she died shortly thereafter of respiratory arrest.

15.278. The abdominal pain in curtain area 3
Rolando gave this patient to Peter.

15.279. The Viking woman
Rolando wheeled this patient, in full Valkyrie costume, through the ER halls. He told Mark, "Don't even ask."

15.280. Yummy Jackson
Twelve-year-old Yummy was a gang member who was brought to the ER with multiple gunshot wounds to the legs and abdomen. He had Tech 9 and Luger handguns on him when the EMTs found him.

When he arrived at the hospital Yummy was still breathing but had no palpable blood pressure. They kept his IVs wide open and proceeded to try and save him.

As the ER staff was working on him, a young boy around ten years old walked into the ER with a handgun and pointed it at everyone who looked at him as he searched the rooms for Yummy.

When he found the right room, he walked in and pointed the gun at Yummy's head.

"You're too late," Peter told him. "He's already dead."

The boy then pointed the gun at Peter, but changed his mind and turned and ran away.

"It's madness," Carter whispered after the boy had left.

15.281. Carter's Rollerblading accident
Carter used this patient's case as his ER presentation to Benton. (See the end of this chapter for the text of Carter's presentation.)

15.282. The hockey referee
This fifty-three-year-old patient was refereeing a hockey game when he grabbed his chest and collapsed.

When he arrived at the ER he was hypotensive with a blood pressure of 80/60, and his heart rate was tachycardic at 120. The EMTs had treated him with 15 liters of oxygen and Ringer's were already running in. They had also given him 8 milligrams of morphine. Susan saw that he was diaphoretic and ordered an EKG, cardiac enzymes, a coag panel, and a chest film.

At this point the patient went into fibrillation and had to be shocked at 200 joules.

He converted to normal sinus rhythm and ultimately was fine, much to the relief of the members of the hockey team who had come to the hospital with the ambulance.

15.283. Haleh's deviated septum
Haleh used this patient to make a point to Peter. This woman was in the ER for causes unknown to viewers, but she had been treated with 5 percent dextrose in normal saline at 100 cc per hour, had had a gastric lavage, and Peter had also ordered a CBC, Chem 7, and amylase tests. He also ordered an NG tube, but Haleh told him the woman had a deviated septum and she didn't feel comfortable doing it (even though she had probably done a thousand of them). Peter got the message.

15.284. Deb's hand laceration
Carter talked Deb through the suturing of this hand laceration. When Carter went to a cabinet to get some more 4 x 4 bandages, he found Harold's pet pit viper.

15.285. Doug's nonexistent six-year-old tetralogy of Fallot
Doug pretended he wanted Sherry Dunphy to look at this nonexistent patient in order to distract her so that Carol and the others could steal back their new crash carts from Cardiology. (See the Glossary for a definition of tetralogy of Fallot.)

15.286. Mrs. Benton
Peter's mother was discussed by Peter and Jeannie after Jeannie's first day with her. Jeannie knew that Mrs. Benton had had a right parietal CVA (cerebrovascular accident) eight months ago and told Peter that his mother was still suffering from left hemiparesis. She was masking well but she had bruises on her left side from the partial paralysis. Jeannie also told Peter he should have told her about his mother's incontinence.

●●●●●●●●●●●●●●●●●●●●●●●●●●●●●●●●●

Original Broadcast Date:
Thursday, February 2, 1995
Written by John Wells;
Directed by James Hayman

"MAKE OF TWO HEARTS"

"That was normal."

—**Mark Greene, to Susan, after they marshaled
all the resources of the ER to save the life of a stray dog**

This Valentine's Day episode opens with Jerry walking through the ER playing "She loves me, she loves me not" with a bouquet of flowers.

Carter accumulates a stack of Valentine cards from young ladies he doesn't even remember, and Mark tells Susan that he slept on the sofa last night.

Peter stashes roses and chocolates for his mother in the lounge refrigerator, but Doug is positive they're for someone Peter is secretly dating.

Doug explains to Mark that he always works on Valentine's Day to avoid any possible dating conflicts, and Deb inadvertently spends the day stoned on acid after she eats LSD-laced chocolates originally belonging to some rather out-of-it cheerleaders.

Dr. Kayson brings Susan a bouquet of flowers and asks her to dinner. She gets out of it by telling him she has already made plans with Mark.

Carol gets frustrated and angry over the way little AIDS patient Tatiana has been abandoned, and Wendy is injured by a violent patient.

Doug *almost* gets fixed up with a faking patient's mother, and later he tries to persuade Carol that she should not get involved with Tatiana's problem and that she

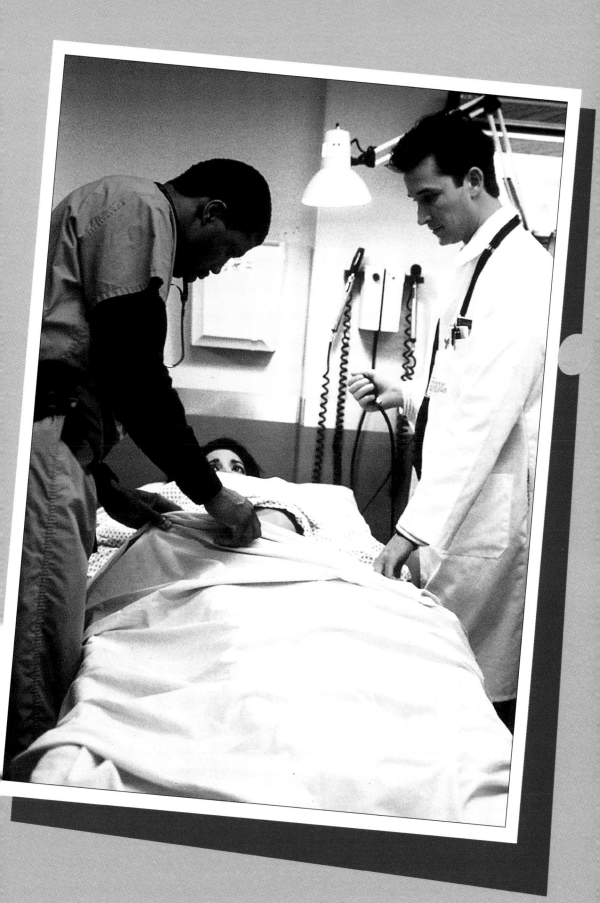

has to let the system handle it.

Peter gets home late and finds the sink running, the refrigerator open, and his mother asleep in front of the TV. He has missed seeing her on Valentine's Day.

In order not to get caught in a lie, Mark and Susan go ice skating, and he tells her about Morgenstern's job offer and that Jenn's mad at him because he accepted it without consulting her.

The episode ends with Carol visiting Tatiana in the foster home. She speaks Russian to her, and they play with Tatiana's doll, Anya, as piano music plays in the background and the scene fades to black without dialogue.

PATIENT HISTORIES

● ●

16.287. Tatiana Hall

This six-year-old Russian girl was adopted in St. Petersburg by a woman who called herself Mrs. Hall. Tatiana had only been in the United States ten days when she was brought to the ER with a cough and a fever of 100°.

Doug diagnosed upper respiratory congestion and an ear infection and prescribed oral amoxicillin.

Shortly thereafter, Tatiana's adoptive mother left the hospital, and Carol discovered that she had given them a fake phone number.

Carol (who could speak a little Russian) took charge of Tatiana and moved her to curtain area 2 so she wouldn't feel so alone. She also wheeled in Bill the dog (Patient 16.290) to keep her company.

It was obvious that Mrs. Hall had abandoned Tatiana at the hospital, and Child and Family Services (CFS) was called. Tatiana's fever remained at 100°, and Doug told McGillis from CFS that Tatiana would have to stay at the hospital for twenty-four hours. McGillis told them that the little girl would then have to be moved to a foster home.

Shortly thereafter Tatiana's fever went to 104°, and Carol gave her 15 milligrams of acetaminophen per kilo of body weight. Tests and X-rays were ordered, and Carol was stunned when the results showed that Tatiana's white count was 2,000 and that she had pneumonia. "She's got AIDS," Carol whispered in disbelief.

The acetaminophen brought Tatiana's fever back down to 100°, and Doug tried to console an angry and distraught Carol about the situation. "It is what it is," he told her, but she was not mollified. Her mood was not improved when "Mrs. Hall" finally returned to the hospital.

Mrs. Hall told Carol that Tatiana had been diagnosed with AIDS the previous Thursday at St. John's. She also told Carol that her husband had died three years ago and that she could not get that close to anyone and lose them again. She gave Carol Tatiana's things and turned to leave. As she was walking out she spotted Tatiana and said to Carol, "I forgot how to say goodbye."

"Dohzvidanya," Carol told her, but Mrs. Hall just turned and walked out of Tatiana's life. [Tatiana's story continues in episodes 17 and 18.]

16.288. The stomachache in 2
Haleh woke Mark from a nap in the doctor's lounge to give him this patient.

16.289. The bounceback migraine in 1
Haleh woke Mark from a nap in the doctor's lounge to give him this patient as well.

16.290. Bill the dog
Officer Grabarsky rushed into the ER with Bill wrapped in a blanket after he accidentally hit him with his patrol car.

Doug, Susan, Mark, and Carter all went to work on Bill and saw that he had a scalp laceration and a fractured left front radius. When Peter arrived, Carter told him they had a "car versus canine" situation, and that was when Peter noticed that Bill had stopped breathing.

They diagnosed a pneumothorax (collapsed lung) and decided to intubate Bill and do a tube thoracostomy (with the help of a veterinary manual on canine anatomy). Until they got him breathing again, Carter performed mouth-to-snout resuscitation on the pooch.

Susan told Lydia to get her a 20 gauge needle on a 60 cc syringe with a three-way stopcock and asked Mark into which intercostal region the tube should be inserted. Mark suggested the eighth, just below the heart, and it worked. The intubation was also successful, and Mark announced, "Bill lives!"

Mark instructed Carter and Deb to sew up the dog's head laceration and put on a cast. Officer Grabarsky was so grateful that he kissed Lydia smack on the mouth. Lydia was surprised but pleased, and they began dating. It isn't known if Grabarsky's new pet Bill accompanied them on their outings.

Carter probably went in search of mouthwash following Bill's treatment.

16.291. The guy who fell off a second-floor balcony
This thirty-nine-year-old was brought to the ER hypotensive and with his abdomen rigid. The EMTs put him in a trauma room.

16.292. Michael Kluge
This seventeen-year-old lost a dare with a freight train and was brought to the ER with crushed legs and head injuries.

He was hypotensive with a pressure of 80/60, and resuscitation was performed in the ambulance. The EMTs gave him 2000 ccs of normal saline, which brought his pressure up to 100. He had a blood loss of 3 to 4 units.

Doug and Peter went to work on Michael and ordered another 10 liters of saline. His pulse was 130 and his puls/ox was 82. His pressure went to 80/40 and continued falling.

Peter ordered an angiogram and O neg, and at this point Michael had a massive seizure. Unfortunately, nurse Wendy Goldman was holding his hand at the time he

seized, and he crushed it pretty seriously. They stopped the seizure by an IV push drug injection, but Wendy's hand had been fractured. (See Patient 16.299.)

Michael was brought to the O.R., but his injuries were too serious and he died during surgery.

16.293–16.295. Cheerleaders on acid Nos. 1, 2, and 3

These three young women unknowingly ate LSD-laced chocolates and were brought to the ER by the high school football player who gave them the candy.

They were kept at the hospital for observation and passed their time watching the green blips on an EKG monitor.

16.296. The bounceback migraine in 6

Haleh had to wake Mark again to give him this patient. When Mark protested that he had already seen him, she told him he saw the one in 1. This was the one in 6.

16.297. Deb Chen

Deb was not technically a patient but it's likely that she was carefully observed by the staff after it became known that she, too, had ingested two LSD-laced chocolates (See Patients 16.293–16.295).

16.298. Dr. Jack Kayson

Dr. Kayson gave Susan flowers and asked her out the day he was scheduled to be released from the hospital after his successful tPA treatment. Susan met with him as he walked on a treadmill, and they discussed her future, both medically and personally. [See episodes 13 and 14.]

16.299. Wendy Goldman

Wendy became a patient at the ER when Michael Kluge (Patient 16.292) crushed her hand during a seizure. She was X-rayed, and the films showed three metacarpal fractures. She was given "a fifth of Demerol" (actually 50 milligrams, but she was too high to remember), and Deb, who was accidentally stoned on acid, applied Wendy's cast. The cast ended up bigger than Wendy's head, and an amused Carter promised to fix it the following day.

16.300. Lorenzo Renzetti

Lorenzo, forty-five, and his son Pauly (Patient 16.301) were both brought to the ER after they got into a violent argument that escalated to "dueling meathooks."

Lorenzo had a meathook firmly embedded in his upper left bicep when he arrived by ambulance at the hospital. His blood pressure was 140/90, his pulse was 96, his respirations were 16, he had a strong distal pulse, and his capillary refill was good. He also had defensive lacerations on both arms, and Peter ordered an IV started, 1 gram of Ancef in an IV piggyback, and his tetanus updated.

Mr. Renzetti survived. His son Pauly did not.

16.301. Pauly Renzetti

Pauly made a derogatory remark about his mother, and his father, Lorenzo, and he ended up fighting with meathooks.

Unfortunately, Pauly did not get a meathook in the arm as did his father. His apparently hit his heart, and shortly after he arrived at the ER he went into fibrillation.

Mark shocked him with the defibrillator three times at 200, 300, and 360 joules, but to no avail.

Pauly didn't make it.

16.302–16.307. The little girls in Valentine's Day heart costumes

These six little girls got hives from the red spray paint they used as makeup for their Valentine's Day show. Doug treated them and told Haleh that little girls with hives were definitely *not* cute.

16.308. Eddie

Middle-aged Eddie was drunk in a hot tub with two hookers when he got lightheaded and nauseous and then threw up. He was brought to the hospital by his "dates," still wearing the flippers he had on in the tub. Mark and Susan told his lady friends that they needed to take Eddie's temperature—rectally—to keep them out of the trauma room. Eddie was eventually admitted to the hospital and even though a heart attack wasn't confirmed, it's likely he had one.

16.309. Mrs. Hayden

Jerry told Peter that Mrs. Hayden was an elderly patient who was a little senile and that she had cut her arm.

Peter found her wandering around an examination room, and when he asked her what she was doing, she replied that there was no starch. She needed starch, she explained, for Joe's uniform.

Peter sutured her right arm, and it was obvious that Mrs. Hayden's condition hit home with him because he was going through the same thing with his own mother. Maybe that's why, when she asked him if he wanted her to iron his uniform, he paused a moment and then said, yes, he would.

Later, Peter checked on Mrs. Hayden and found her ironing a towel with a box of Kleenex, completely oblivious to her surroundings.

"I guess you found the starch, huh?" Peter said softly as he watched her iron.

16.310. Jake Leeds

Jake, Diane Leeds's son, showed up in the ER complaining of a pain in his side and a stomachache.

Doug took him to curtain area 2 and ordered a CBC, a urinalysis, and an ultrasound. Jake's temperature was normal, and both Carol and Diane believed that he was faking it. (He was.)

Diane told Doug that Jake had pulled this stunt before in order to try and fix her up with single doctors.

16.311. The chicken pox in 3

Jerry gave Doug this patient.

16.312. Mrs. Goodwin

Mrs. Goodwin was brought to the ER by helicopter in anaphylactic shock after eating some kind of seafood.

She had upper-airway obstruction with stridor and she was hypotensive with a blood pressure of 45 palp.

Mark, Susan, and Haleh went to work on Mrs. Goodwin and tried to intubate her with a 6.5 endotracheal tube. Her throat was so badly swollen, however, that Susan decided she needed a crike (cricothyroidotomy).

Mrs. Goodwin was given a 1–10,000 solution of epinephrine IV push; Benadryl 50 milligrams IV; and 300 milligrams Cimetidine IV. Her pressure went to 100/80 and her puls/ox was 96. Mark ordered an epinephrine drip, 1 milligram to 250 at 10 micrograms per minute, and that was when Mrs. Goodwin began hemorrhaging out of her mouth and her blood pressure began crashing.

Mark ordered her blood typed and crossmatched for 6 units and a CBC, lytes, LFTs, and amylase.

Susan couldn't see down Mrs. Goodwin's throat with an endoscope because of bleeding varices and she asked Mr. Goodwin if his wife was an alcoholic. (The veins become enlarged and bleed in alcoholics.) He nodded yes, and Susan asked for the catcher's mask, a device that allowed a tube with two balloons attached to be positioned securely in the throat. The balloons are inflated and they put pressure on the enlarged veins in order to stop the bleeding.

Susan and Mark successfully inserted the tube and inflated the balloon in the stomach to 200 cc and the esophageal balloon to 40 milliliters.

Mrs. Goodwin survived.

● ●

Original Broadcast Date:
Thursday, February 9, 1995
Written by Lydia Woodward;
Directed by Mimi Leder

"THE BIRTHDAY PARTY"

ER 17

"One more won't make any difference now."

—Mr. Thornberg, an end-stage lung cancer patient,
responding to Carol, after she chastised him for smoking a cigarette

"I couldn't be at my mother's birthday party because I had to save a man with 'Die Nigger Die' tattooed on his forearm."

—Peter Benton, to Jeannie, after showing up after the party was over

This episode begins with Doug waking up in bed with a woman whose name he does not know. He calls her Natalie (it's Pamela), she calls him Don, and Doug decides he'll go in to work early that morning.

At the hospital, everyone reminds him that he's early, and Doug uses the time to relieve an exhausted Carol and watch Tatiana for a while.

Peter has stayed the night at his sister Jackie's house and promises his family that he will be back there by seven that evening for his mother's seventy-sixth birthday party. But he can't find anyone to trade shifts with, and later, Dr. Hicks tells him in no uncertain terms that he either stops the shift-swapping or he takes a hiatus to care for his mother. "That won't be necessary," he coldly tells her.

Deb and Carter discuss next year's elective choices, and Carter is stunned to learn that he has to actually apply to stay at the ER and that twelve med students are already in line ahead of him. Later, when he asks Benton what his chances are of getting next year's surgical sub-internship (sub-I), Peter tells him "one in thirteen." (Mark tells Carter that he walked right into that one.) Carter further antagonizes Benton by inappropriately hiring belly dancers for a "birthday" show for Peter on the basis of misunderstood eavesdropping.

Carol and Tag look at the church where he wants them to get married. She hates it. "It's a mausoleum," she tells him.

Susan confides in Mark that she doesn't think she'll ever get married because all the marriages she knows are "pretty rocky." Mark knows she's talking about him and Jenn and says, "Thank you very much." Later, when Mark shows up late for his daughter, Rachel's, birthday party, he and Jenn have an argument and Jenn drops the bombshell that she's going to clerk in Milwaukee again next year.

Peter turns down Jeannie's request for a ride to his mother's birthday party, and Diane Leeds witnesses Doug's assault on a patient and then waits for him to make sure he's all right.

Peter finally makes it home for the party, an hour after it ends, and Jeannie gets a glimpse into how tortured Peter actually is about neglecting his family for his career.

PATIENT HISTORIES

17.313. Tatiana Hall
[We first met Tatiana in episode 16 (Patient 16.287). In that episode, Carol learned that the little girl had AIDS and immediately bonded with her.]

In this episode, Tatiana was taken to the Sunrise House Hospice by Mrs. Brown from the Department of Child and Family Services.

Tatiana did not want to leave Carol, but she finally was persuaded that she had to go with Mrs. Brown. Carol and Doug watched in silence as she walked out holding onto her doll, Anya.

Carol later suggested to her fiancé, Tag, that the two of them adopt Tatiana, but he was against it: "We could be watching a child die for years," he told her.

Carol later visited the little girl at the hospice and it was obvious she was not willing to give up the idea of adoption.

17.314. All of Mort's hemorrhoid cases
In order to attend his mother's birthday party, Peter offered to trade with fellow resident Mort for his shifts on Christmas, New Year's, Thanksgiving, the Fourth of July, Flag Day, as well giving him his first born, *and* taking all his hemorrhoid cases for a year. Even with such an enticing offer, Mort couldn't help him, and Peter missed the party.

17.315. Mr. Halgrim
Mr. Halgrim walked into the ER, doused himself with gasoline, and threatened to set himself on fire.

Carter tried to talk him out of it by telling him that he'd just set off the sprinkler system and then he'd be nothing but a bald guy with a really bad sunburn. The only problem with this tack was that Mr. Halgrim knew that, much to Carter's surprise, the ER did not have a sprinkler system.

Carter then tried to persuade Mr. Halgrim to put down his lighter by offering to be his friend.

During their conversation, Peter walked right up to Halgrim and matter-of-factly covered him in foam with a fire extinguisher. He then called Carter Dr. Freud and told him that, when he was through making new friends, "Sparky" would need an eyewash and a shower (as well as a Psych Services consult).

17.316. Gus

Young Gus was brought to the ER after he got his head stuck in a wall-mounted tiger's head trophy after seeing *The Lion King* nine times.

Gus's father's great-grandfather was a Rough Rider and had bagged the tiger riding with Teddy Roosevelt in 1910. This didn't really impress Doug. He told Malik to go to Ortho and get a bone saw. Doug cut off the jaw of the stuffed tiger in order to free Gus's head.

17.317. René Franks

René was one of the ER's "regulars," a suicidal, alcoholic junkie who dated a guy named T. J. who the ER staff disgustedly referred to as "the Creep."

The *first* time René showed up at the ER in this episode, her blood pressure was 90/60, her pulse was 108, and she had been found by her father with empty bottles of vodka, brandy, Valium, Flexeril, and Darvon.

Susan ordered a CBC, Chem 7, Path 7, tox screen, and a blood alcohol. Mark told René that she was definitely not getting any Demerol and asked Susan if she wanted to do a gastric lavage. Susan said yes, and Mark told René that they were going to pump her stomach, which they immediately began doing, using a nasogastric tube. Susan ordered 3 liters of saline and charcoal, and René survived.

René's tests showed the presence of cannabis, opiates, benzodiazepines, and a blood alcohol level of 375. Her overdose had been a suicide attempt because she had had a fight with the Creep. The lavage worked, and her father reluctantly signed her out.

René returned later that evening because she had overdosed again. Her pulse was 50, her pressure was 80/50, and her respirations were 14. Her father did not know what she had taken so Susan ordered another tox screen and a BA.

René had no gag reflex, so Susan intubated her and told her "René, we haven't lost anyone today. We are not starting with you."

Susan ordered René prepped for yet another gastric lavage and her father turned and walked out of the room.

17.318. Mr. Kazuo

This patient amputated a finger of his left hand while boning a fish. Peter ordered an IV started, 5 milligrams of morphine, a CBC, an Ancef IV, a DTP (diptheria-pertussis-tetanus injection), and an X-ray.

Mr. Kazuo's coworkers had brought the big tub of fish into which the amputated digit had fallen to the ER, so Peter ordered the transplantation team to the hospital. He also ordered Carter and Deb to dig through the fish tub and find the finger. The good news was that it was on ice; the bad news was that it was in a mountain of fish.

Deb found the digit, and it is assumed Mr. Kazuo was soon back boning halibut to his heart's content.

17.319. Kyle Thomas's brother

This six-year-old boy was the son of a cop and was shot in the back and neck by his older brother Kyle.

Officer Thomas told Doug that he always locked up his guns but that this time he must have forgotten. Kyle found one of his daddy's guns and accidentally shot his brother with it.

When the boy was brought to the ER, his blood pressure was 70/50 and his pulse was 112. The EMTs had given him 15 liters of O_2 by mask and had started two large bore IVs, which were running wide open.

Peter and Doug went to work on him, and Doug confirmed bilateral breath sounds.

Peter ordered the boy's blood typed and crossmatched for 4 units as well as a CBC, and c-spine, and chest films. He also ordered a flow sheet started, and an NG tube and Foley catheter inserted.

When Malik brought in the boy's X-rays, traumatic injuries to the C7 and T1 vertebrae (the bottom vertebra of the neck and the first thoracic vertebra parallel with the shoulders) were confirmed. The boy had a serious spinal-cord injury.

To reduce spinal-cord swelling, Peter ordered a bolus of 600 milligrams of methylprednisolone, and the boy's head was placed in a Gurner-Wells clamp to prevent movement.

Peter said to call Neuro and book an O.R., and Doug went out to talk to Mr. Thomas. Doug told him that they would have to do exploratory surgery on his son and that the boy had reflex activity and anal sphincter tone, which were both hopeful signs. When Officer Thomas asked Doug if his boy would live, though, Doug replied, "It doesn't look good."

17.320. Kyle Thomas

Kyle came to the ER with his brother and was in shock when Doug saw him standing covered with blood and crying in the trauma room. Doug placed him on a gurney and ordered him put on a mask and an IV of saline started. Kyle, who looked to be around eight, later cried to his father that he had shot his brother.

17.321. Mike Thornberg

This patient was brought to the ER with end-stage lung cancer with altered mental status. Carol saw him and told Lydia to do a CBC, lytes, calcium level, and an EKG.

Mike was diagnosed as being hypercalcemic, which meant the cancer had caused too much calcium to build up in his system, and that's what was causing his disorientation and agitated state of mind. (Lung tumors produce PTH-like [parathyroid hormone] peptides that increase serum calcium concentrations.)

Susan put Mike on an IV of 300 ccs of normal saline an hour and ordered him diuresed with 40 milligrams of Lasix IV.

Mike quickly came around and Carol found him later wandering the halls, wheeling his IV pole, smoking a cigarette. As his lady friend and roommate said, Mike was "a real character."

17.322 and 17.323. The two women with "abdominal pain" in curtain area 2

Lydia summoned Peter to curtain area 2 to examine these two sisters. When Peter entered the room, Malik urgently told him that their pressure was bottoming out at 50/0. That was when they began manifesting undulating abdominal seizures that Peter had never seen before.

The "seizures" were actually belly rolls and the "patients" were actually the two belly dancers Carter had hired because he believed it was Peter's birthday. It most definitely was *not* Peter's birthday, and Dr. Benton was less than thrilled with the two ladies' "performance."

17.324. The baby who "fell" out of a second floor window

This little girl was brought to the ER by her father who said she had fallen fifteen feet off a second-floor balcony and had been unresponsive since the fall.

The EMTs reported that her skin was warm and dry, and that they were unable to get an IV going.

The baby's pulse was strong, and she moved all her extremities to pain. Doug ordered a head CT and a cross-table c-spine X-ray. He also ordered her blood typed and crossmatched for 2 units and, because he heard no bowel sounds, an abdominal CT. "Tough day to be a kid," Doug mused.

Later, Malik came for Doug and told him there was something he needed to see. The X-rays had shown no injury to her neck, so they had removed her back board and cervical restraint. When Doug rolled her over to examine her back, he saw the imprint of a workboot in vivid detail in the middle of her back.

Doug exploded and ran out into the waiting room, where he punched the father in the mouth and had to be restrained by Malik and Jerry. Later, two detectives from Domestic Violence came to the hospital to talk to the father. Outside the ER, Mark told Doug that because of his assault on the father he was probably looking at inkblots, couch time, and an appearance before the Resident Review Committee.

17.325. The rule-out MI in 1

Mark took care of this man, who presented with a possible heart attack on his sixtieth wedding anniversary. As Carol was leaving for the day she asked Rolando to check on this patient's lab results.

17.326. Olin

Peter asked Jerry for this patient's chart.

17.327. The MVA in 4

Peter asked Jerry where this patient's lab results were.

17.328. The MVA on its way

Jerry told Peter that this MVA would be arriving at the ER in six minutes.

17.329. Billy Larson

Mrs. Larson brought Billy to the ER because he had a cold and kept falling asleep in school. Doug examined him and determined he was anemic, malnourished, and badly needed a dentist.

Doug told Mrs. Larson (who had three other children) to go to food banks and shelters to get the food for her children any way that she could.

17.330. The Skinhead

This kid took a crowbar to a black kid on West Avenue, and, in retaliation, another brother jumped him with a knife.

He was brought to the ER with defensive wounds on his head and forearm, and a knife sticking out of his heart.

His blood pressure was 110/70, his pulse was 108, his respirations were 24, and his GCS was 15. He had been given 15 liters of oxygen by mask, but he was on some kind of drugs and had to be restrained.

Peter ordered his blood typed and crossmatched for 8 units of packed cells, a CBC, .8 of Narcan, and his glucose checked. He also ordered a portable X-ray. (This patient, by the way, had a swastika tattooed on one arm and DIE NIGGER DIE on his other arm, and Malik voiced the opinion that the knife in his heart should have gone all the way through. Peter got angry at that and told them all to do their damn jobs.)

It was determined the boy needed surgery and Dr. Hicks gave Peter the assignment. As they were scrubbing, she explained the procedure:

> The muscles of the left ventricle are holding the knife in place. We'll begin with a medium sternotomy to expose the structures around the knife. Then we'll open the pericardial sack, extract the knife, tamponading the wound with your finger, as you make horizontal matrice sutures to avoid the coronary arteries.

Not to everyone's delight, this charming patient survived.

17.331. Doug Ross

Doug injured his hand when he punched out the father who kicked his daughter out a second-floor window (Patient 17.324). Diane Leeds told him to get his hand looked at. It was not told whether he did or not.

● ●

Original Broadcast Date:
Thursday, February 16, 1995
Written by John Wells; Directed by Elodia Keene

"SLEEPLESS IN CHICAGO"

ER-10

"Dr. Benton, I think there's more to patient care than just cutting them open."

—John Carter

"That's what nurses are for."

—Peter Benton

"Please, no dead kids today."

—Doug Ross

This episode begins with an exhausted and surly Peter snapping and yelling at his ER comrades. A week ago he had traded shifts to be with his mother and now he has been on for forty-eight hours straight. Susan tells him, "Hey, Peter, those Dale Carnegie classes are really starting to show!"

Carol visits Tatiana in the hospice and is told that her adoption application passed with flying colors. Later, however, Carol is rejected as an adoptive mother when it is learned that she had attempted suicide several months before.

Mark tells Doug that Jenn has agreed to clerk for the judge in Milwaukee again next year. Peter argues with Dr. Hicks about his trading shifts and not getting enough sleep, and she orders him to get some rest.

A visiting "researcher" suggests that Mark and Jenn move to Kenosha and each commute an hour to their respective jobs.

Carter takes a personal interest in a terminally ill patient, resulting in Peter's questioning his suitability as a potential surgeon.

Diane Leeds comes to the ER and tells Doug she now has to defend him a second time because of the incident with Mrs. Howe (see Patient 18.343). Doug then asks her out, but she turns him down. Later she agrees to go out with him, but it's obvious she's not sure she's making the right decision.

Dr. Morgenstern tells Mark that he's taking over Brigham's residency program at Harvard and that Mark's attending job is "almost a lock." The new guy (who hasn't arrived yet) has to approve it, but Morgenstern doesn't think there'll be any problems. Mark is taken aback by this new development.

Peter finally goes home and promises Walt he'll get up early enough to give his mother her medicine.

A distraught and vulnerable Carol visits Doug looking for emotional support. To his credit, when she tries to kiss him, he turns away, knowing he shouldn't take advantage of her in the state she's in.

At home, Mark makes the Kenosha suggestion to Jenn, but it falls on deaf ears. Jenn tells him she can't go on like this anymore and that she's leaving him.

The episode ends with Peter's mother being rushed to the ER after she falls down the stairs because Peter didn't wake up in time to give her her medicine.

PATIENT HISTORIES

● ●

18.332. The crash ileectomy
Dr. Jagman operated on this patient (much to Peter's displeasure) and removed two feet of necrotic bowel (which Carter kept in a jar at the admitting desk while waiting for Research to pick it up).

The patient infarcted during the procedure, perfectly illustrating the old maxim about the operation being a success, but the patient dying anyway.

18.333. The diabetic woman with pressure sores
Susan asked Peter why he didn't admit this woman. The woman needed to be debrided, Susan told him, or she was not going to heal. Peter adamantly told her that maybe Medicine could take her, but the patient was *not* a surgical candidate and she was not coming onto his service.

18.334. The Code Brown in 2
Peter yelled to Carter to get a nurse and clean up this Code Brown. (A patient did not make it to the bathroom in time.)

18.335. Tatiana Hall
Tatiana was still living at the Sunshine House Hospice when Carol visited her and

asked her if she wanted to come and live with her. (The first thing Tatiana wanted to know was if Carol had a VCR.)

Carol had obviously convinced Tag that adopting Tatiana was the right thing to do, and Carol's application passed with flying colors—until the Family Development Department dug a little deeper and learned about Carol's suicide attempt less than a year ago.

Carol's adoption of Tatiana was immediately called off, and the little AIDS patient was left at the hospice.

18.336. The drug test subject

This young college student hired himself out as a drug test subject to make extra money.

He showed up at the ER with a two-day-old rash that had started on his chest and then spread, as well as a fever. Two of the drugs he was taking were P43B and ZX7.

He told Malik that the experiment in which radioactive isotopes were injected into his brain paid very well. Malik was curious and asked him how much he made a year.

18.337. Mr. Primmer

Peter asked Carter if he had stuck this patient for blood gases. When Carter replied, "Stuck him," Benton told him to discharge him.

18.338 and 18.339. Jagman's two bowel infarctions

Peter told Dr. Hicks that since Jagman had already done two bowel infarctions, *he* should have been the one to do the next procedure. Dr. Hicks was not persuaded and blasted Peter for turning his residency into a competition.

18.340. The burn in 1

Carol gave Doug this patient.

18.341. The knee laceration in 5

Peter took this patient.

18.342. Joyce Warner's sickle cell case

Mark referred to this case as he was buttering up Dr. Warner in an attempt to convince her to take a look at the drug test subject (Patient 18.336) Susan was treating.

18.343. Bonnie Howe

This little girl was brought to the ER with a second-degree burn on her right palm in the shape of a star.

Her mother told Carol and Doug that the knob had come off the radiator and Bonnie had grabbed the metal part and burned herself. As Doug was examining her, Bonnie kept moaning, "It's my fault. It's my fault."

Carol and Doug were immediately suspicious, and Carol decided to call around to the other area hospitals and inquire as to whether Bonnie had been treated for the same type of injury elsewhere.

Carol learned that Bonnie had previously been treated at Mercy General for the same type of burn. Carol took Mrs. Howe outside the room and asked her to explain

how this happened. "Most people don't understand," Mrs. Howe told Carol, to which Carol replied, "I'm pretty understanding." Carol then lied to Mrs. Howe and told her she would not tell the doctor anything she told her.

Bonnie touches herself "down there," Mrs. Howe explained, and after three chances, she puts a star-shaped paperweight on the stove, and when it's extremely hot, makes Bonnie hold it in her hand.

Carol and Doug reported Mrs. Howe to the police and she was arrested. Bonnie was taken into the custody of Child and Family Services.

18.344. Art Moss (a.k.a. Sam Hart; a.k.a. Gene Finch)

This elderly man was dragged into the ER by the manager of the restaurant where he had been eating. After finishing the thirty-five dollar champagne brunch (complete with steak and eggs) Art/Sam/Gene keeled over and started shaking and shivering. His eyes then rolled back, and that was when the manager decided to bring him to the hospital.

Susan told Lydia that it sounded like a grand mal epileptic seizure. However, the patient had no tongue abrasions and no sign of incontinence but he was unresponsive, so they put him in curtain area 2.

Upon examination, they found that Art/Sam/Gene's blood pressure was 120/80, and that even though he had a slightly irregular heartbeat, his reflexes were normal.

That was when Mr. Moss/Hart/Finch opened his eye and peeked at Susan. It turned out that he was a world-class con artist and petty thief and had faked a seizure to get out of paying his meal tab. While at the hospital, he picked Mark's pocket and stole six dollars out of his wallet, then flim-flammed Jerry out of twenty dollars of petty cash.

18.345. Joseph Klein

This old man fell down a flight of stairs and was brought to the ER with a collapsed lung, tracheal shift, possible broken rib, and congestive heart failure. As Mark so colorfully put it, "This guy's a train wreck."

Mr. Klein's blood pressure was 80/60, his capillary refill was poor, he had pedal edema, and his heart rate was racing at 128. The EMTs had not been able to find a vein to start an IV, so Mark ordered Malik to prep him for a central line.

Mr. Klein also had an NG tube, and during his examination it was discovered that his voice box had been removed during previous cancer surgery.

They gave Mr. Klein 5 milligrams of morphine, some normal saline, and 400 milligrams of dopamine. His pressure was only 60 palp, so Mark ordered the dopamine increased 10 micrograms per minute. Peter started putting in a chest tube, but Dr. Hicks came in and took over, telling Peter to go get some rest. She successfully inserted the tube, and Mr. Klein's puls/ox went from 82 to 90, and they registered breath sounds.

Mark joyfully exclaimed, "The train is back on the track!", and that was when Carter told him that Mr. Klein's old chart revealed that he had terminal cancer and had signed a DNR (do not resuscitate) order the last time he was at the hospital.

Mark ripped off his gloves in disgust and left the trauma room.

Carter was greatly affected by Mr. Klein's case and learned that the old man hadn't spoken to his son in twenty years and that he was all alone in the world. Carter began reading to him and spending time with him, and was with him when he died.

Peter scolded Carter for spending too much time with one patient and asked him why he wanted to be a surgeon when he didn't think like one.

18.346. Marty (a.k.a. John Koch)

This dapper young man introduced himself to Mark as "John Koch, MIT, Sloan School of Management" and told him that he was working on the Andover Project, a study focusing on building a new hospital for the twenty-first century. He was working on a team approach to medicine and envisioned a hospital without departments, one in which each floor had teams of professionals all working together for the patient. He told Susan that the current system's territorialism and friction between departments was "all part of an outdated patriarchal system based on confrontation where he who yells the loudest wins even though he may be totally wrong."

Susan was impressed with Koch and was surprised when he offered her a job in the new hospital he was building. It was right after she told him she was interested that an orderly and a psychiatric nurse showed up to take "Marty" back to the institution. It seemed that Marty liked to impersonate medical professionals and once even passed himself off as an OB and delivered two babies before he got caught.

18.347. The lacerated liver

This patient was in a two-car accident, and when he arrived at the ER, Jagman got to do the surgery to repair his liver because Benton was on his mandated rest period. Peter was upset that he did not get to do the procedure and told Carter to bring him anything surgical, and that he did not want to wait to be called for a consult.

18.348. Mrs. Von Avery

Conni asked Jerry for twenty dollars for cabfare to send Mrs. Von Avery home.

18.349. Mr. Furst

After his pain worsened for two days, this patient arrived at the ER in agony. Carter gave Peter the rundown on Mr. Furst:

> Patient is a fifty-two-year-old male with a history of calcium oxalate stones. Intravenous pylogram showed a 6 millimeter kidney stone in the calyx consistent with obstructive uropathy. Lithotripsy unsuccessful, urology's been paged. We started an IV for hydration, gave him 5 milligrams of morphine for the pain.

After listening to Carter, Peter took it upon himself to order Furst to the O.R. for removal of the stone.

Mark, who had not even examined Furst yet, was livid with Peter's presumptuousness and told him he was supposed to wait until he was called for a consult. Peter said, okay, examine him, but Mark signed the order anyway and shouted at Peter, "Don't pull this crap again!"

Mr. Furst did not end up needing surgery. He passed the stone naturally as they were preparing to anesthetize him.

18.350. Doug Ross
Doug received three deep scratches on his neck struggling with Mrs. Howe as Carol carried away her daughter Bonnie. Carol cleaned and bandaged Doug's injuries.

18.351. The GSW to the neck
This sixteen year old was shot by a cop as he was robbing a store. When he arrived at the ER he was bleeding profusely, and his blood pressure was only 60/40. Carol bagged him, and they prepared to intubate him.

Doug ordered the kid loaded up with O neg and told someone to get Benton. The kid had been shot in the carotid artery and was bleeding into his lung. Peter used a vascular clamp on the bleeder, which stopped the hemorrhaging.

18.352. The drunken slob
Peter fell asleep suturing this patient's arm. The drunk, who also had fallen asleep, heard Benton's beeper and woke him up.

18.353. The cop
This officer took a bullet straight to the heart, and when he arrived at the ER he was bleeding out. Mark ordered another liter of saline and a thoracotomy tray.

Peter arrived and identified a hole in the guy's ventricle. He ordered acetylcholine and a macrochromatic needle. He closed the hole using horizontal matrices, explaining that the trick was to seal the wound without closing off the artery.

Peter's suturing worked, and Dr. Hicks commented that the rest she had ordered apparently did him some good.

18.354. Mrs. Benton
Peter's seventy-five-year-old mother fell down the stairs after Peter failed to hear her when she called for her medicine.

The EMTs diagnosed a possible hip fracture, and when she arrived at the ER her blood pressure was 90/60 and her heart rate was 110. The EMTs told Susan and Carter that they had started an IV of normal saline and given her 10 liters of O_2 by nasal cannula. Her GCS was 3–5–4 and Susan ordered calls made to Radiology and Neurology.

Susan told Carter to check her pupils and response to pain, and when she asked Peter what had happened, he was so stunned he couldn't even respond.

Mrs. Benton was admitted to the hospital.

● ●

Original Broadcast Date:
Thursday, February 23, 1995
Written by John Wells;
Directed by Christopher Chulack

"LOVE'S LABOR LOST"

"I have never seen such a chain of errors in judgment!"

—OB Attending, Dr. Coburn

"What do you mean? I did what you said."

—Mark Greene

"You miss a preeclampsia, you underestimate the fetal weight . . ."

—Dr. Coburn

"I was expecting OB backup!"

—Mark Greene

". . . you miss a placental abruption . . ."

—Dr. Coburn

"What?"

—Mark Greene

"Blood clot. [points to X-ray] Right there. You do an ill-advised forceps delivery on a baby that's too big and then you do a hack job of a c-section."

—Dr. Coburn

"Hey, look. It was me in the barrel with a baby going down the tubes."

—Mark Greene

"The only thing that saved you from disaster was dumb luck!"

—Dr. Coburn

"Yeah? Well, if it wasn't for me the mother'd be dead and the baby, a vegetable."

—Mark Greene

• • •

"It was my fault she went sour. She's my patient."

—Mark Greene, to Susan

"Dr. Greene, I just wanted to tell you that I thought what you did was a heroic thing."

—John Carter, after Jody O'Brien died

eclampsia: n. a rare and serious condition, affecting women either at the end of pregnancy or shortly after childbirth, in which the whole body is affected by convulsions and the patient eventually passes into a coma. Eclampsia is a threat to the life of both baby and mother.

—*Bantam Medical Dictionary*

"It's like joining the circus."

—Mark, to Carter, on working at the ER

Usually Mark and company treat over a dozen patients in a single episode, and several more are often mentioned but not seen, but in this episode, there's only one patient: Jody O'Brien. Oh, sure, a gangbanger is treated for a gunshot wound, Mrs. Benton is operated on, and a tattooed man is looked at for a skin abrasion, but the only patient who really matters is the very pregnant Jody.

"Love's Labor Lost" begins with Mark and Doug passing a football and ends with Mark riding home alone on the train after Jody O'Brien has died.

In another continuing story arc, Peter now has to deal with the guilt he feels over his mother's fall down the stairs while he was sleeping.

Other than a few other run-of-the-mill patients and emergencies, the remainder of this episode is concerned with the young mother-to-be Jody O'Brien, who came to the ER because she was urinating a little too often and ended up leaving the hospital in a body bag.

"Love's Labor Lost" might well be the single best ER episode of the first season.

PATIENT HISTORIES

19.355. The kid thrown out of the car
Doug and Mark were passing a football outside the ER when a car sped by and threw this kid out of the backseat.

The kid's pulse was thready and weak, and he was bleeding. They gave him 15 liters of O_2 and started a flow sheet. His blood pressure was 60/30, and Mark ordered his blood typed and crossmatched for 8 units and a saline IV wide open.

Mark asked Carter and Deb what he should do next, and Carter said .8 Narcan.

It was then that the kid began going down the tubes. He had a single gunshot wound, his heart rate was 108, and they could barely feel a pulse. He went into arrest, and Carter started CPR. Mark decided to do a thoracotomy because the boy had a penetration trauma and was in full arrest.

Susan used the rib spreader, and they found his pericardium dry. Mark found the hole in the kid's aorta and was able to get a faint pulse. The kid was eventually stabilized and sent to surgery.

19.356. The three-month-old baby with the 105° fever
Lydia asked Doug to take a look at this infant.

19.357. Mrs. Benton
Mrs. Benton was brought to the ER with a broken hip sustained when she fell down the stairs at Jackie's house.

When she arrived at the ER her blood pressure was 140/90, and Susan ordered her given another 3 milligrams of morphine, which Peter raised to 5. Shortly thereafter, in the examination room, Peter ordered yet another 5 milligrams of morphine; and a Chem 7, U/A, and EKG; as well as hip, chest, and pelvis X-rays.

Peter also ordered a call made to the chief of Orthopedics.

Haleh made Peter leave the room when they undressed his mother because she did not want to be naked in front of her son.

Dr. Wilson, the chief of Orthopedics, arrived and told Peter that he would scrub in on the surgery, but that he was going to have a resident do the actual procedure. Peter was livid and insisted that Wilson himself do the operation, to which Wilson finally agreed. But he told Peter, "Look, I know this is your mother, but you are way over the line, son."

Peter tried to scrub in and assist on his mother's operation, but Wilson threw him out of the O.R., coldly telling him, "Don't test me."

Mrs. Benton came out of Recovery at 11:47 that evening. She had lost approximately 500 cc of blood and she was brought to room 604.

19.358. Mr. Longét, the Tattoo Man

This patient presented at the ER with a severe abrasion on his right bicep. Mr. Longét, a diabetic, was covered with tattoos and had tried to remove one of his body decorations with a power sander.

Mark ordered Carter to give Mr. Longét a gram of Ancef, update his tetanus, and give Plastics a call. As he was examining the rest of Mr. Longét's body, Mark mused that perhaps they'd be able to do a skin graft by moving a serpent head from his left arm onto the injured area.

Mr. Longét was shocked: "Onto the body of a goddess!?"

19.359. Jody O'Brien

Thirty-year-old Jody O'Brien was pregnant and due in two weeks when she was brought to the ER one afternoon by her husband, Sean, because her stomach hurt and she had to urinate every thirty seconds.

Mark thought that it sounded like a bladder infection and took a fetal weight measurement. He determined that the baby's weight was five or six pounds (this was Mistake Number 1) and Jody told him that she had had no medical problems with the pregnancy until now. He asked her about cramping and vaginal bleeding, and ordered a fetal microphone so he could hear the baby's heart sounds. Jody broke into laughter when Mark asked her if she thought she could give him a urine sample.

When the test results came back, Mark discussed Jody's case with Carter and Deb. Mark felt that even though Jody had said she was thirty-eight weeks along in her pregnancy, he thought her dates were off because the baby was small on exam. Jody's initial blood pressure had been 130/90, but it had dropped to 120/80. (Mark's perfunctory dismissal of Jody's initial high blood pressure reading was Mistake Number 2.) He noted that she had no cramps or spotting and that her urinalysis test showed white cells too numerous to count as well as the presence of bacteria. It also showed a 2 plus protein result (an indication of possible kidney disease or trouble). Jody's CBC was normal, though, and she had no fever.

Deb volunteered a diagnosis: simple cystitis (Mark concurred). And she suggested fluids, rest, and a course of Bactrim. (At this point Sean asked who Deb and Carter were, and when told they were med students, Jody commented, "They're so young," to which Mark replied, "I know. It's disgusting.")

Mark decided on Macrodantin as the antibiotic of choice and told Jody to rest, drink plenty of fluids, and follow up with her doctor in the morning.

He then released her in the late afternoon.

(Mark told Carter and Deb that he chose Macrodantin over Bactrim because the sulfa drugs, of which Bactrim is one, compete with bilirubin for the binding sites on albumin and that this increases the risk of neonatal jaundice.)

7:15 P.M.: At 7:15 that evening, Sean O'Brien came running back into the ER shouting for Mark. His wife, Jody, was unconscious in the car. She had had a seizure in the parking lot. (As Susan later said to Mark, "Oops.")

Mark, Haleh, Carter, Deb, and Carol immediately went to work on Jody. They started a flow chart and Mark ordered a stat. BP, a second IV, and 15 liters of O_2 by mask. Her blood pressure was up to 160/100, and Mark ordered 4 grams of Proclamptin by IV, a coag panel, and a fetal monitor. Jody had eclampsia, and, when she seized again, Mark ordered a bite block, 4 milligrams of magnesium sulfate, and 2 milligrams of Ativan. He decided to do an external jugular. A bed pan was placed beneath her.

Jody's seizure stopped, and Mark ordered her hyperventilated. He also requested a Doppler ultrasound, blood gases, and did a quick pelvic exam. Mark heard strong fetal heart tones on the Doppler at a rate of 140 and determined that Jody was 2 centimeters dilated, 80 percent effaced, and that the membrane was intact. He ordered 30 cc of saline and asked that a call be made to OB. He then explained to Jody's husband that eclampsia was a condition in which the blood vessels go into spasm, causing a lack of oxygen to the brain, which leads to the seizures.

Mark then briefed Susan on the case and told her he was going to stay at the hospital even though his shift was over. He felt a little guilty because he had seen Jody earlier, and he wanted to make sure she was going to be all right.

Jody's blood pressure remained steady at 120/70, and Mark graded the baby's physical profile at an 8 (2 each for movement, breathing, tone, and amount of fluid). He explained that anything less than a 6 was cause for worry. As Jody and Sean discussed baby names (Thurman, Jason, and Patrick were all considered) Mark had Carter estimate the baby's weight by dividing the abdomen into four sections and finding the deepest pockets of fluid without fetal parts or umbilical cord. He instructed Carter to mark each corner of the quadrant, measure, and add up the numbers. Jody's AFI was 14. Mark also told the O'Briens that the baby's heart rate should be between 120 and 160. At that moment their son's was 140, which Mark assured them was excellent.

Mark discussed Jody's case on the phone with Dr. Coburn, the OB attending, who was busy at St. Luke's Hospital. He gave her Jody's numbers and confirmed that her cervix was favorable for delivery. He assured Dr. Coburn that he felt very comfortable handling an induction of labor and delivery and she told him she'd get there as soon as she could.

9:00 P.M.: Jody's repeated blood pressure readings had all been normal, and Mark decided to start the induction and do a trial of labor. He ordered Carol to give Jody .5 milligrams of Pitocin IV (see the Glossary).

10:12 P.M.: Jody's contractions were coming every ten minutes, she was 5 centimeters dilated, 90 percent effaced, at station minus 2, and her membrane was still intact. (During Mark's examination, Jody bemusedly asked Carter if he wanted to look too, and he eagerly said yes.)

Names were still being discussed, and the choices had been narrowed to Ian, Patrick, Dermott, Hunter, and Jared. Jody and Sean asked Mark's opinion, and while reviewing the choices, he noted that Jared was on both of their lists. "Jared it is," he told them.

12:45 A.M.: Jody was now in full labor with contractions two to three minutes apart. She decided that she had had enough "natural childbirth" and requested an epidural. EKG tracings were showing decreased rate activity of the baby's heart, and Mark explained that babies sleep in twenty-minute cycles in utero and that the little guy needed to be awakened. He accomplished this by giving Jody's belly a little electrical shock, which woke the baby up and caused his heart rate to rise. At this point, Dr. Urami, the anesthesiologist, arrived to give Jody her epidural.

2:30 A.M.: At this point Jody was 8 centimeters dilated and completely effaced, and Mark assured her that it wouldn't be too much longer. Susan took a pressure reading inside the uterus and also an EKG off a fetal scalp electrode, which showed repeated D cells and a rate that was variable with a late component. Mark ordered Jody infused with 500 cc of normal saline through the uterine catheter.

3:15 A.M.: Mark demanded to know why he couldn't send Jody up to Obstetrics. Her epidural was wearing off, and he told someone to find Drake, the OB resident. Jody had just about had it with her labor at this point and told her husband, "You know that fantasy you have about me quitting work, staying home, and having a bunch of kids? Forget it! This is it!"

Mark decided that the time had come for Jody to deliver. She was fully dilated and 100 percent effaced, and they couldn't wait any longer.

Mark instructed Jody to start pushing and told Carter to *run* and get Carol as well as a baby warmer and newborn resuscitation unit STAT.!

Jody's labor continued, but the delivery was not progressing. The baby's heart rate was dangerously low, and Mark told Carter to go up to OB and *drag* Drake down there and make sure he brought some forceps with him. In the meantime, Mark decided to start the pudendal block (used when an episiotomy is planned and during forceps deliveries).

4:13 A.M.: Carter told Mark that OB had two c-sections and three imminent deliveries. Susan told him to wait for OB, but Mark decided that the baby monitor said it was now or never. "Why put your ass on the line?" Susan asked him, but Jody's BP was 150/100, and the baby was breaking down. Mark decided to go for a delivery.

To prevent breaking the growth plates, Mark told Susan to cut a medium episiotomy, and almost immediately the baby's head delivered.

But then the trouble began. The baby's shoulders got stuck on Jody's pelvic bone (shoulder dystocia, see the Glossary), and Mark ordered the leads off and initiated a McRoberts maneuver. He told Carter to apply fundal pressure by pushing down on Jody's abdomen as he tried to free little Jared's shoulders. He ordered the episiotomy extended and tried to rotate the infant's posterior shoulder medially and deliver that first. It didn't work, and he then decided to do a "splash and crash": He pushed the baby back inside the uterine canal and called for a cesarean tray. He also told someone to get Benton.

Mark told Sean O'Brien that he needed his consent to do the c-section, but that if they waited five more minutes his baby would be brain dead. Sean anxiously consented and Mark ordered a call made to Respiratory stat.

Jody's abdomen was painted with Betadine. Her pressure was now 170/120, and Mark decided there was no time for anesthesia and that he would throw in a local. As he was preparing to begin the cesarean, Jody had a seizure. Mark ordered a bite block and instructed that she be paralyzed and intubated with 4 milligrams of Versed and .10 of Norcuron (vecuronium). He used a 7.5 endotracheal tube to intubate and ordered her given 15 liters of oxygen. He instructed that she be bagged and that they type and crossmatch her blood and do a coag panel.

Jody's blood pressure was now sky high at 200/130, and the panic in the trauma room was palpable. After Deb Chen knocked over a tray covered with instruments, Mark told everyone to stop and take a deep breath.

He then ordered that Jody be given 10 milligrams of hydralazine and another bolus of magnesium sulfate. He also told someone to call the NICU (Neonatal Intensive Care Unit) and have them come down for the baby. He also once again told someone to go up to OB and physically drag someone down to the ER.

Mark began the cesarean with Susan assisting. Neither of them was sure of the exact surgical procedure, and Mark was especially concerned about not cutting the baby with his scalpel.

As soon as he cut through the uterine wall and exposed the cavity, another complication reared its ugly head. Jody had had a placental abruption and there were 2 liters of blood in her uterus. Jody was bleeding out, and Mark knew he had to get the baby out immediately or both the mother and the baby would die.

He ordered 8 units of O neg stat. When he got the baby out, its blood pressure was 120/80 and he was much bigger than Mark had estimated.

They suctioned his nose, and it was then that they saw that Jared O'Brien, less than one minute old, was not breathing.

4:42 A.M.: Doug took over caring for the baby and Mark instructed Carter to reach into Jody's chest, feel for her aorta, push down on it, and not let go. (See Patient 19.365 for details on the treatment provided to Jared O'Brien.)

At this point, Jody's blood pressure was 80/50, her pulse was 112, a Foley was in, and she had had three units of normal saline.

Dr. Coburn finally showed up and demanded to know what was going on. Mark gave her the bullet: "I intubated, baby went bad; I tried forceps, he got a shoulder dystocia, she seized; I para-lyzed and did a crash section. Got in there and there are two liters of blood in her uterus." Coburn then asked Mark if he had known the patient had abrupted, and he admitted that he had not known until he got in there. (This was Mistake Number 3.) Coburn then saw Carter with his hand in Jody's chest and asked who he was and what he was doing. Carter told her, "John Carter, med student, and I'm pressing on the aorta." Coburn saw the incision and said, "It's a damn mess, What'd you use, a chainsaw?"

5:30 A.M.: The NICU baby transporter arrived and took charge of Jared. Coburn and Mark worked on Jody and achieved hemostasis (cessation of bleeding). They gave her transfusions, and Mark went out to tell Sean that his wife was stable.

As Coburn argued with Mark about his judgment during this crisis (see the dialogue excerpt leading off this chapter), Deb came running to tell Mark that Jody was crashing.

Jody's capillary refill was bad, and they immediately started an arterial line and put her on a rapid effuser transducer to supply her with blood. Mark ordered a milligram of atropine and a dopamine drip. He then took her off the respirator and had her bagged manually.

It was at this point that Jody went into DIC (disseminated intravascular coagulation—no blood clotting). Mark ordered 100 milligrams of lidocaine IV push and another 10 units of blood. Jody's EKG began showing multifocal PVCs and she lost her pulse. Mark grabbed the defibrillation paddles and shocked her three times, once at 260 joules, once at 300, and once at 360, but to no avail. At this point she had been "down" for thirty-three minutes. Mark then performed external heart massage, but Jody's blood gases were bad and her EKG was showing flat line.

6:45 A.M.: Mark continued external heart massage and ordered another 7 milligrams of epinephrine. Susan told him it was thirty minutes past too late and that Jody was gone. Coburn stepped in and called Time of Death at 6:46 A.M. Mark refused to accept this and said she wasn't flat line, that her EKG showed fine defibrillation, and he again ordered the epi.

No one moved as Susan looked him straight in the eyes, silently communicating to him the undeniable truth that Jody was dead.

Mark ripped off his gloves, walked out of the ER, and got right on an elevator that he took up to the NICU.

Mark found Sean O'Brien in the nursery holding his new son and told him his wife was dead. (This is seen through the nursery's glass wall, the conversation is not heard.) Later, Carter found Mark staring down at Jody's body and attempted to offer some solace, but it didn't help.

On the train home, Mark cried for a dead mother who would never see her son take his first step, a tragedy for which he obviously accepted full blame.

The almost unanimous opinion of OB and ER people with whom I've discussed this episode is that it's medically realistic in the way Jody is treated as each of her crises manifest, but it's a little unrealistic in its basic premise. My sources say there is no way Mark would have been put in the position of having to induce labor and deliver Jody's baby in the ER because OB and the OB attending were just too busy.

19.360. The old man with dentures

Carter did a physical examination on this gentleman which included the following:

1. Follow my finger with your eyes
2. Squeeze your eyes shut tightly
3. Press against my hand with your face
4. Show me your teeth

When Carter got to number four, the patient reached inside his mouth and removed a full set of dentures, which he proffered to a surprised Carter.

19.361. Joey Paige

Joey's father found Joey passed out in the greenhouse at the nursery where Mr. Paige worked. The EMTs gave him Narcan, glucose, and saline, and, when he arrived at the ER, his blood pressure was 90/60 and he had a low pulse rate.

While under observation, Joey crashed with a pulse that went down to 40, and a blood pressure of 70/50. He was also incontinent and frothing at the mouth.

Mark and Doug learned that Joey's blood results showed a negative drug screen (no presence of drugs in his blood), and they ordered 1 milligram of atropine IV push, and a 1 milligram per hour drip.

It was eventually determined that Joey had been poisoned by the phosphate insecticide that had been sprayed in the greenhouse that morning. His father was relieved that Joey had not been taking drugs or drinking since he had lost other children to alcohol and drugs.

19.362. The weak and dizzy in 3
Doug told Deb Chen to work up this patient.

19.363. Sadie Hubbell
This woman asked Carter and Mark to sign a "get well" card for herself.

19.364. The hemorrhoids case
Jerry offered this chart to Mark, but when Mark heard it was a hemorrhoids case, he pointed to Carter, who resignedly took it.

19.365. Jared O'Brien
Jody and Sean O'Brien's son, Jared, was delivered by emergency cesarean section, and after his nose was suctioned and his umbilical cord clamped, Mark saw that he was not breathing.

Mark intubated him with a 2.0 tube, and they started CPR on him. They did a glucose stick, which showed his blood sugar was 20 and his tone was flaccid.

They pumped in the O neg (10 cc per kilo), bagged him, and hyperventilated him. They also gave him D10 (10 percent dextrose solution) and .04 milligrams of epinephrine. Mark did an umbilical line and with the O neg, the glucose, and the saline, Jared began pinking up.

Once he was stabilized, Jared was transported to the NICU where he was presumably observed until his father took him home.

19.366. The little girl who thanked Susan
This young lady thanked Dr. Lewis as she was leaving the ER. It was not said what she had been treated for.

19.367 and 19.368. OB's two c-sections
These were two of the cases that had OB so busy they could not take Mark's ER patient Jody O'Brien into their service.

19.369–19.371. OB's three imminent deliveries
Likewise, these three cases.

• •

Original Broadcast Date:
Thursday, March 7, 1995
Written by Lance A. Gentile;
Directed by Mimi Leder

"FULL MOON, SATURDAY NIGHT"

"Rita, you cheating bitch! I'll kill you!"
—PCP Gurney Man

"Full moon, Saturday night."
—Susan Lewis

"Cool."
—John Carter

"It feels like a bag of worms."
—John Carter, the first time he felt a live heart

"People die, Mark. You do the best you can. You're human."
—Jenn Greene

"I'm not supposed to be."
—Mark

"Sure you are. You're the only one who doesn't know it."
—Jenn

"You may change your mind when you see the dress."
—Carol Hathaway, after Susan agreed to be one of her bridesmaids

This episode begins with a plaintive saxophone playing over scenes of the Chicago skyline at night.

We then see Mark standing in an empty trauma room staring at the bed where Jody O'Brien died. Susan suggests he take the night off and, uncharacteristically, Mark agrees to and leaves the hospital.

Doug is now dating Diane Leeds on a regular basis and spending nights at her apartment.

Susan prepares Carter for his first "full moon, Saturday night" while the ever-competitive Deb sneaks a look at Carter's procedure book.

Mark meets the new ER chief at a diner, but doesn't know who he is and is rude to him.

Peter fights with Tag about releasing Mrs. Benton from the hospital too early. Carol and Tag look through bridal books, listen to tapes of wedding bands, and discuss their honeymoon.

Wild Willy, the new ER chief, pulls a surprise drill and calls a meeting, and Mark shows up when it's all over. Later, on the train home, Doug tries to convince Mark that Jody's death was not his fault.

Mark gets off at his stop (800N, 300W), sits down on a bench, and that is where Jenn finds him the next morning.

Back at the hospital in the morning, Carol and Susan joke that every full moon should be lady's night. Carol muses that they were like Thelma and Louise last night, but Susan says they were more like Lucy and Ethel.

The episode ends with Carter calling in a request for "Twist and Shout" to the local radio station and dedicating it to Susan. As the new day begins, Carter, Carol, and Susan dance to the song as life in the ER goes on around them.

PATIENT HISTORIES

● ●

20.372. The PCP Gurney Man

Doug described this guy as a "jilted boyfriend on PCP, twenty-two, six foot eight, strapped to his own gurney."

Susan got the assignment to handle him, but Gurney Man went nuts before she had a chance to examine him. He stood up and started screaming and, still strapped to his gurney, crashed through a window, trashed several rooms of the ER, and then stalked out of the ER like some bizarre medical Frankenstein's monster.

This was the last we saw of PCP Gurney Man.

20.373. Mrs. Benton

In this episode, Peter's mother continued her stay in the hospital as she recovered from hip-replacement surgery.

Her mental state was still forgetful and occasionally disoriented. After a long enough period had passed, Tag was the orthopedist who had to break the news to Peter that his mother could no longer stay in the hospital (Medicare wouldn't pay for any more time) and that he had better get his family together and find a good nursing home.

Not characteristically, Peter angrily refused to accept what Tag (and everyone else for that matter) was saying and adamantly insisted that his mother was going home, *no matter what.* Ludicrously, he even said that *he* would take care of her.

Physical therapist Jeannie Boulet had agreed to sit with Mrs. Benton in her hospital room, and one day Peter went to visit his mother and found her restrained to the bed, and Jeannie nowhere in sight. When Jeannie returned, he confronted her, and she told him that she had been the one who had asked that Mrs. Benton be restrained.

Peter then "fired" her and spent all his off-shift time in his mother's room. He also removed her restraints.

When Peter got paged to the unscheduled meeting with the new ER chief, he left his mother alone. When he returned a few hours later, he found her on the floor next to the bed. She had tried to get out of bed by herself, had fallen, and could not get up.

This apparently convinced Peter that everyone was right about her needing skilled nursing care for the rest of her life, and, at the end of the episode, Peter made an apologetic visit to Jeannie's house, where he also met her husband, and asked her to help him find some good nursing homes for his mother.

20.374. Louie

Louie was an elderly man who had a severely enlarged prostate and was a tad senile.

The first time we saw Louie, Conni was chasing him through the halls as he sat on a rolling porta-potty. (He was yelling that she was trying to kill him.) Conni told Carter to catch him and then told Carol that Louie had drunk a six-pack and that she had been trying to put in a Foley catheter, but he wouldn't let her.

Carol took over, assured Louie that she would use a lot of lidocaine, and successfully got the catheter inserted.

The next time we heard about Louie was when Haleh told Carol that someone called from the Tiki Torch about a guy down there on a porta-potty with the hospital's name on it. Carol told Haleh to send a cab for Louie, and when he returned to the ER she saw that he had been drinking and that his urinary bag had six pints in it and needed to be changed.

20.375. Dr. Foster

When Mark went home "with the flu," Susan told Carol to call Dr. Foster in, but Carol told her he had broken his leg skiing.

20.376. David Kersletter

This intoxicated eighteen-year-old had played chicken with a car driven by Hank Travis (Patient 20.378) and lost.

When he arrived at the ER, he had a serious chest laceration, his blood pressure was 140/90, and his heart rate was tachycardic at 160.

He had minimal blood loss considering the severity of his chest laceration, his mental status was alert, his GCS was 15 (as good as it could be, considering the nature of the trauma), and the EMTs had already given him 300 ccs of normal saline.

Susan told Malik to get chest and abdominal films, do a head CT, and notify Kersletter's family. She then asked Carter what he wanted to do. Carter immediately replied, "Check for pneumothorax, do a quick neuro exam, rule out abdominal trauma, get an EKG to screen for a cardiac effusion." Susan concurred and instructed Carter to count out the "one, two, three" transfer to get the patient onto the trauma room bed. Susan then additionally ordered a tox screen, a BA, and a cross-table c-spine.

Kersletter's puls/ox was 76, his reflexes were intact, his pupils were equal and responsive to light, and his abdomen was soft and apparently nontender.

Susan ordered him given 60 milligrams of Toradol because she didn't want to mix morphine with alcohol.

After Kersletter was stabilized, Susan told Carter and Deb to work on opposite sides of his chest laceration and suture to the middle.

20.377. The gangbanger in the suture room
Haleh gave this unseen patient to Susan.

20.378. Hank Travis
Middle-aged Hank Travis was driving the car that hit the intoxicated David Kerlsetter (Patient 20.376) and he insisted on staying at the ER as David was sutured.

As Hank watched from the hall as Deb and Carter worked on Kersletter, he suddenly collapsed with chest pain and went from being an ER visitor to being an ER patient.

Susan immediately identified an early diastolic murmur and was alarmed to learn that Travis's blood pressure was dangerously high at 230/160. At first, they were all concerned about an aortic rupture, but his crit reading was 46, which indicated that he was not bleeding internally.

Susan decided that they had to do a section before Hank ruptured or stroked out and ordered a bolus of 3.5 milligrams of Esimil and a transesophageal echocardiogram to check out the damage to his heart. She also ordered the Cardiac Unit paged.

At this point the new ER chief, Dr. Swift, arrived and Susan (assuming he was the floater Carol had called) told him to "Glove up and get your butt over here."

Mr. Travis's blood pressure was now 190/130 and Susan performed the TE (transesophageal) echo and identified a type A dissection of the descending aorta.

She then ordered Travis sent to the O.R., and it is assumed he was successfully operated on and that he survived.

20.379. The lice case
Carol got the short stick in a three-way "pick" between her, Haleh, and Malik and got the task of delousing and treating this unseen patient.

20.380. Timmy Falco
Timmy came to the ER with his fiancée because he had been hiccuping for more than two days and hadn't slept in two nights.

He had tried holding his breath, sipping ice water, being tickled, breathing into a bag, and watching scary movies, but nothing had worked.

He and his fiancée were getting married in two weeks, and Susan initially figured his hiccuping problem was just prewedding jitters. To be safe, however, she ordered blood tests, abdominal X-rays, and an ultrasound; and prescribed Thorazine to stop his hiccups.

The Thorazine worked on the hiccups, but Susan informed Timmy that there were some potentially serious findings in his CT and ultrasound. The films showed pockets of bacteria invading his liver. These were inflaming his diaphragm and causing his hiccups. He needed to be admitted and treated aggressively with IV antibiotics.

Susan also had to ask Timmy some very personal questions, and even though she suggested she talk to him alone, he insisted his fiancée stay with him. Susan asked him if he had ever done IV drugs or had had high-risk unprotected sex with men or prostitutes, both of which he answered no to.

From the test results, there was the possibility that Timmy was HIV positive. He might even have had AIDS.

Later, his fiancée came to Susan to inquire about the possibility of her being sick herself. (See Patient 20.397.)

20.381. The "weak and dizzy after sex" eighteen-year-old female
This unseen patient showed up at the ER ill after having sex for the first time.

20.382. Arlena the astrologer
Arlena the astrologer came to the ER complaining of acute abdominal pain. Susan told Carter to do a focused H and P on her and be sure to include a pelvic and a rectal.

Carter examined Arlena and when she admitted there was a possibility she could be pregnant (the moon, after all, *was* in the fifth house), Carter ordered a pregnancy test.

The test came back positive, and Carter did an ultrasound that showed that Arlena was pregnant with twins, and that one of them was an ectopic pregnancy.

Arlena was admitted, and the ectopic was surgically removed.

20.383. The wheezer
This patient needed blood gases, and Deb volunteered to do it.

20.384–20.387. The Popsicle pledges
The EMTs brought in these four naked college students. They had frostbite to all extremities, and Susan ordered blankets to warm them up. Shortly thereafter, a cherry bomb exploded in the trash can, a stunt that Carol and Susan both blamed on the pledges.

20.388. The woman with the broken ankle
Tag and Carol bandaged this woman's left leg as they discussed their honeymoon plans. Tag liked Hawaii; Carol always wanted to see Paris. While they were working, Haleh interrupted to tell Carol about Louie (see Patient 20.374) and when she left, the ankle patient asked, "Where were we?"

20.389. Dr. Mark Greene
Susan told Dr. Swift that Mark had gone home with a touch of the flu, when in reality he had gone to an arcade to get his mind off the death of Jody O'Brien.

20.390. Dr. Swift's fictitious third-degree-burn patients

On his first night on duty as ER chief, Wild Willy (Dr. Swift) staged a drill in which the ER was told to expect fifteen to thirty night-club fire victims, all of whom had third-degree burns.

He used this drill to clock how long it took his residents to mobilize. Doug arrived twenty-nine minutes, thirty-two seconds after being paged; Mark showed up so late he scored a new record at one hour, forty-seven minutes.

20.391. Mr. DeNardo

This patient showed up at the ER drunk and with a smashed finger. Deb asked Carter for help with him because Mr. DeNardo was obnoxious and kept pawing her.

At first he didn't want them treating him, but when Carter told him it was them or nobody, he consented.

As Carter was numbing DeNardo's finger with ethyl chloride, Deb recklessly approached the injured finger with a cautery needle, causing the ethyl chloride to ignite into a giant fireball that Carter extinguished with a pillow.

Deb asked Carter not to tell anyone about her potentially deadly mistake.

20.392. The patient with ptosis, myosis, and hidrosis

During a "get acquainted" staff meeting, new ER chief, Dr. Swift, presented the hypothetical case of a patient who presents at the ER with ptosis, myosis, and hydrosis (anhidrosis) and asked what this sounded like. Doug immediately endeared himself to Wild Willy by saying, "The Osis sisters. I dated the short one." He somewhat redeemed himself by then giving the correct answer: Horner's syndrome.

20.393. Mr. Talbott the werewolf

This guy claimed to be a real werewolf and said he had scraped the upper right side of his face while climbing a cliff chasing cats.

As Carol was dressing his injury, he asked her to put him in restraints until sunrise. She good-naturedly told him she'd get him a doctor.

When she turned to leave the room, Mr. Talbott shrieked a guttural werewolf howl at her and lunged out of the bed. Carol retreated, and he then told her, "Never turn your back on a werewolf."

Carol slowly backed out of the room, and when Carter heard the howling, she nonchalantly told him there was a werewolf in the ER.

Carter went to take a nap.

20.394. The drunk burglar

This guy accidentally broke into a neighbor's house and was shot in the lower chest with a 12-gauge shotgun.

He was in bad shape when he arrived at the ER, and Susan, Mark, Haleh, and Carol immediately went to work on him. They started two IVs and intubated him with a 7.5 ET tube. His pulse was 40 palp and his heart rate was bradycardic. Susan ordered calls made to Respiratory for a ventilator and to Radiology for a chest film and instructed Haleh to type and crossmatch his blood for as many units as possible.

In the meantime, they hung some O neg.

As Susan was starting a central line, the patient went into arrest, and they gave him an amp of epinephrine, and Carter started external compressions.

They gave him 4 units of O neg, and Susan said to call Dr. Swift. Carol said she would also call in Tag.

The patient was registering no pulse when Tag arrived. He successfully performed a thoracotomy and clamped off a bleeding artery. The burglar's heart started, and Susan made Carter do internal cardiac compressions. The patient again arrested, and Susan shocked him twice with the internal paddles, which restarted his heart.

He finally stabilized and they took him to the O.R.

20.395. The baby in the trash bag

This three- to four-week-old male infant was found by the police in a trash bag, and when he was brought to the ER he was hypothermic, his blood pressure was 60 palp, and his heart rate was 80. His heart showed no arrhythmias, and his body temperature was 89°. Susan ordered heated and humidified O_2, a dextrose stick, and told Haleh to start an IV with saline heated to 110°. Dr. Swift arrived, and Susan told him to check the baby's lytes for acidosis. The baby's temperature slowly rose to 92°, and the consensus was that he would survive.

Susan ordered Haleh to call Children and Family Services for a foster placement.

20.396. Deb's shaved-head laceration

Deb shaved the left side of this patient's head and sutured his head laceration. But instead of shaving just the area immediately around the laceration, Deb trimmed a huge, oval-shaped area that looked to be a good six by eight inches in size.

When Carter stopped in to check on her, he was stunned by her tonsorial "skills" and asked her if she had shaved the gentleman's scalp all by herself, which she said she had.

The wary patient had not yet seen Deb's handiwork.

20.397. Timmy Falco's fiancée

This young girl asked Susan if she herself could be sick after learning that her fiancé, Timmy, might be HIV positive (see Patient 20.380). The girl told Susan she had the feeling that Timmy had not been completely honest with her. Susan suggested that she be tested to be sure.

• •

Original Broadcast Date:
Thursday, March 30, 1995
Written by Neal Baer;
Directed by Donna Deitch

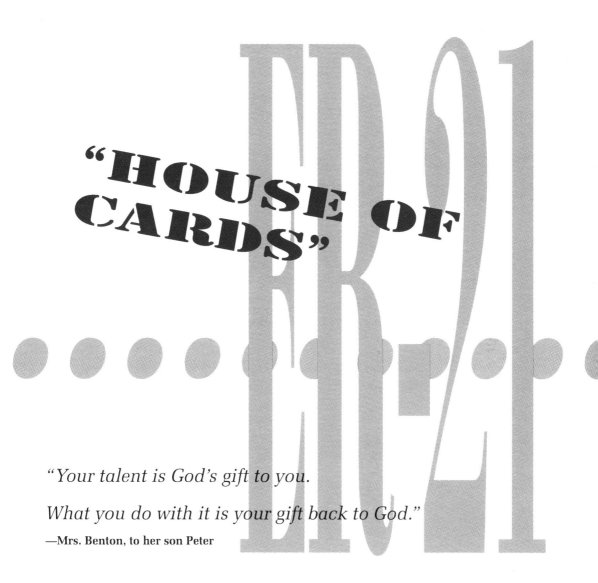

"HOUSE OF CARDS"

ER-21

"Your talent is God's gift to you.

What you do with it is your gift back to God."

—Mrs. Benton, to her son Peter

This episode opens with Doug being shooed out of Diane Leeds's bed before Jake wakes up. Doug soon learns, however, that Jake has known all along that he's been spending nights with his mother.

Peter works on the sub-I evaluations, and Deb and Carter discuss their prospects. Carter tells her he's already done four or five intubations, so many chest tubes he's lost count, and a femoral cutdown. This panics Deb and directly influences a terrible decision she makes later.

Peter and Jackie put their mother in a nursing home, and Mark once again butts heads with Dr. Swift, prompting Swift to make Mark present his disastrous eclampsia case at a case conference later in the day.

Mark discusses his marital problems with Susan and tells her that he's going to Milwaukee to talk to Jenn over the weekend. Susan convinces him to go that evening instead. ("That's so like a guy to wait four days," she tells him.) Mark agrees but is upset when, later, Jenn tells him not to come until Saturday.

Peter visits his mother at the Melville Home, and Deb tells Carter she's quitting medical school. She admits she doesn't like taking care of patients and tells him that the difference between them is that he cares about the patients as people and she is unable to.

Susan arrives home to find her prodigal sister Chloe sitting in the hall outside her door, and the episode ends with Chloe crying on Susie's shoulder, as Susan comforts her and tells her they'll be okay.

PATIENT HISTORIES
● ●

21.398. Peter's shingles patient
Peter told Carter to go to Radiology and pick up the film on this unnamed shingles patient.

21.399. Mrs. Baba
This patient of Peter's was scheduled for gall bladder surgery and was on an NPO (nothing by mouth) order. Carter mistakenly gave her a glass of water, and her surgery had to be canceled. Carter was busy doing something else, and she kept telling him she was thirsty. To shut her up, he gave her a cup of water without looking at her chart, and, thus, Peter could not operate. Dr. Benton was not pleased.

21.400. Mr. McDowall
This patient presented at the ER with abdominal pain and was placed in Mark's service.

Mark examined him and ordered a CBC, Chem 7, LFT (liver function test), and an abdominal ultrasound. Susan questioned the ultrasound order, and Mark replied that it could be appendicitis, to which Susan countered that it could be gas.

At this point, Dr. Swift arrived and intervened. After hearing Mr. McDowall's symptoms, he canceled all of Mark's test orders and asked him for his diagnosis. "Probable gastroenteritis," Mark told him. Swift then wanted to know why, if Mark thought this patient had a stomach flu, he was ordering a thousand dollars worth of tests. Mark explained that Mr. McDowall had pain in the right lower quadrant and that he wanted to rule out appendicitis.

"It's ruled out," Swift brusquely said, and then told the patient to go home and take nothing by mouth for six hours and then just sips of clear fluid. "If it gets worse, come back," he told him.

Mark was livid that Swift overruled him in front of another doctor (Susan), a nurse (Lydia), and, most insultingly, a patient.

21.401. Mrs. Benton
In this episode, Peter finally agreed with his sister Jackie and the doctors that his mother could not go home and that she needed round-the-clock care.

Peter assumed the responsibility of telling her that she'd be living out her days at the Melville Home. Mrs. Benton looked at Peter and sobbed, "Do I have to go, Peter?" to which Peter replied, "Yeah, Ma. You do." Mrs. Benton turned to her son Peter, not Jackie, the daughter she had been living with for years, for the final answer as to whether or not she had to go.

21.402. The electrical worker

This young man fell twenty feet from a utility pole and suffered high current burns.

He had full-thickness burns on both arms that prevented Mark from starting the necessary IVs, and they concluded that he needed a central line. Susan decided Carter should do it, and she ordered a long 14 gauge needle on a 6 cc syringe.

The patient's puls/ox was 92, his blood pressure was 120, and they gave him 300 ccs normal saline and a tetanus shot.

Carter successfully inserted the central line under Susan's supervision, and when Peter arrived, Mark filled him in: The patient had circumferential third-degree burns to the upper extremities; he showed no cardiac ST changes and his c-spine, chest, and pelvis X-rays were all negative. He had no long bone fractures. Peter decided they could do the Foley catheter upstairs and ordered the patient sent to the Burn Unit.

21.403. Janette Ryan

This young lady, approximately seven years old, was brought to the ER by her mother. Janette did not have a fever, but she was complaining of a headache, dizziness, and nausea. Doug told Mrs. Ryan that it was probably just a flu bug, but because Janette's heart rate was a little fast, he wanted to put her on a heart monitor and check her rhythm. At this point Mrs. Ryan told Doug that they didn't have any health insurance and that she was concerned about the costs of the tests, but Doug promised her that they would work something out.

While under observation, Janette went into tachycardia and her pressure dropped to 70/50. Doug ordered her given 15 liters of oxygen and 3 milligrams of adenosine IV and asked that her lytes be checked. He then told her to blow on her thumb (a diagnostic action known as the Valsalva maneuver, see the Glossary) in order to achieve maximum intrathoracic pressure. Janette then lost her pulse and went into fibrillation. Doug shocked her twice with the pediatric defibrillator paddles at 100 joules. After the second jolt, her pulse was restored and her pressure went to 100/60.

Doug later spoke to Janette's mother and told her that her daughter had supraventricular tachycardia and that she needed to be admitted to Cardiology. He also told her that someone from Social Services would help her with her application for Medicaid and then assured her that Janette would be fine.

21.404. Anita Salazar

Mrs. Salazar was an illegal alien who came to the ER because she had been coughing up blood for a week.

Mark immediately suspected tuberculosis and told Lydia to put her in an isolation room. He ordered a chest X-ray and a sputum culture, put her on oral cefotaxime, and told her he needed to see the rest of her family as soon as possible.

Anita tested positive for TB, and when Mark told her she needed to be admitted to the hospital or she would infect everyone she came in contact with, she began to dress, telling Mark she would not stay. (She was afraid of getting caught by the Immigration and Naturalization Service.) Mark began shouting at her, and Susan had to step in and stop him. "How do you expect her to trust you if you're screaming at her?" she asked. He explained that Mrs. Salazar was leaving AMA (against medical advice) with infectious TB, but then he just gave up and said, "She leaves, she leaves."

Mrs. Salazar did leave, and Mark later told Lydia to ask the health department to go out and try and find her.

Mark's impassioned and emphatic attempts to get Anita Salazar to stay must have worked, however, because later that day Lydia called Mark out of the doctor's lounge, telling him he had visitors.

Mrs. Salazar was back with her mother and three children, one of whom was visibly ill (see Patients 21.419 through 21.422).

21.405. Shirley
This elderly twosome, Shirley and her combative sister Sari (Patient 21.406) were in a five-mile-per-hour motor vehicle accident and were brought to the ER by ambulance. Shirley had a nose laceration but otherwise had stable vital signs. Susan dressed and bandaged Shirley's nose.

21.406. Sari
Sari and her argumentative sister Shirley (Patient 21.405) were in a five-mile-per-hour motor vehicle accident and were brought to the ER by ambulance. Sari was dizzy and had a headache, but otherwise had stable vital signs. Carol treated Sari by giving her her proper eyeglasses.

21.407. Mrs. Blum
Mrs. Blum came to the ER specifically to be examined by "Dr. Carter." There was nothing actually wrong with her, although she came in complaining of cramps. She and her husband Dan wanted to have a baby and they believed that Carter had "the magic touch." A while back, Carter had examined Mrs. Blum's friend Barbara, and the following week Barbara had gotten pregnant. Mrs. Blum was hoping for the same results.

21.408. The pregnant woman in 3
This woman was eight months pregnant and came to the ER complaining of stomach cramps and frequent urination. Dr. Swift wanted Mark to see her, but he refused and gave the chart to Susan (see Patient 19.359).

21.409. Barbara
This was Mrs. Blum's (Patient 21.407) friend who Carter examined and who later became pregnant, thanks to Carter's rumored "magic touch."

21.410. Carter's suprapubic tap

This infant was brought to the ER by his mother because he had a temperature of 102° and hadn't been urinating. Doug determined that they needed to do a suprapubic tap, and tapped Carter to do the procedure (which was one he needed for his procedure book). They had given the baby eight ounces of clear liquid and there had been no urine production. Doug explained to the baby's mother that they were going to use a small needle to get a urine sample.

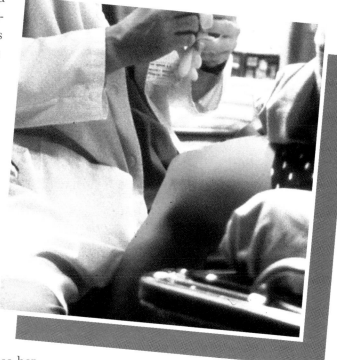

Doug talked Carter through the procedure, cautioning him not to press too hard on the baby's belly while inserting the needle.

Carter then asked Doug how one knew when one was pressing too hard, and, at that point, the baby let loose and urinated all over Carter.

Doug told Carter, "That's probably too hard."

21.411. Mary Gitlitz

This patient came to the ER because her husband believed that she had paranoid psychosis with highly elaborate delusional systems, although Mary believed that he read too much.

Susan Lewis questioned her, and Mary told Susan that she did not hear voices, she did not have frightening thoughts, but that she did believe that people were trying to harm her because the streets weren't safe.

She also told Susan that she had seen a shrink in the past and as she was rummaging through her pocketbook for his number, she pulled out two handguns, a .228 and a 9 millimeter double action with a thirteen-round clip. She let Susan take them to Security because she still had the Baretta.

21.412. The finger lac in 2

Carol gave this finger laceration to Carter after Deb refused to do it because she had to finish Peter's med renewals. Carter sarcastically asked her if she had enough finger lacs in her book.

21.413. Peter's small bowel

Peter ordered Deb to scrub in on this surgery after Carter mistakenly gave an NPO patient water and Peter could not operate (see Patient 21.399). Deb closed the incision

A Transcript of Mark Greene's Case Conference on the Death of Jody O'Brien

CONFERENCE MEMBER: Do you know the diagnostic criteria for preeclampsia?

MARK: Blood pressure greater than 140 over 90; persistent proteinuria; and edema.

CONFERENCE MEMBER: She had hypertension, proteinuria.

MARK: Which I attributed to a urinary tract infection, and her pressure was high on only one occasion.

CONFERENCE MEMBER: You should have taken it again in six hours.

MARK: My index of suspicion should have been higher.

CONFERENCE MEMBER: She seized in the parking lot.

MARK: I treated her seizure aggressively with magnesium sulfate and Ativan.

DR. COBURN: Have you have a chance to review the ultrasound findings?

MARK: I missed the placental abruption.

DR. COBURN: Did you know what you were looking for?

MARK: The AFI and biophysical profile were excellent. There was a normal fundal placement.

DR. COBURN: Yet she abrupted.

MARK: I had no clinical reason to be suspicious. There was no vaginal bleeding, abdominal pain, or fetal distress.

CONFERENCE MEMBER: What are the criteria for operative vaginal delivery?

MARK: Mainly a favorable fetal lie and a small baby, under 4,000 grams.

CONFERENCE MEMBER: The baby was 9 pounds, 3 ounces. That's macrosomic.

MARK: I used the Leopold maneuver and fundal height to estimate baby weight and size. I was off.

CONFERENCE MEMBER: What risks do you run using forceps on a macrosomic baby?

MARK: A 23 percent chance of shoulder dystocia.

CONFERENCE MEMBER: Which happened.

MARK: Yes.

DR. COBURN: What qualifies you to manage high risk OB in an ER?

DR. SWIFT: We're not here to question Dr. Greene's training. Stick to the case.

DR. COBURN: Why a c-section in an ER?

MARK: The baby was hypoxic and bradycardic. Had to do it in minutes or we ran the risk of brain damage.

DR. COBURN: How many crash c-sections have you done?

MARK: I've scrubbed in on several.

DR. COBURN: Oh, and that qualifies you?

DR. SWIFT: I give Dr. Greene credit for crashing her when he did.

CONFERENCE MEMBER: Knowing the outcome, what would you have done differently?

MARK: I should have taken her up to OB myself. Immediately. I've induced before, delivered babies before. I assumed that I could handle the situation. I was wrong.

during this surgery.

21.414. Smiley

Smiley was drunk when he was involved in a motor vehicle rollover that threw him twenty feet. When he was brought to the ER he had no ID on him, had already yanked out two IVs, and did not want to be touched.

Carol, Peter, and Mark went to work on Smiley and ordered a BA, a cross-table c-spine, a CBC, and his blood typed and crossmatched for 4 units. His pressure was 90/50, his cap refill was slow, and he was hypovolemic (see the Glossary).

Smiley's lungs were clear, but his abdomen was rigid, and they prepped for a lavage. (They were concerned about a ruptured spleen.) They intubated him with an 8.5 ET tube and hung a 500 cc bag of IV saline. They also gave Smiley 1 percent Xylocaine with epinephrine.

At this point Smiley began bleeding out. They needed to know what the source of the bleed was and ultimately determined that Smiley's femoral artery had been cut. Peter applied manual pressure to the pumper, ordered a call made to Vascular, and had Smiley sent to the Cath Lab.

21.415. Deb's laparotomy

Deb assisted on this surgery.

21.416. Thoreau

This junkie was the patient that convinced Deb Chen to leave the ER and resign from medical school, although the guy probably never even knew Deb's name.

Deb was asked to help Wendy get an IV started on this drug addict. His veins were so torn up, however, that there was no place to start the IV. Wendy decided to go get Susan, but Deb told her that she would start a central line herself, a procedure she was neither authorized nor qualified to do. (The extremely competitive Deb was thrown by the fact that Carter had already done a central line—with Susan's supervision and guidance—and wanted to "catch up.")

Deb began the procedure, lost the guide wire inside the patient (requiring surgery to remove it), and fled the hospital in terror.

Later that evening Deb told Carter she was quitting her medical education.

21.417. Billy Shmoo

Twelve-year-old Billy was hit while riding his bike and thrown twenty feet. When he arrived at the ER his pressure was 60/40 and he had a left pneumothorax. His reflexes were normal and his lacerations were superficial. His pulse was thready at 150, his puls/ox was 65, and Doug ordered a CBC, Chem 7, and a flow sheet started.

They did a cross-table c-spine with a portable unit, and Doug decided to do a chest tube, using a 28 French tube.

Billy's breath sounds were good, but as Doug was working on him, his pressure crashed, he developed dilated neck veins, and Doug ordered the team to prepare for pericardiocentesis (removal of excess fluid from the pericardium).

Billy's pressure dropped to 40 palp, but following the procedure, it went to 60/40, his rhythm returned to normal, and Doug assured him he'd be fine.

21.418. Chloe

Susan found her sister Chloe sitting outside her apartment door when she arrived home from work one night. Her boyfriend (and the father of her child) had dumped her, and Chloe was several months pregnant and filthy. (She looked like she hadn't bathed or washed her hair in days.)

Susan took her in, fed her, and tacitly agreed to let her live with her until she had the baby. [Susan had not seen Chloe since episode 12, "Happy New Year."]

21.419. Christina Salazar

This young daughter of Anita Salazar came to the ER with her mother when she returned after being diagnosed with tuberculosis. Of the three Salazar children, Christina was the one manifesting symptoms consistent with tuberculosis.

21.420. Maria Salazar

This young daughter of Anita Salazar came to the ER with her mother when she returned after being diagnosed with tuberculosis.

21.421. The Salazar boy

This twenty-five-year-old son of Anita Salazar also came to the ER with his mother when she returned after being diagnosed with tuberculosis.

21.422. Anita Salazar's mother

Anita brought her mother with her when she returned to the ER after being diagnosed with tuberculosis.

● ●

Original Broadcast Date:
Thursday, April 6, 1995
Written by Tracey Stern;
Directed by Fred Gerber

"MEN PLAN, GOD LAUGHS"

ER-22

"Why are you taking a picture of my head when my leg hurts?"
—Charlie Caffee

"Because I'm the doctor and that's what I wanna do."
—Doug Ross

(Curiously) "Why do nurses wear colors and doctors wear white?"
—Susan

(Sarcastically) "Because doctors are pure and good."
—Carol

This episode begins with Mark waking up alone at 5:46 in the morning with brochures about Milwaukee area hospitals scattered on his bed. It is obvious that he has been looking for a job near Jenn.

At the hospital, Susan tries to persuade her mother to loan Chloe some money and help her out now that she's pregnant.

Later, Susan talks to Mark about Jenn, and he tells her that Jenn did not want him to go to Milwaukee early, but that he's going tonight. (He unwisely refuses to honor Swift's request to stay after his shift because of this trip.)

Carter studies a book called *Emergency Medical Secrets*, and Carol and Susan both tease him about his odds on passing his medical boards.

Carol tells Susan she's having nightmares about getting married in a peach wedding gown and later asks Mark if Rachel can be the ring-bearer.

Jeannie Boulet tells Peter she still visits his mother at the home, and we learn that she is studying to be a physician's assistant (which is a grueling twenty-seven-month full-time program). Jeannie asks Peter to dinner, and he says yes.

Peter goes out of his way to be compassionate and kind to his patients, while Carter asks Mark if he'll give him a recommendation for an ER sub-internship. Mark says he will, but tells him he's not sure it'll help coming from him.

Carter completes Peter's charts when Peter goes out looking for a neurosurgeon for a critically ill teenager, a good deed for which Carter later makes Peter thank him twice.

In Milwaukee, Jenn adamantly tells Mark that their marriage is over, but he tells her he wants to see Rachel more. When he goes in to read Rachel a story, Jenn bursts into tears in the living room.

During dinner, Peter and Jeannie talk about their childhoods, their medical educations, and their parents, and the episode concludes with the two of them smiling and laughing together in a diner booth.

PATIENT HISTORIES

● ●

22.423. Mrs. Benton

In this episode, in response to his feelings of guilt and powerlessness concerning his mother, Peter lashed out and argued with a staff doctor at the nursing home over the care Mrs. Benton is receiving. Peter complained that she wasn't getting enough exercise and that they were not moving her to the dining room to eat. The doctor explained that they couldn't move every patient for every meal and that his mother was still recovering from hip surgery and they would gradually increase her exercise regimen as she improves.

Peter foolishly threatened to take over the supervision of his mother's care, but the doctor brought him back to reality by reminding him that his mother broke her hip and it simply would not heal overnight.

22.424. Chloe

Chloe came to the hospital for an ultrasound (performed by Dr. Nancy Coburn, the OB/GYN who excoriated Mark for Jody O'Brien's death) and learned that she was having a girl and that it was a little underweight but that overall the baby was fine (considering that Chloe had been living on Twinkies and popcorn).

Chloe had no medical insurance, and Susan tried to persuade their mother to lend Chloe two hundred dollars, but she refused.

Later Chloe put three hundred dollars of baby supplies on Susan's charge card.

22.425. Rolando

Emergency Service Coordinator Rolando originally thought he had a cold but then came to the conclusion that he had the flu. Dr. Swift told him to call in a replacement and go home, but he was unable to find someone to take his place.

22.426. Isadore

Isadore was accidentally caught in a metal press, and when he arrived at the ER he had multiple lacerations, his pressure was 80/30, his pulse was 135 and thready, and he had sustained a 500 cc blood loss. His GCS was 3–4–4, he had back pain, and his watch had stopped eighteen minutes earlier. Doug ordered a cross table c-spine, and Carter noted diminished breath sounds bilaterally. Isadore's puls/ox was 85. They started a flow sheet, and Doug decided to intubate with a size 7 ET tube.

Isadore's pulse weakened further, and his blood pressure began falling. Doug ordered two large bore IVs of normal saline wide open and told Conni to bag him. He also told Carter to immediately get Benton, since Isadore now had no distal pulse.

Peter arrived and immediately identified Isadore's problem: posterior dislocation of his right hip, a traumatic condition characterized by flexion (usually mild), internal rotation, and abduction (shortening) of the leg.

Peter got up on the table, told Carter to hold Isadore's pelvis down and instructed Doug to stabilize his neck. He then pulled the hip joint back into place. "I felt it pop!" Carter exclaimed. Isadore's distal pulse returned immediately and Peter instructed them to call Ortho.

"You saved his leg," Carter said in amazement, to which Peter replied, "Yeah, well, legs are something I *can* save."

22.427. Katie Nemeth

Katie went with her mother to work on Take Your Daughter to Work Day and ended up with a sudden hearing loss because she took her ear muffs off on a firing range. Her mother, Lieutenant Nemeth, worked at the Great Lakes Naval Base and took Katie to morning gunnery exercises.

Doug tested Katie's ears with a tuning fork and told Wendy to call ENT (Ear, Nose, and Throat) for audiometry to rule out middle-ear damage.

22.428. Henry Offenbach

Little Henry was brought to the ER by his anxious parents because his lips turned blue at night, and they were worried about his heart. Henry's father, Leonard, told Mark that heart problems ran in his family. Mark immediately identified bounding pulses and a heart murmur and ordered a chest X-ray and an EKG.

Henry's tests showed the possibility of a hole between his aorta and pulmonary

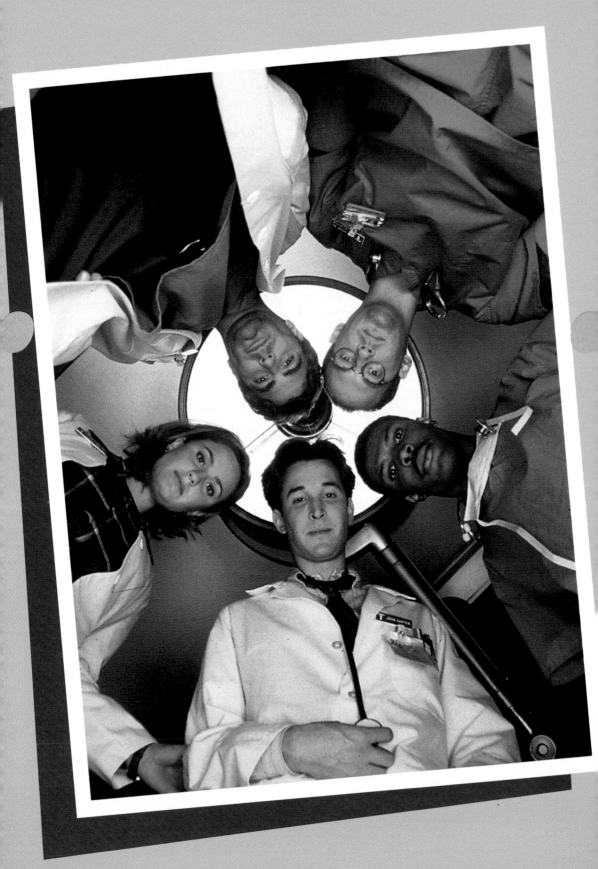

artery, and Mark told his parents that he would probably need open heart surgery to repair it. Mark explained that Henry was turning blue because there wasn't enough oxygen in his blood. He also assured Leonard that it was not an hereditary condition.

22.429. Samantha

Sam was brought to the ER with a head trauma because she slipped and fell in the hall at school. Her homeroom teacher brought her in. She was hypotensive with a pressure of 60 palp and cyanotic. Her pupils were equal and reactive to light.

Peter asked Carter for his diagnosis, and he suggested a blood clot or a seizure disorder. Peter then ordered a head CT, a CBC, and a Chem 7. It was then that Haleh told Peter that Sam's pressure had gone to 60 over nothing, and the girl went into v-fib (ventricular fibrillation). Peter shocked her with 100 joules and she converted.

Samantha's glucose was "through the roof" at 600, and her blood pressure was still down. Peter ordered IV loading of 10 units regular insulin and a infusion of 5 units of insulin an hour. Peter told Carter to smell Sam's breath, and he noted it was fruity. Carter then correctly identified ketoacidosis and realized that Samantha was in a diabetic coma. Peter ordered blood gases and a liter of saline wide open.

The homeroom teacher told Peter that Samantha had eaten chocolate cake and ice cream, and she revealed that she had not known that her student was diabetic.

Peter told Haleh to let him know when the Chem 7 was back and to do a potassium reading every thirty minutes. Haleh offered to turn Samantha over to Doug since she was not a surgical patient, but Peter insisted she contact him with the results.

Later, Samantha's blood pressure returned to normal and her PH level went to 7.3. Peter told Haleh to give her 20 millequivalents Kay Ciel wide open. It was obvious that Samantha had not taken her insulin all week. When she recovered enough, Peter told her, "You have an illness. You want to pretend you don't. Where's that gonna get you? You have to accept the way things are. So maybe you won't be exactly like everybody else, but if you don't take your insulin, you'll die."

Carter complimented Peter on the way he spoke to Samantha, but it isn't certain that his message sank in.

22.430. Mrs. Dibble

Mrs. Dibble was a bipolar psychotic who stopped taking her lithium and was found sweeping sidewalks in Bryant Park. She wandered the halls in the ER rambling about all manner of important philosophical topics. Mark told Malik to take her to 3.

Later, after she was back on her meds, she told Mark, "It's hard to be happy. You can't try. It comes or it doesn't." Mark found himself pondering this nugget of wisdom from a supposed mental case.

22.431. Doug Ross

Doug technically became a hospital patient when he agreed to see the staff psychiatrist because of his assault on a child-abusing father. [see episode 17, Patient 17.324.]

Dr. Murphy saw Doug and told him he was a reasonably normal guy with "sloppy impulse control." He made Doug tell him he'd never do it again and released him.

When Doug told him he hadn't been very happy lately, Dr. Murphy suggested he try therapy.

22.432. "Dr." Lyle Strong

Susan was happy to treat a fellow healer when this urologist in town for a convention came to the ER complaining of kidney pain and flank tenderness.

He explained that he often got kidney infections, and when she asked him why he didn't take Bactrim, he replied, "Physician heal thyself. We never do."

His temperature was 98.9°, and Strong told Susan to give him 100 milligrams of meperedine for the pain. Susan told him she was sure his diagnosis was correct but she'd prefer to confirm it first. She then ordered a urinalysis and told Dr. Strong to wait for the test results.

Later, Dr. Strong's urinalysis results showed the presence of blood in his urine— *chicken* blood. Susan also noted that he signed his name "Dr. Lyle Strong, M.D." (Physicians only use the *M.D.* after their name.)

Susan was certain that Strong was a drug addict looking for Demerol and decided to expose him by telling him that his tests showed he had an aplastic bicystic renal neoplasm. When "Dr." Strong said that that was impossible, she told him he was right, because there was no such thing. She then asked him if he knew the penalties for trying to illegally acquire narcotics, and he jumped off the bed and fled the ER still wearing his hospital gown.

22.433. Lew Reicher

Lew was brought to the ER drunk and bleeding from his mouth. His pressure was 60 and his pulse was thready at 145. Mark ordered a CBC, Chem 7, a coag panel, and an EKG. He also ordered an IV started, a Foley catheter inserted, and he prepped to perform an endoscopic examination.

Mark identified a bleeding ulcer and sent Lew to surgery to have it repaired.

Later, Lew's wife brought a bag of clothes for him, but would not see him. She told Mark that he lived on the street, and that she just wanted to see if he was alive.

22.434. Ronson

Mark told Rolando that this patient was discharged.

22.435. Loomis

Mark told Rolando to send this patient to X-ray.

22.436. Charlie Caffee

This young man, age sixteen, came to the ER because his leg felt "funny" and he couldn't move his arm. He had had the flu recently and was also complaining of headaches. He had fallen the previous Saturday.

Peter checked Charlie's eyes and briefed Doug when he arrived, telling him the boy was manifesting left-side hemiparesis with an onset of twenty-four hours.

Doug took over and, after a brief physical examination, sent the boy for an MRI (magnetic resonance imaging), telling Malik to make Radiology push him ahead of everyone not critical. Doug also told Malik to find Charlie's parents and decided he wanted Peter to look at the MRI. He also wanted a Neuro consult.

When Doug got the MRI results, he told Carol to have Peter meet him in Radiology. Charlie's MRI showed that he had an aneurysm at the juncture of the basilar and vertebrial arteries,

and that it was pressing on his spinal tract. Doug determined it could go immediately, or in a week. Neurologist Dr. Seymour Lassally arrived and, as soon as he saw the X-ray, asked when the paralysis had begun. He told Peter that it needed to be surgically repaired and that they could not do it there. Hypothermia was needed, and Dr. Lassally told Peter to call Mike Dyer over at Mercy.

Dr. Dyer was out jogging, so Peter borrowed Carter's jeep to find him and have him review the MRI. Later that day, Charlie was shipped to Mercy, and it is assumed his aneurysm was repaired successfully.

22.437. Dr. Seymour Lassally's astrocytoma
Dr. Lassally could not spend a lot of time looking at Charlie Caffee's (Patient 22.436) MRI results because of this scheduled astrocytoma surgery.

22.438. Peter's hydrocele
Peter scrubbed in on this surgery after he tried to convince Samantha (Patient 22.429) to take her insulin.

22.439. Chloe's daughter Susan
Dr. Coburn performed the ultrasound on Chloe in which it was revealed that she was having a girl and that the baby was a little underweight.

22.440. The woman with the dog bite
Mark treated this woman (who was concerned that the dog that bit her had been rabid) and later told Doug that he thought she had been hitting on him. Doug quizzed him on the details and confirmed that she had, indeed, been hitting on Mark.

22.441. The gangbanger with the GSW to the chest

This kid came in with a gunshot wound to the chest. He had lost 500 ccs of blood, his pressure was 50 palp, and his pulse was 140.

Mark and Susan intubated him and identified an entry wound to the upper left chest with an exit wound below the scapula, and a second entry wound in the abdomen with an exit from the left flank.

While being examined, the boy went into fibrillation, and after he was shocked twice at 300 joules, he converted to sinus rhythm. Susan ordered him given lidocaine IV push, and Mark identified a tension pneumothorax and, using a 16 gauge needle, inserted a chest tube.

At this point, to Mark's surprise, the boy's mother impassionedly told him to let her son die. She then explained that he had killed three boys already, but Mark and company continued their efforts anyway.

22.442. Garrison

This patient had hypocalcemia, and as Mark was leaving for the train station, he told Susan to check on him.

22.443. The orbital fracture in 3

This girl had been hit in the eye with a softball. Mark told Susan to try and get a consult.

22.444. The back pain in 6

Mark told Susan that this patient could have a herniated disk.

22.445. Leslie Nesbitt

This patient was hit by lightning and was cyanotic and in full arrest when she arrived at the ER.

The EMTs had started CPR and given her 2 amps of epinephrine and 2 milligrams of atropine. Dr. Swift identified feathering burns and made Carter handle the trauma treatment.

Carter ordered a CBC, Chem 24, and cardiac enzyme tests, and when he was told that her pupils were fixed and dilated (usually a dreadful sign) he responded that it didn't matter: He knew that that happens temporarily with lightning injuries. Carter also ordered 400 milligrams of dopamine; 500 D5W (500 cc of 5 percent dextrose in normal saline); a cross-table c-spine; and a head CT, non-contrast.

After Leslie was shipped to the ICU (Intensive Care Unit), Swift told Carter, "Well done," to which Carter replied that he had good teachers.

• •

Original Broadcast Date:
Thursday, April 27, 1995
Written by Robert Nathan;
Directed by Christopher Chulack

"LOVE AMONG THE RUINS"

"Tell me that you didn't just get into a

pissing match with Swift and walk out of a trauma."

—Doug Ross

"I did."

—Mark Greene

This episode begins with Mark standing at a window in Jenn's Milwaukee apartment watching her sleep. Their marriage is still on the rocks, and it's obvious it's tearing him apart.

Mark commutes back to Chicago, and, when he arrives at the ER, he and Doug discuss his situation.

Later, Peter learns from Dr. Swift that Carter applied for the ER sub-internship, and when Swift asks Peter for a recommendation, Peter tells Carter to write his own and he'll sign it.

Carol can't seem to find the time to get together with Tag to write their wedding vows (uh-oh), and finally Tag gets disgusted and writes them by himself. In the meantime, Carol impulsively invites Diane Leeds to the wedding, knowing that she'll bring Doug with her (uh-oh, again).

Doug continues to coach Jake's Little League team and tries to pull him out of

189

his slump by making him wear his socks inside out.

Mark continues to butt heads with Swift and is almost totally convinced that he'll never get the ER attending job. Swift confronts him about his attitude, and Mark tells him that he generally does not have a problem with authority. "But when it's enforced arbitrarily and undermines *my* authority," he tells Swift, "I resent it." Swift then reveals that Dr. Morgenstern had told him that Mark was the most impressive resident he'd ever seen, but that he keeps asking himself if Mark is the same guy Morgenstern was talking about.

We learn that Susan owes $85,000 in medical school student loans; Mark owes $110,000; and Peter is three months behind on *his* loan payments. After Jerry learns that Carter's family is wealthy, Peter sarcastically asks Carter if it's nice not having to worry about loans.

With two weeks to go before her wedding to Tag, Carol talks to Lydia and learns that Lydia's first husband, Earl, left her after four years. Carol then ponders a religious novice's dilemma about whether to become a nun or get married.

Carter tries writing his own evaluation but can only come up with "conscientious, hard-working, earnest, and ever punctual," which Susan says sounds like a recommendation for a train conductor.

At one of Jake's softball games, Doug deliberately overlooks Jake's not touching first base and lets his home run stand. Later, he explains to Jake that he had lied and that it was wrong. They agree not to tell Diane.

Carter gives Benton his recommendation, and Peter signs it without even reading it. Carter angrily asks him what he wants from him, and Peter asks him why he's applying for an ER sub-I if he wants to be a surgeon. Carter then tears up the recommendation.

Tag reads the first draft of his vows to Carol:

Carol, before we were together, I'd been in love many times, or so I thought.
But now I know that you're the only one I've ever truly loved; the only one
I can imagine spending my life with; the one I can't imagine spending my
life without.

Carol tells him the vows are beautiful, and he then asks her if she feels the same way, to which she replies yes.

At the Melville Home, Walt tells Peter that he starts talking like Barry White whenever Jeannie is around, and he then sings "Can't Get Enough of Your Love, Baby" to Peter.

Susan arrives home to find Chloe smoking and watching *Love Connection* and learns that she didn't go to her obstetrician's appointment. Susan explodes and tells Chloe she can't stay with her after the baby is born. "You're thirty-four years old, Chloe," she tells her sister. "Figure something out."

Back at the ER, Carter gets hit on by a gorgeous radiologist (thanks to Kovalev's "Singles" book—see Patient 23.447) and they go out together.

Mark takes the train back to Milwaukee and, for some reason, finds Jenn in a romantic, conciliatory mood. Just as they start going at it hot and heavy, Rachel comes in and wants her daddy to fix her tummy. The episode ends with the three of them snuggling together in bed. When Rachel whispers to her father, "Daddy, I'm glad you're home," Mark whispers back, "So am I."

PATIENT HISTORIES

● ●

23.446. The roomful of drunks
In the ER, Dr. Swift rousted these itinerant imbibers by donning a New Guinea tribal mask and scaring the bejesus out of them. Swift asked Jerry if he would like to participate, but Jerry was in his Shakespearean mode and declined.

23.447. Kovalev
This cabbie sustained a laceration over his right eye when he was robbed. Susan, Carter, and Malik treated him.

Kovalev ran a dating service from his cab and kept a book of snapshots and biographical profiles of his clients. Kovalev put Carter in the book for free because he treated him, and later Melanie Graff, a gorgeous radiologist came down to the ER and asked Carter out after she saw his picture while X-raying the cabbie. (Also, Susan was dismayed to find a picture of Div in the cabbie's book with a woman who Kovalev told her owned a chain of mortuaries.)

23.448. Peter's patient that Carter wrote the aftercare for
Peter and Carter had just finished treating this patient when Swift revealed to Peter that Carter had applied for the ER sub-internship.

23.449. The kid in 3 who hit his head
Dr. Swift, running the ER board against Mark's wishes, gave this patient to Doug.

23.450. The knee lac in 5
After Dr. Swift gave Patient 23.449 to Doug (a job that Mark should have been doing), he told Mark to take this knee lac patient. Mark was very sarcastic as he agreed to take the patient.

23.451. Chloe
Chloe had an 8:30 appointment with her obstetrician after which she was to visit Social Services to apply for AFC (Aid to Families with Children) food stamps, and other assistance.

Later that evening, Susan came home to find Chloe smoking and learned that Chloe had not stayed for her doctor's appointment. This pushed Susan over the edge, and she angrily told her sister that she would no longer support her and the baby.

23.452. Doug's bogus malpractice suit
We were not told the details of this lawsuit but we do know that Diane Leeds helped Doug beat it.

23.453. Donny (Donald) Costanza
Thirty-four-year-old Donny was brought to the ER unconscious after a high-speed

automobile collision with a tree. His blood pressure was 110/85, his pulse was 88, and he showed a positive response to pain. His pupils were equal, round, and responsive to light, and Mark ordered a lateral c-spine X-ray. Donny's abdomen was not rigid and his bowel sounds were normal. His puls/ox was 92, his crit count was 44, his coma score was 9, and they were concerned about possible borderline brain damage.

Mark ordered Norcuron, Dilantin, and mannitol, and Carol found a suicide note to a woman named Amy among Donny's belongings. The letter read: "I gave up everything because you were all that mattered. Without you I'm already dead."

Dr. Swift then entered the trauma room and Mark gave him the bullet. Swift immediately decided that Donny needed to be intubated, but Mark explained that he was waiting for the X-ray results because he wanted to clear the c-spine first. "That's the wrong choice," Swift told him. He then told Mark he was not going to argue with him and took over.

Mark disgustedly ripped off his gloves and left the room.

Susan later told Swift that Donny's X-ray showed a small subdural bleed. The patient remained unconscious as Amy made her way to the hospital.

When Amy arrived, Susan told her that Donny had a severe concussion and some brain swelling and was in a coma. Amy told Susan that this was not his first suicide attempt and that the last time he had used pills. She also explained that he was a gambler and a master manipulator and that she was getting on a plane in three hours to get away from him.

Donny eventually regained consciousness, and Susan was surprised and a little saddened to see Amy sitting with him and telling him she wasn't going anywhere.

23.454. Howard Davis

This patient was *the* Howard Davis of the hospital's Davis Cardiac Wing, and when Dr. Swift arrived, he made sure that everyone in the ER knew it, and that Davis got the red carpet treatment.

Davis showed up at the ER with a superficial hand laceration. He had been cutting a bagel and the knife slipped.

Peter had initially examined Davis's hand and determined it was a superficial cut and that it was something Carter could easily attend to. He told Carter to irrigate and stitch the laceration, and that was when Carter told Peter who the patient was. It seems that Carter had gone to prep school with Davis's son and knew him and his family.

Dr. Swift stepped in at this point and took over. First, he told Jerry to call Bissell, the chief of hand surgery to come and take a look at Mr. Davis's hand, and to also get Plastics down to look at it.

He then asked Mr. Davis if there was anything else he was concerned about, and Davis pointed to a small bump at the corner of his eye. Swift then told Jerry to get Zimmerman from the Eye Institute and ordered Peter, a *second-year surgical resident*, to stitch up a superficial hand laceration that any med student (such as Carter) could have handled.

Peter, of course, complied with Swift's order, and it was during the procedure (which Carter assisted at Davis's insistence) that Peter learned that Carter came from a very wealthy family.

Later Jerry found out that Carter's father was Roland Carter and that his family was worth a cool $178 million. This did not do much to endear Carter to Benton, especially since Peter was three months behind on paying back his enormous med school student loan.

23.455. Brenda
Brenda was part of a girls' basketball team and was brought to the ER (with all her teammates *and* her basketball) because she had severe pain in her head and her neck.

Brenda could not touch her chin to her chest when asked to (a classic symptom of meningitis), and Doug immediately ordered a CBC, Chem 7, and cultures times 3. He also told Brenda's Mother Superior that he wanted to do a spinal tap on the teen and put her in isolation.

Doug's suspicions of bacterial meningitis were proved correct when Brenda's test results came back. He put her on antibiotics and admitted her to Intensive Care.

Doug then informed the rest of the team that they would all need to be put on an antibiotic because of their exposure to Brenda. (See Patients 23.456, 23.457, and 23.458–23.472.)

23.456. Elizabeth the Novice
Elizabeth was preparing to become a nun, but had not yet taken her final vows when she accompanied Brenda, Mother Superior, and the St. Josephine's girls' basketball team to the ER because Brenda didn't feel well.

Because of their exposure to Brenda, Elizabeth and the others needed to take rifampin, an antibiotic that could harm an unborn fetus, and so Doug ordered pregnancy tests for everyone. (Rifampin can cause the birth defect spina bifida during fetal development.)

Mother Superior told Doug that she and Elizabeth could be exempt from the pregnancy test but that all the girls should definitely take one.

Later, Elizabeth came to Carol and told her that there was a chance that she could be pregnant and she needed to take the test, too. She told Carol that she'd been seeing a man and that she was confused about what God wanted her to do.

Elizabeth's test came back negative, and she was a bit dismayed: Her decision, she told Carol, would have been made for her if she had been pregnant.

23.457. Mother Superior
Mother, who was head of St. Josephine's convent, had been a nurse before she became a nun. She accompanied Brenda, Elizabeth, and the girls' basketball team to the ER when Brenda became ill.

23.458–23.472. St. Josephine's girls' basketball team
These fifteen girls were all exposed to bacterial meningitis when their teammate Brenda contracted the disease, and they all had to take rifampin, a powerful antibiotic, as a precautionary measure.

Because of this drug's potential harm to an unborn fetus, Doug made them all take pregnancy tests. None of them were pregnant, and they were all able to begin taking the drug.

23.473. Taylor
Carter picked up this patient's X-rays for Dr. Benton.

23.474 and 23.475. Dumb and Dumber
A young man Haleh referred to as Dumb put a billiard ball in his mouth. It got stuck, and he could not remove it. When the EMTs arrived and asked Dumb's friend how it happened, he demonstrated by putting a billiard ball in *his own* mouth, where it, of course, also got stuck. Haleh christened this second youth Dumber.

23.476. Santi
Murphy's Law states that if something can go wrong, it will. In the case of children, Murphy's should be modified to state that if there's any way at all that something can be used by a kid to hurt himself, it will.

Santi was brought to the ER by his hysterical father, who burst into the hospital carrying his screaming son. To add to the confusion, Santi's father did not speak English.

Santi had been playing with a coat hanger and had somehow got the curved steel hook part of the hanger embedded into the roof of his mouth, with the wooden triangle of the coat hanger thrusting out of his mouth like some bizarre antenna.

Mark saw that Santi had pierced his posterior oral pharynx with the hanger, and that it was near his carotid artery. The boy's throat was swelling up, and Mark decided to do a needle crike (a cricothyroidotomy—see the Glossary). Dr. Swift arrived and told Malik to get the bolt cutters.

Santi's puls/ox was falling at 88 and his throat ultimately became completely swollen shut. Mark performed the crike and used a number 3 ET tube to bag him. Swift told Mark to throw in a figure 8 and close off the incision, and Santi's puls/ox began improving.

Mark and Swift then sent Santi to the O.R. to have the remaining piece of metal removed, and Wendy translated their assurances that his boy would be just fine to his distraught father.

23.477. Peter and Jeannie's nosocomial infection case
As part of her physician's assistant degree program, Jeannie was assigned to write a paper on nosocomial infections (infections contracted while in the hospital) and she asked Peter if he could give her a case or two.

Peter, ever eager to please Jeannie in any way he could, agreed to give her a few cases from which she could choose one to write about.

23.478. Mrs. Benton
By this episode, Mrs. Benton was settled in at the Melville Home, and when Peter went to visit her one night after work, her door was closed because she was getting a sponge bath. Peter sat in the lounge with Walt and waited until they could go in to see her.

• •

Original Broadcast Date: Thursday, May 4, 1995
Written by Paul Manning; Directed by Fred Gerber

"MOTHERHOOD"

ER·24

"There's a horse in my parking space."

—Doug Ross

This Mother's Day episode begins with a birth and ends with a death.

As Carol and Susan coo over Susan's new niece, Susie, Carol reveals that she's so stressed out over her wedding that she and Tag are barely speaking. The caterer canceled, the bridesmaids' gowns are late, and the parents are early, she complains to Susan. (Later Tag hangs up on her when she tells him she does not want to have dinner with his mother for the third night in a row.)

Mark tells Carter that he's got the ER sub-I if he wants it, but Carter says he wants to wait until he hears about the surgical sub-I before he accepts Mark's offer. Carter thinks surgery is what he wants, and, later, foolishly jumps the gun by turning Mark down before he has heard about the surgical sub-I.

Diane Leeds stuns Doug by informing him that she's going house hunting and that she'd like him to move in with her and Jake.

Susan and Chloe's mom, Cookie, visits with deli food and balloons and is so thrilled with little Susie that she tells Chloe, "It almost makes me glad you got yourself knocked up." Susan, in the meantime, is under the impression that everything is on track with the plans to have Chloe live with their parents, Cookie and Henry. She is shocked to find out that Cookie has changed her mind and will not take in Chloe and Susie.

Linda Farrell shows up at the ER and asks Doug to join her for Manhattans at

Shaw's. Doug turns her down, and she reminds him that even though he's being good now, she knew him when he was bad.

Carol and Susan lay out on lounge chairs in sunglasses and discuss their respective situations. Carol muses about separate honeymoons, and Susan thinks she might go to Hawaii with Carol and stay there.

Dr. Hicks finally informs Carter (who is shaken by the news) that he did not get the surgical sub-internship.

Peter is urgently summoned to the nursing home, where he learns that his mother has died, while Doug and Mark shoot hoops and discuss Doug's fears of commitment.

Later, Diane arrives at Doug's apartment to see him coming out with Linda Farrell. Diane angrily breaks up with him and refuses to give him another chance.

At the ER, Jenn Greene eats pizza with Carol while waiting for Mark, and the two women talk about their respective weddings. (Jenn reveals to Carol that she survived her wedding thanks to drugs.)

Jeannie shows up at the nursing home to find Peter still there and still in shock. He thought he'd be more prepared, he tells her, and when he breaks down, she holds him, and their embrace turns into a passionate kiss, which *she* initiates.

The episode ends with Susan holding little Susie and singing "Blackbird" to her in Chloe's darkened hospital room.

PATIENT HISTORIES

● ●

24.479. Chloe

Early Mothers' Day morning, Chloe woke Susan and told her it was time for the baby. Susan was shocked to hear that Chloe's contractions were two minutes apart and shouted at her for waiting so long. Chloe insisted on taking her enormous boom box and the Beatles' *White Album* with her to the hospital.

It was 4:30 A.M. when they arrived at the ER. Carter handed Susan a mug of coffee, and Susan called Dr. Janet Coburn, Chloe's obstetrician. Chloe's membrane had already ruptured, however, and her contractions were now ninety seconds apart.

Chloe was rushed to the delivery room with the baby crowning. She screamed at Carter to put on the Beatles "Blackbird," but all he could manage to find was a rap tape.

Susan ended up delivering her own niece, singing along with Chloe in an a capella rendition of "Blackbird," as Carter observed and assisted.

24.480. Susie

Little Susie was born on Mother's Day, and even though her mother, Chloe, did not take very good care of herself, Susie was apparently in good health. Carol told Susan that the baby looked like her and it was obvious that Susan had already bonded with her namesake niece, probably even before Chloe did.

24.481. James Schaffer

Fifteen-year-old James was playing around on a construction site when he fell from the second floor and landed on a long steel rebar, impaling himself and puncturing his interior vena cava (one of the large arteries to the heart).

When the boy arrived at the ER, he was in shock, his pulse was thready, and his pressure was 50/30.

Peter immediately ordered his blood typed and crossmatched for 8 units and asked Carter if they should just yank out the rebar. Carter correctly answered no and, when prodded, suggested a laparatomy, to which Peter replied, "Right again."

Peter performed the surgery and, after he had surgically opened the pericardium, allowed Carter to pull out the bar.

After Carter acknowledged that the surgery had been "very cool," James went into ventricular fibrillation and Carter began cardiac massage. Peter shocked James once, but he did not convert to normal sinus rhythm. Shortly thereafter, the boy died.

Peter then had to inform James's mother that they had tried for thirty-three minutes to resuscitate her son, but to no avail. He told her, "We used all our capabilities."

24.482–24.488. Palmer and 6 other Ranger Scouts with diarrhea

These charming little urchins were brought to the ER by their troop leader, Dolores Minky, because they were all complaining of abdominal cramps, vomiting, diarrhea, and excessive flatus.

One of the youths, a lad named Palmer, was held in especially low regard by his fellow Scouts because, as they complained, he had farted all the way to the hospital.

Ms. Minky told Doug that it was probably a giardia infection (on a recent camping trip they had all drunk stream water), and then one of the boys threw up on Doug.

24.489. Michelle's boyfriend

This young man had mixed ammonia with bleach and ended up in the ER critically ill with chlorine poisoning.

Susan ordered 125 milligrams of Solu-Medrol IV push, a nebulizer treatment, and a portable chest film. She also ordered him given humidified oxygen at 15 liters per minute and a blood gas test.

Mark arrived, Susan filled him in and told him that Respiratory was coming down, and he told her to call him if she needed him.

24.490. Joanie Lafferty

Seven-year-old Joanie was brought to the ER by her mother because she had been running a high fever and vomiting.

Doug suspected Joanie might have a problem outside of his pediatrics expertise and asked Mark to take over.

Joanie was dehydrated, running a fever of 102°, and had a faint heart murmur. Mark ordered administration of fluids via a saline IV of 100 ccs an hour. He also ordered a CBC, Chem 7, and asked that Joanie be prepped for an LP (lumbar puncture, a spinal tap).

Joanie's pressure was 80/50, her resps were 36, and her murmur registered 3 over 6. Mark suspected either pneumonia or early heart failure and told Mrs. Lafferty that her daughter might have endocarditis, which is inflammation of the inner lining of the heart. Shortly thereafter, Joanie developed pulmonary edema, and Mark ordered 5 milligrams of morphine, a nitro drip, and a blood gas drawn.

Ultimately, Mark called for a cardiac consult. He and Dr. Netzly concluded that

Joanie urgently needed a mitral valve replacement, and it is assumed the young lady came through the three-hour operation successfully.

24.491. The guy who impaled himself on a TV antenna and punctured his gall bladder

The surgeon who assisted Peter on his laparatomy on James Schaffer (Patient 24.481) told him about this patient he had once treated.

24.492. Peter's appendectomy

After Carter successfully assisted on a laparatomy (although the patient died anyway), Peter allowed him to scrub in on an appendectomy.

24.493. Kaitlin Sandburg

This young lady was brought to the ER by her apprehensive mother because she had been stung by a bee.

Doug examined Kaitlin and told Mrs. Sandburg that he was confident that her daughter was not allergic to bee stings and that she probably would not have a reaction. Mrs. Sandburg told Doug that *she* was allergic to bees, and when Doug told her that the condition was not genetic, she sarcastically asked Doug how could he be so sure.

When Doug left the room, Mrs. Sandburg told her daughter Kaitlin that she didn't like Doug.

24.494. The Asian woman who drank too many Mimosas

Carter stitched up this woman's ear after she drank too many Mimosas and fell in the restaurant parking lot. She was so drunk that she fell asleep as Carter was sewing her up.

24.495. Ada

This elderly woman was brought to the ER by her daughter, Ethyl, with a cut on her arm. When Carter went in to see them, Ada fell off her chair in apparent cardiac arrest, and Carter had to call a Code Blue.

24.496. The old man who swallowed his dentures

This elderly man was eating in a restaurant when he suddenly turned blue and collapsed. The EMTs tried the Heimlich maneuver on him but it didn't work.

When he arrived at the ER he was cyanotic, his pulse was 58, and his pressure was 50 palp (which quickly dropped to 40 palp). The EMTs had already given him a 500 cc bolus of normal saline in two IVs and Peter ordered 1 milligram of atropine and a dopamine drip.

Peter ordered Carter to intubate him, but he couldn't because of some type of obstruction, which Susan verified.

Susan then told Carter to get the McGill forceps quickly because the patient's puls/ox was falling.

Carter rooted around in the old man's throat and finally pulled out a complete set of dentures. Peter had one word for the food-encrusted bridge: "Nasty."

Peter ordered the patient hyperventilated and his blood gases taken, but the crisis was over.

24.497. Doug's referral to Dr. Metcalf

Doug sent this patient to O.R. 3 with assurances that Dr. Metcalf was on his way.

24.498. The teenage girl who overdosed

This young lady was brought in comatose after taking a speedball (heroin and cocaine) and some downs. Not much else is known about her, not even whether or not she survived.

24.499. Rosario

Rosario was a gangbanger who was stabbed in the chest by Angelina Figueora (Patient 24.500). When she arrived at the ER she was cyanotic, her pulse was 140 and thready, her pressure was 50/30, and she had decreased breath sounds on the left. Mark identified a tracheal shift and a tension pneumothorax.

At this point Rosario woke up screaming, and Susan ordered her given a total of 5 milligrams of meperedol in her IV.

Shortly thereafter, a young lady burst into the trauma room screaming that Rosario had cut her ear off. This gangbanger then leaped up onto the gurney and punched Rosario in the face. Carter just stood there stunned until Doug shouted at him to "Focus!" Malik then pulled One-Ear off and put her in a suture room in restraints. It wasn't told if Rosario survived.

24.500. Angelina Figueora

Angelina was the gangbanger who stabbed Rosario (Patient 24.499) in the chest (with Rosario's own knife) and was subsequently shot in the head.

When she arrived at the ER her pulse was 60, her blood pressure was 90/60, and her GCS was 5. Her pupils were blown, and there was gray matter in her hair.

Susan ordered 75 grams of mannitol, 1 gram of Ancef, a CBC, Chem 7, a chest film, a CT, and her blood typed and crossmatched for 2 units.

Angelina didn't make it.

24.501. The girl whose ear was cut off by Rosario

This gangbanger burst into the trauma room and began beating up Rosario as she was being treated.

One-Ear was put in restraints in a suture room, and it is assumed her ear was reattached.

24.502. Mrs. Benton

The doctor on duty at the Melville Home told Peter that his mother arrested at 5:15 P.M. and that they worked for twenty-five minutes, using all their capabilities to resuscitate her, but her heart was too weak and she died. Jackie was with Mrs. Benton when she passed away.

● ●

Original Broadcast Date: Thursday, May 11, 1995
Written by Lydia Woodward; Directed by Quentin Tarantino

"EVERYTHING OLD IS NEW AGAIN"

"I don't know what to say. I don't know what the future holds but I guess I'm just lucky to be alive and to have so many good friends who care for me. It's been a wonderful year because of all of you."

—Carol Hathaway, at her wedding reception
after the wedding was called off

"You're gonna make a good doctor."

—Peter Benton, to Carter, on the last
day of Carter's ER rotation

"I'm coming back in the fall."

—John Carter, on the last day of his ER rotation

This final episode of ER's first season opens exactly the way its first episode opened, with someone sleeping.

In episode 1, it was Mark who was asleep. In this episode, it is Carter. Malik wakes Carter because a GSW to the head is coming in and everyone else is busy. It's Carter's last day in the ER, and, after a very traumatic ordeal in which Carter almost does a crike on the GSW, Peter coldly tells him to turn in his lab coat when he leaves and he'll get his deposit back.

At home, Carol wakes up and sees that it is raining, and we can tell she interprets this as a sign that her pending marriage is wrong.

Susan rushes around getting ready for work and tells Chloe to do the laundry. The wedding is at five, so Susan has to be home by three to get ready.

At the ER, Mark suggests that Doug tell Diane how he feels. Doug doesn't know how he feels, and Mark asks him if his and Diane's breakup might be for the best. Doug sees his point, but admits that it's been hard on Diane's son, Jake.

Carter has to do an evaluation of his ER rotation and is thrilled to learn that he gets to grade Benton. With Haleh's prodding, he spitefully gives Peter a 16 out of a possible 40 and then turns the evaluation in to Dr. Hicks.

Jeannie stops Peter in the hall and tells him not to call her at home anymore. They agree to meet for lunch to talk things over.

Later Peter tells Carter that Wilkins took the orthopedic sub-internship and that the ER surgical sub-internship is his if he wants it. Carter is ecstatic, but realizes he needs to "reevalauate" Peter before Dr. Hicks reads his scathing review.

In the meantime, Dr. Swift tells a stunned Mark that he has decided to give him the attending job. Mark walks out of his office in shock, but then returns to shake Dr. Swift's hand and say thank you.

Peter and Jeannie confront their feelings for each other, and Jeannie tells him she can't continue to see him. She tells him that she thinks their passionate kiss in the nursing home was about him losing his mother. Peter responds, "We'd like to think that, wouldn't we?"

Susan arrives home late in the afternoon to find Chloe gone and the baby alone.

Carter asks Dr. Hicks if he can take another crack at his evaluation of Benton, and she then reads him Peter's evaluation of him. (See the end of this chapter for what Peter said about Carter.) She allows him to redo the evaluation, and they agree he'll give Benton a 38 out of 40.

Carol arrives at the church to wed Tag, only Tag is nowhere to be found. She locates him on a bench outside the church, and he tells her he's not sure she loves him enough. She ultimately admits that she does not love him as much as he loves her. He then kisses her, thanks her, and leaves.

Back at the ER, Jake comes to see Doug, and Doug explains to him that he did a bad thing to his mother and that it had nothing to do with Jake. Doug apologizes to Jake, and Jake walks away, saddened and feeling betrayed by Doug.

At the wedding reception, the guests decide that it would be a shame to waste

all the terrific food (lobster Newburg!) and drink and they start to eat. (Jenn orders a
gin and tonic while Susan asks for a Chivas straight up.)

Doug visits a distraught and tearful Carol in the church and assures her that
someday she will be happy. "You will," he tells her. "You will." They then join the
reception, where Carol receives an ovation and makes a heartfelt speech thanking
them all for their support. Afterward they all dance to "Tequila."

At the hospital, Carter cleans out his locker and thanks Benton for everything he
did for him over the past several months. Benton tells him he's going to make a good
doctor. Carter then turns in his lab coat (and gets his deposit back) and tells Rolando
he's coming back in the fall. Sarah Hahn then calls him "Dr. Carter" and thanks him
for making a difference in her brother Caleb's life.

The episode (and the season) ends with Carter walking away from the hospital
as the ambulances and the police cars arrive and life in the ER goes on.

PATIENT HISTORIES

25.503. Mark's MI

Mark was treating this patient when Patient 25.504, the attempted suicide, came in.
Carter ended up having to take charge of the suicide attempt.

25.504. The self-inflicted GSW to the head

This young man attempted suicide by taking his mother's .357, putting it in his
mouth, and pulling the trigger.

The EMTs started two large bore IVs and gave him 15 liters of oxygen, and when
they arrived at the ER, the boy's blood pressure was 80/50, his pulse was 56, his GCS
was 6, and he was cyanotic.

He was put on a ventilator, and it was noted there was gray matter (brains) in his
hair. The boy's pupils were midrange and sluggish, and when Malik asked, "Where's
his face?", an EMT replied, "He left it on the dining room wall."

Because his puls/ox was bad, it was obvious he needed an airway. The problem
was there was no one to do it—except Carter, a third-year med student who had only
done one under strict supervision by a surgeon.

Carter tried to intubate the boy instead of doing the cricothyroidotomy, but it
didn't work. At this point, the boy's PCO_2 was 60, his puls/ox was 65, his PH was
7.20, he had diminished breath sounds, and he was "hypoxic as hell." It was clear
that without a surgical airway, the boy would die.

Carter finally decided to do it and refused both Versed and Norcuron because if
he paralyzed him and did not get the airway on the first shot, the boy would die.

Lydia told Carter to make a vertical incision through the skin and then a horizontal
cut through the membrane, and right after Carter made his first cut, Benton arrived.

Carter informed him that the boy had been given 4 units of blood, that his pressure was 70/50, and his pulse was 54, and Peter went to work, quickly establishing an
airway.

Dr. Benton's Final Evaluation of Med Student John Carter

Carter, John Truman

An exceptional student; well-trained; superior diagnostic skills; fast learner; dedicated; selfless; excellent bedside manner with patients; far more successful at dealing with the patient's emotional needs than this instructor. Highly intelligent. One of the finest students I've ever had the opportunity to work with. Recommend high honors.

Peter then asked Carter if he was going to do the crike, and when Carter acknowledged that he was, Peter made a grunting sound. Carter then asked him if it was the wrong choice, and Peter said simply, "Nope."

The patient's mouth was then packed with gauze and he was sent to the O.R.

25.505. Bonnie Curtis

Middle-aged Bonnie was drunk and not wearing a seat belt when she hit a parked car and bent the steering wheel of her Buick with her chest at seven o'clock in the morning.

When she arrived at the ER, her pulse was 120, her resps were 36. She was shocky with a pressure of 70/50 and her puls/ox was 85.

She was also wide awake and shouting for a cigarette.

Mark ordered a CBC, Chem 7, cardiac enzymes, EKG, a BA, and a cross-table c-spine X-ray. Bonnie's abdomen was soft and nontender, there was no rebounding or guarding, and she had normal bowel sounds. Her PO_2 was 70 on room air and her resps were high. Dr. Swift then arrived and Mark filled him in on Bonnie's condition.

Swift suspected a mild myocardial infarction, but Mark feared a pulmonary embolism. Swift argued that her readings were indicative of alcoholic cardiac myopathy. Mark stood firm and wanted a V/Q (ventilation perfusion, see Glossary) scan. Swift told him he was grasping at straws and ordered thiamine folate and hydration with 5 percent dextrose in normal saline. He also said to handle her blood pressure with dopamine and ordered her sent to telemetry for a serial EKG and enzymes.

He then left the trauma room.

Mark then reordered the V/Q scan but told them to do Swift's orders too.

Later, in the X-ray lab, Swift confronted Mark about doing the V/Q scan anyway and asked Mark if he ordered pulmonary angiography (indicative when the patient has a pulmonary embolism). Mark defended his decision by telling Swift that her PCO_2 was rising, her PO_2 and PH were falling, and she showed S1Q3 on her EKG.

Swift smiled and said, "Good work," and Mark realized that Swift had been trying to get him back on his game by challenging and confronting his decisions.

It is assumed Bonnie sobered up and survived.

25.506. Caleb Hahn

Caleb was a young leukemia patient (He had ALL, acute lymphoblastic leukemia) who was brought to the ER by his worried sister, Sarah, when he began running a fever of 101°.

Caleb had no cough or abdominal pain, and Doug ordered a CBC plus differential, blood cultures times three, a urine culture, throat swab, and a chest film.

Doug then asked Carter what else he should do, and Carter replied that he'd do an LP (a spinal tap) on Caleb. Caleb exploded at hearing this and said he didn't need one. Doug then explained that Caleb was manifesting early signs of meningitis, which include irritability and lethargy.

Doug told Caleb that they would try antibiotics for a while, and if he was still being a "pain in the ass" later, they'd give him the tap.

Doug then ordered 80 milligrams of gentamicin, 1 gram of oxacillin, 15 grams of piperacillin IV, and an oncology consult.

Dr. Weiss, the resident oncologist, ordered 300 micrograms of Nupogen to stimulate white blood cell growth, and Carter volunteered to keep an eye on Caleb. Caleb, however, was surly and rude to Carter, so Carter left him alone.

Eventually Caleb's fever went down to 99°, and they determined he had an infection and that his fever was not due to his recent chemotherapy.

Carter befriended Caleb by playing Mortal Kombat with him (Caleb was Johnny Cage) and telling him about the death of his brother Bobby. He then used their new friendship to show Caleb that he was mistreating his sister by being arrogant and mean to her. Later, Caleb's sister, Sarah, thanked Carter for caring.

25.507. Thomas Allison

Susan gave Peter the bullet on Thomas. She told him that Thomas, a male in his thirties, was an end-stage AIDS patient on multiple meds with a fever of 101°. His heart rate was tachycardic and he had a history of GI lymphoma, PCC pneumonia (pneumocystis carinii), Kaposi's sarcoma, AIDS dementia, oral thrush, and cryptococcal meningitis. He also had high-pitched bowel sounds, tenderness and distention, and hepatosplenomegaly. Susan also told Peter that Thomas had had no recent stool or gas, that he was vomiting blood and bile, and that she had started him on a 300 cc fluid challenge.

Thomas's companion, Mr. Warner, told Susan that Thomas was taking DDC, Bactrim, AZT, Fluconazole, and Rifabutin.

Peter ordered a KUB; lateral decubitus chest films; blood cultures times three, including microbacterial and fungal; CBC; Chem 24; urine culture; an NG tube; 4 milligrams of morphine IV; and 25 milligrams of Compazine IV.

Susan told Thomas's companion that Thomas had a possible bowel obstruction from enlarged lymph nodes due to recurrent lymphoma, and that he might need surgery, although they would try drugs and hydration first.

Thomas was running a fever of 102° and his blood pressure was 70/50. Peter decided that Thomas needed an emergency colostomy, and was told that his mother had power of attorney.

Shortly after she arrived, Thomas's mother, Marjorie, refused permission for the emergency surgery. She said she did not want to put her son through any more pain, and Peter reluctantly accepted this, telling her they'd try and keep him comfortable. He then ordered another 4 milligrams of morphine and went out to talk to Mr. Warner.

Warner knew that Marjorie would not allow the surgery, because that was what Thomas would have wanted. He told Peter that they had already said their goodbyes, but "I guess you're never really ready." He asked Peter if he could take Thomas home, but Peter advised against it, because if he regained consciousness, it would be rough, and in the hospital they could control his pain.

Later, when Peter went in to check on Thomas, he noted his pressure was 65/50 and his fever had gone to 103°. Peter sat by the side of the bed, held Thomas's hand, and silently cried. It was clear that he was using Thomas's pending death as a way to say goodbye to his recently deceased mother.

25.508. The unconscious geezer in 2
This patient was one of two charts (the other was Patient 25.509) that Conni gave Doug. Doug took this patient and gave the drunk in 5 to Carter.

25.509. The four-martini lunch with a bellyache in 5
This patient was one of two charts that Conni gave Doug. Doug immediately gave this one to Carter.

25.510. Carter's brother, Bobby Carter
Carter told Caleb (Patient 25.506) the story of his brother, Bobby, who had had AML (acute myeloblastic leukemia) as a child. Bobby did not survive, but Carter explained to Caleb that he had ALL (acute lymphoblastic leukemia), which Carter assured him was much more treatable than Bobby's disease.

25.511–25.512. The last two patients
As Carter was walking out of the ER at the end of the last day of his ER rotation, two patients were brought in, one by ambulance, and one in the backseat of a police car.

The patient in the ambulance was a GSW to the head, Her pressure was 90/50, her pulse was 120, and she had been given 10 liters of O_2.

The other patient was removed from the police car and put on a gurney as Carter walked away from the ER.

● ●

Original Broadcast Date:
Thursday, May 18, 1995
Written by John Wells;
Directed by Mimi Leder

WHAT'S YOUR ER I.Q.?

WHAT'S YOUR ER I.Q.?

This 101-question quiz tests your knowledge of all things *ER*.

Try to answer as many questions as you can from memory, but if you can't get some of them, you can search for the answers in the episode summaries and patient histories in this volume. (And here's a hint: The questions are generally in chronological order, beginning with the first episode and continuing through to the season finale.) The Answers section follows this quiz. Let the quizzing begin! Stat.!

1. How many hours a week did ER residents (like Peter and Mark) work?

   A. 40   **B.** 60   **C.** 90

2. What would Mark's starting annual salary have been if he had taken the plush job with the Harris Medical Group?

   A. $50,000   **B.** $120,000   **C.** $75,000

3. What was the name of the flirtatious ER patient who gave Carter a sexually transmitted disease?

4. **TRUE OR FALSE:** The first time we see Dr. Doug Ross in *ER*, he is drunk.

5. How did Carol Hathaway attempt to commit suicide?

   A. She took an overdose of depressant drugs.

B. She hanged herself.   **C.** She tried to drown herself.

6. **TRUE OR FALSE:** After Carol's suicide attempt, Doug visited her at home every week until she came back to work.

7. What were Mark and Jenn celebrating when they got caught having sex in an examination room?

    A. Jenn's father decided to give them the down payment for a house.
    B. Mark finished paying off his student loan.
    C. Jenn passed her bar exam.

8. What was the name of the liquor store owner who was repeatedly held up and who ended up fatally shooting a young robber?

9. **TRUE OR FALSE:** Carol wanted to go to work in a doctor's office after her suicide attempt, but her shrink insisted she go back to the ER.

10. What was written on the orthopedic brace Mark gave Carol at her Welcome Back party?

    A. "Welcome Back"   **B.** "Welcome Home"
    C. "A Mind Is a Terrible Thing to Waste"

11. TOUGH ONE: What year did Mr. and Mrs. Packer go on their honeymoon? (*Hint*: It was the year they saw Mary Cavanaugh sing.)

    A. 1948   **B.** 1953   **C.** 1955

12. **TRUE OR FALSE:** Little Huey's father passed out when he learned that his infant son had to undergo a spinal tap.

13. How many hours of sleep did Dr. Benton like to get each night?

14. What specific car repair did Walt perform on Peter's car on Walt and Jackie's tenth anniversary?

    A. New brakes   **B.** A transmission repair   **C.** A water pump

15. What did ER patient Harry Stopeck sell?

    A. Jewelry   **B.** Wholesale meats   **C.** Office equipment

16. What was the name of the naked blonde who was brought to the ER handcuffed to a guy who was having a heart attack?

    A. Priscilla   **B.** Rachel   **C.** Heather

17. What date was "Dr. Greene Day?" (*Hint*: See Patient 4.75.)

18. Why did Jennifer Greene move to Milwaukee?

    A. She wanted to be near her ill mother.
    B. She was given a job as a law clerk for a federal judge.
    C. She and Mark put Rachel in a special school, and Jenn wanted to be near her.

19. What was Peter *really* listening to when he told Carter he had Snoop Doggy Dogg in his cassette player?

    A. *Advancements in Liver Transplantation*
    B. *Multiple Casualty Management in the Emergency Department*
    C. *Trends in Cardiac Surgery, Volume 2*

20. **TRUE OR FALSE:** Mark's patient Sam Gasner, the builder, finally received the heart transplant he needed so desperately.

21. What was the name of the babysitter Mark and Jenn used for Rachel in Chicago?

    A. Tommy   **B.** Ronny   **C.** Connie

22. A delivery man once crashed his car through the front door of the ER. What did the driver deliver?

    A. Pizza   **B.** Flowers   **C.** Chinese food

23. What drug company did hotshot sales representative Linda Farrell work for?

    A. Kline   **B.** Novell Pharmaceuticals   **C.** McKesson Drugs

24. **TRUE OR FALSE:** Emergency Service Coordinator Jerry (played by Abraham Benrubi) was a vegetarian.

25. COMPLETE THE MED STUDENT'S MAXIM: "See one, do one, _____."

26. How many medical residents were given a Starzl Fellowship (to study with surgical transplant teams) each year?

    A. 30   **B.** 40   **C.** 50

27. **TRUE OR FALSE:** ER nurse Lydia Wright began dating Officer Grabarsky after she met him in the ER.

28. Who was "Dr. Intercom"?

29. What is a "champagne tap?"

30. TOUGH ONE: Lovable Patrick appeared in three episodes of *ER*, but only twice was he there for a medical reason. Can you name the two injuries that brought Patrick to the ER?

31. What was Mookie's street name?

    A. Blade   **B.** Slice   **C.** Edge

32. How did Susan learn to hot-wire a car?

    A. One of Chloe's criminal boyfriends taught her.
    B. Her brother Earl taught her.
    C. Chloe taught her.

33. **TRUE OR FALSE:** Peter won the Starzl Fellowship.

34. What was Mookie's first assignment at the ER. (*Hint*: This "assignment" was given to him by Peter.)

    A. Peter made him clean out the refrigerator in the doctor's lounge.
    B. Peter made him clean up a Code Brown in trauma room 3.
    C. Peter made him hold a retractor during an MVA trauma.

35. What animal part did Carter use to practice his sutures on?

36. **TRUE OR FALSE:** Carter had a sister.

37. **TRUE OR FALSE:** Tag knew how to pluck turkeys.

38. What kind of car did Linda Farrell drive?

    A. A Porsche   **B.** A Mercury Sable   **C.** A Lexus

39. What size and cut was Carol's engagement ring from Tag?

    A. Two carat marquis   **B.** Two carat oval   **C.** One carat round brilliant

40. Match the following Disaster Protocol color codes with their proper definition.

A.	Black	**1.**	Walking Wounded
B.	Red	**2.**	Urgent
C.	Green	**3.**	DOA
D.	Yellow	**4.**	Critical

41. What takeout food did Linda Farrell order delivered to the ER during the big blizzard?

    A. 24 containers of Kung Po chicken   **B.** 30 pizzas   **C.** 100 Big Macs

42. **TRUE OR FALSE:** As a prank, Mark and Susan once put a cast on Carter's left arm while he was sleeping.

43. What do the ER staff call motorcycles?

44. Who was Susan's Secret Santa?

    A. Haleh   **B.** Carter   **C.** Doug

45. What did Susan's Secret Santa give her for Christmas?

    A. A grand piano music box   **B.** A muffler and scarf set   **C.** A bottle of Giorgio

46. Why did the cat walk on sand?

47. What article of clothing did Susan give Chloe before Chloe moved to Texas?

    A. A pair of jeans   **B.** A winter coat   **C.** A silk blouse

48. **TRUE OR FALSE:** The Piano Showroom was on the Eisenhower Expressway.

49. TOUGH ONE: According to Dr. Morgenstern, there were three "requisite qualities" of a good ER specialist. Name them.

50.   What kind of car did Susan Lewis drive?

      A. A Honda Accord   **B.** A Buick Regal   **C.** A Volkswagen Bug

51.   What was the name of the diner where everyone from the ER often ate after work?

      A. The Pit Stop   **B.** Uncle Henry's   **C.** Doc Magoo's

52.   What are the odds of getting infected from a needle stick if the patient has HIV or AIDS?

      A. 1 in 100   **B.** 1 in 250   **C.** 1 in 1,000

53.   TRUE OR FALSE: Malik once accidentally hit Carter with the defibrillation paddles.

54.   FILL-IN-THE-BLANK: Mr. Desmond was a sociologist at the University of Chicago studying violence. He would go around the city insulting and provoking people until they assaulted him. His methodology was to ask two questions to probe for insecurities and then use this information to antagonize the person to the point of violence. He defined this period between provocation and assault as the PVA, which stood for Provocation to _____.

55.   TRUE OR FALSE: Tag and Carol liked to play with edible body oils.

56.   Approximately how many pediatric patients did Doug see in the ER in a given year?

      A. 1,500   **B.** 3,000   **C.** 4,500

57.   Complete this old hospice joke: "Life goes on."

      A. "Says who?"   **B.** "Just not here."   **C.** "And then sometimes it doesn't."

58.   How long did it take Carol to acquire two new crash carts for the ER?

      A. Six weeks   **B.** Six months   **C.** A year

59.   Who initially offered Mark the ER attending job, Dr. Morgenstern or Dr. Swift?

60.   What department of the hospital did Diane Leeds work in?

      A. Risk Management   **B.** Physical Therapy   **C.** Prostheses

61.   What did Peter give his mother for her last Valentine's Day?

      A. A heart locket   **B.** A new walker   **C.** Roses and chocolates

62.   TRUE OR FALSE: Deb Chen once worked a day at the ER while stoned on acid.

63.   What was the name of the stray dog that Mark and company saved in the ER and who was later adopted by Officer Grabarsky?

      A. Bill   **B.** Bob   **C.** Frank

64. WHO SAID IT?: "I couldn't be at my mother's birthday party because I had to save a man with 'Die Nigger Die' tattooed on his forearm."

    A. Peter   **B.** Jeannie   **C.** Malik

65. How old was Mrs. Benton when she died?

    A. 74   **B.** 75   **C.** 76

66. **TRUE OR FALSE:** Little AIDS patient Tatiana lived at the Sunrise House Hospice while Carol tried to get approval to adopt her.

67. What did Doug find on the back of a little girl who had fallen out of a second-floor window that provoked him to punch her father in the mouth?

    A. Cigarette burns   **B.** A boot print   **C.** Dozens of purple bruises

68. How did Carter commemorate Peter's "birthday"?

    A. He hired two belly dancers to come to the ER.
    B. He sent Peter a singing telegram.
    C. He completed all of Peter's charts while Peter napped.

69. Why was Carol's pending adoption of Tatiana rejected?

70. A visiting researcher from MIT (who turned out to be an escaped mental patient) came up with an intriguing compromise solution for Mark and Jenn regarding her job in Milwaukee and his in Chicago. What was it?

    A. He suggested Mark get a helicopter license and lease a chopper that he could park on the hospital roof.
    B. He told them to move to Kenosha because it was halfway between Chicago and Milwaukee.
    C. He suggested that Jenn file motions to have all of the cases assigned to the judge she was clerking for moved to Chicago.

71. **TRUE OR FALSE:** Dr. Morgenstern took a job at Harvard, resulting in Dr. Swift's having final approval on Mark's attending job.

72. What was Dr. Swift's nickname?

    A. Wild Willy   **B.** The Terminator   **C.** The Boss

73. Which of the following errors did Mark make during his treatment of Jody O'Brien? (Choose as many as apply.)

    A. He missed a placental abruption on the ultrasound.
    B. He underestimated fetal weight.
    C. He blew off a borderline high blood pressure reading.
    D. He used forceps on a macrosomic baby.
    E. All of the above.

74. WHO SAID IT?: "Dr. Greene, I just wanted to tell you that I thought what you did was a heroic thing."

75.   Mr. Longét, the Tattoo Man, presented at the ER with a severe abrasion on his right arm. How did he acquire this injury?

      A. He tried to remove a tattoo with hydrochloric acid.
      B. He tried to remove a tattoo with a power sander.
      C. He fell off his Harley and scraped his arm.

76.   Jody O'Brien and her husband, Sean, considered several names for their soon-to-be-born son, including Thurman, Jason, Patrick, and Jared. Which name did they finally decide on (with more than a little help from Mark)?

77.   What descriptive metaphor did Carter use to explain what a live heart felt like the first time he handled one?

      A. A bag of fish   **B.** A bag of mud   **C.** A bag of worms

78.   What song did Carter once call in to a radio station and request be played and dedicated to Susan?

      A. "Twist and Shout"   **B.** "You Are So Beautiful"   **C.** "Doctor My Eyes"

79.   What are "Popsicle pledges"?

80.   **TRUE OR FALSE:** Carol once treated a werewolf.

81.   **WHO SAID IT?:** "Your talent is God's gift to you. What you do with it is your gift back to God."

82.   Deb once botched a procedure she wasn't even supposed to be doing, resulting in the patient requiring emergency surgery. What procedure did Deb try to perform?

      A. An intubation   **B.** A cricothyroidotomy   **C.** Insertion of a central line

83.   What does NPO mean?

      A. Nothing By Mouth   **B.** Nasogastric Tube   **C.** Normal Saline Only

84.   Mrs. Benton was placed in a nursing home named for a famous American author. What was the name of the home?

      A. The Twain House   **B.** The Melville Home   **C.** The Faulkner Residence

85.   "Why do nurses wear colors and doctors wear white?"

86.   **TRUE OR FALSE:** Because of their marital troubles, Mark and Jenn refused Carol's request to let their daughter Rachel be ring bearer at Tag's and her wedding.

87.   **FILL-IN-THE-BLANK:** Jeannie Boulet was studying to be a _____.

      A. Surgical Nurse   **B.** Physician's Assistant   **C.** Master Phlebotomist

88.   What did Susan sarcastically say was Chloe's diet when she was pregnant?

      A. Pop-Tarts and pizza   **B.** Twinkies and popcorn   **C.** Tacos and Pez

89. What specific drug was "Dr." Lyle Strong (who was not a doctor) seeking when he came to the ER with a phony kidney ailment?

    A. Demerol   **B.** Percocet   **C.** Valium

90. Match Mark and Susan with their student loan balances:

    A. Susan   **1.** $110,00
    B. Mark   **2.** $85,000

91. How much was Carter's family worth?

    A. $78 million   **B.** $100 million   **C.** $178 million

92. Haleh nicknamed two ER patients Dumb and Dumber. What specific stupidity were they both guilty of?

    A. They both got their hands stuck in pickle jars.
    B. They both got billiard balls stuck in their mouths.
    C. They both fell asleep on tanning beds and got second-degree burns.

93. WHO SAID IT?: "It almost makes me glad you got yourself knocked up."

94. What specific cassette did Chloe insist on bringing with her to the hospital when she was in labor?

    A. *Frampton Comes Alive!*
    B. The *Saturday Night Fever* soundtrack
    C. The Beatles' *White Album*

95. What famous film director directed the second-to-the-last episode of *ER*'s first season?

    A. Quentin Tarantino   **B.** Martin Scorsese   **C.** Spike Lee

96. **TRUE OR FALSE:** Carol and Tag's wedding was at ten o'clock in the morning.

97. What was Carter's initial scoring (out of a possible 40) of Dr. Benton on his ER rotation evaluation?

    A. 16   **B.** 2   **C.** 40

98. What Mortal Kombat character did young leukemia patient Caleb Hahn want to be in his competition with Carter?

99. **TRUE OR FALSE:** End-stage AIDS patient Thomas Allison's mother agreed to allow Peter to do an emergency colostomy on her son.

100. What was the name of Carter's brother who died of leukemia?

    A. Ronnie   **B.** Tommy   **C.** Bobby

101. WHO SAID IT?" "I'm coming back in the fall."

ANSWERS

● ●

1. C.   **2.** B.   **3.** Liz.   **4.** True.   **5.** A.   **6.** False. After eight weeks, he still had not been to see her even once.   **7.** C.   **8.** Ivan.   **9.** False. Her shrink suggested she work in a doctor's office, but Carol insisted on going back to the ER.   **10.** B.   **11.** A.
12. True.   **13.** "Anything more than three hours and I'm sluggish all day."
14. B.   **15.** C.   **16.** A.   **17.** August 25.   **18.** B.   **19.** C.   **20.** False. Sam died before Mark could find him a heart.   **21.** A.   **22..** A.   **23.** B.   **24.** True.   **25.** "teach one."   **26.** A.   **27.** True.   **28.** Doug Ross, according to Susan. She angrily called him this after Div Cvetic told Doug that he and Susan were dating.   **29.** A "champagne tap" is a successful lumbar puncture the first time a medical student attempts one, so-called because the supervising resident has to, by custom, buy the student a bottle of champagne.   **30.** First, he came in for an injured elbow, and the second time, for a head laceration.   **31.** B.   **32.** A.   **33.** False. It went to his rival, Dr. Sarah Langworthy.   **34.** A.   **35.** Pig's feet. (He had a refrigerator full of them at home.)
36. True. (His parents visited her in Switzerland for Thanksgiving.)   **37.** True. (See episode 9.)   **38.** C.   **39.** A.   **40..** A,3; B,4; C,1; D,2.   **41.** B.   **42.** False. They did put a cast on him but it was on his right leg, not his left arm.   **43.** Donorcycles, for obvious reasons.   **44.** B.   **45.** A.   **46.** To get "sandy claws!" (This was Patrick's Christmas riddle for the ER staff.)   **47.** B.   **48.** True.   **49.** "Confidence, composure under pressure, assertiveness."   **50.** C.   **51.** C.   **52.** B. (Note: The most recent edition of Current Emergency Diagnosis and Treatment states: "Exposures as the result of needlestick injuries carry a 1:200 risk of HIV infection.")   **53.** False. Deb was the one who shocked Carter and knocked him out cold.   **54.** Provocation to Assault Interval.   **55.** True. We learned this in episode 14 when Tag accidentally left his bag of oils and sex toys under the admitting desk at the ER.   **56.** B.   **57.** C.   **58.** B. ("And a couple thousand requisition forms.")   **59.** Dr. Morgenstern, but Dr. Swift was the one who signed off on the appointment.   **60.** A.   **61.** C.   **62.** True. She ate two LSD-laced chocolates by mistake.   **63.** A.   **64.** A.   **65.** C.   **66.** True.   **67.** B.
68. A.   **69.** Because the agency learned that she had recently attempted suicide.
70. B.   **71.** True.   **72.** A.   **73.** E.   **74.** Carter, after Jody O'Brien died.
75. B.   **76.** Jared.   **77.** C.   **78.** A.   **79.** College students pledging a fraternity who are stripped naked and left on the outskirts of town. They usually ended up being picked up by a cop and brought to the ER frostbitten and humiliated.   **80.** True. (At least he claimed he was a werewolf and he could howl pretty good, if truth be told.)   **81.** Mrs. Benton, to her son Peter.   **82.** C. (She lost the guide wire inside the patient.)   **83.** A.   **84.** B.   **85.** "Because doctors are pure and good." (See episode 22.)   **86.** False. They were thrilled to be asked.   **87.** B.   **88.** B.   **89.** A.
90. A,2; B,1.   **91.** C. **92.** B.   **93.** Chloe (and Susan's) mother, Cookie, to Chloe, upon seeing Chloe's new daughter, Susie.   **94.** C.   **95.** A.   **96.** False. It was scheduled for five o'clock in the afternoon.   **97.** A.   **98.** Johnny Cage.   **99.** False. She refused permission, telling Peter she would not put him through any more suffering.   **100.** C.   **101.** Carter, to Rolando, on the last day of Carter's ER rotation.

IV

MEDSPEAK

THE ER MEDICAL GLOSSARY

MEDSPEAK: THE ER MEDICAL GLOSSARY

Most of the medical terms used in *ER* are defined in this glossary and it should answer any questions that might arise as you read through the Patient Histories. Slang ER terms ("crispy critter") are also included. If a word is in **boldface** within a definition, it means that that term is also a glossary entry and you should read that entry for more information. I've tried to use plain language when possible, but sometimes the only way to explain a specialized technical term is with technicalities.

abduction: To move a limb or some other body part away from the midline of the body.

ABG: An arterial blood gas reading.

acetaminophen: A nonsalicylate analgesic-antipyretic, e.g., Tylenol.

ACE: angiotension-converting enzyme.

acidotic: Abnormally high acidity of body fluids and tissues.

adenosine: A drug used to help a patient with **tachycardia** convert to normal sinus rhythm.

agonal: A word used to describe a major negative change in a patient's condition, usually preceding immediate death, such as a complete cessation of breathing or a dire change in the patient's EEG or **EKG**.

albuterol: A bronchodilator drug used on asthma patients and patients having bronchial spasms to dilate the bronchia and improve breathing.

Alzheimer's Disease: A progressive disease with specific brain abnormalities marked by memory loss and progressive inability to function normally at even the simplest tasks.

AMA: Against medical advice; also, American Medical Association.

amitriptyline: A tricyclic antidepressant.

amoxicillin: An antibiotic.

amp: Abbreviation for *Ampule*, which is a sealed plastic or glass capsule containing a single dose of a drug in a sterile solution for injection.

anaphylactic shock: An extreme allergic reaction that usually involves heart failure, circulatory collapse, and sometimes results in death.

Ancef: A cephalosporin antibiotic.

aneurysm: A balloonlike swelling in the wall of an artery.

angina pectoris: A severe acute attack of cardiac pain.

angioplasty: Plastic surgery of blood vessels during which a balloon is passed into the artery and inflated to enlarge it and increase blood flow.

anhidrosis: The abnormal absence of sweat.

anterior: Word used to describe the front surface of an organ, muscle, etc.

Antivert: A drug prescribed for nausea and dizziness.

aortic calcification: Hardening of the aorta, the main artery coming out of the left ventricle of the heart, usually from cholesterol deposits or some other organic substance.

aortic coarctation: A dangerous narrowing of the aorta.

aortic rupture: A tear in the aorta.

arterial stick: Insertion of an IV line into an artery.

ASA: The abbreviation for acetylsalicylic acid (aspirin).

astrocytoma: A slowly growing tumor of the glial tissue of the brain and the spinal cord.

asystole: A condition in which the heart no longer beats and usually cannot be restarted.

Ativan: A minor tranquilizer drug (lorazepam) used for anxiety, tension, agitation, or fatigue.

atypical angina: A form of **angina pectoris** that does not manifest the typical angina symptoms of chest pain, shortness of breath, etc., but which comes on suddenly and occurs without a predisposing cause.

AZT: An antiviral drug (zidovudine) prescribed for the treatment of AIDS.

Babinski's reflex: Also known as the plantar reflex; the movement of the big toe upward instead of downward; used to test injury to, or diseases of, the upper motor neurons.

Bactrim: The trade name for cotrimoxazole, an antibacterial agent particularly useful for urinary infections.

bagging: Manual respiration for a patient having breathing trouble that uses a hand-held squeeze bag attached to a face mask.

Barlow's syndrome: Infantile scurvy.

Betadine: Trade name for povidone-iodine, a preparation used as a surgical scrub that is available in liquid and aerosol forms.

bilateral hemothorax: Blood in both sides of the pleura, the membrane covering the lung.

blood culture: Incubating a blood sample so that suspected infectious bacteria can multiply and thus be identified.

blood gas: A test to determine the gas-phase components of blood, including oxygen, carbon dioxide, pH balance, etc.

blood swab: A blood sample taken with a cotton-tipped stick.

body packer: A drug courier who swallows condoms filled with cocaine or heroin in order to smuggle them into a country and then passes them rectally after he's safe.

bolus: A large dose of a drug that is given (usually intravenously) at the beginning of treatment to raise blood-level concentrations to a therapeutic level.

bounceback: A patient who returns to the ER with the same complaint shortly after being released; e.g., "The bounceback migraine in 6."

bowel disimpaction: Manual removal of impacted fecal matter from a patient's rectum.

BP: Abbreviation for blood pressure.

bradycardic: A slowing of the heart rate to less than 50 beats per minute. (Interestingly, some athletes with extremely efficient cardiovascular systems have normal bradycardic resting heart rates of as low as 35 beats per minute. The normal heart rate is 60–80 beats per minute.)

breath sounds: The sounds heard through a stethoscope placed on the chest over the lungs. Experienced medical people can tell a great deal from the quality of a patient's breath sounds.

bronchoscopy: The use of an endoscope to examine and take biopsies from the interior of the bronchia.

BUN: Abbreviation for blood urea nitrogen.

c-section: Shorthand for **cesarean section**, which is surgical delivery of a baby through the abdominal wall.

c-spine: Shorthand for cervical spine, or the neck.

calcium oxalate stone: A kidney stone.

Calot's triangle: The cystic duct, the common duct, and the liver.

calyx: A cup-shaped part of the kidneys.

capillary refill: When a fingernail is pressed, the nail bed turns white. Capillary refill refers to the return of the nail bed to a pink color. Good cap refill is two seconds or less.

Capoten: See **captotril.**

captotril: An antihypertensive and **ACE** inhibitor prescribed for high blood failure and congestive heart failure. It is also sold under the trade name **Capoten** (captotril is the drug's generic name).

carboxyhemoglobin: A substance formed when the poisonous gas carbon monoxide combines with hemoglobin in the blood. Carboxyhemoglobin is incapable of transporting oxygen to the body's organs. Large amounts of this compound are found in carbon monoxide poisoning.

cardiac effusion: See **pericardial effusion**.

cardiac enzymes: Creatine kinase, lactate dehydrogenase, and aspartate transaminase.

cardiomyopathy: A disorder of the heart muscle that can often be fatal.

cardiac tamponade: Compression of the heart.

CAT scan: Computerized axial tomography.

catcher's mask: A device used for a patient with bleeding varices in the throat that allows a tube with two balloons attached to be positioned securely in the throat and inflated. The balloons then put pressure on the enlarged veins in order to stop the bleeding.

CBC: Abbreviation for complete blood count, which is an all-purpose blood test; combining diagnostic evaluations of red blood cell count, white cell count, erythrocyte indices, hematocrit, and a differential blood count.

cc: Abbreviation for cubic centimeters.

cecum: A pouch at the junction of the large and small intestine. The lower end bears the vermiform appendix.

ceftriaxone: A cephalosporin antibiotic.

cellulitis: Inflammation of the connective tissue between organs and adjacent soft tissue, usually due to a bacterial infection.

cephalosporin: An antibiotic.

cesarean section: Surgical delivery of a baby through the abdominal wall.

champagne tap: A successful lumbar puncture the first time a medical student attempts one. So-called because the supervising resident has to, by custom, buy the student a bottle of champagne.

Chem 7: A battery of blood chemistry tests; the seven parts of a Chem 7: sodium, potassium, chloride, bicarbonate, blood urea nitrogen (BUN), creatinine, and glucose.

chest film: A chest X-ray.

claudication: Limping caused by impaired blood supply to the legs.

coag panel: A blood test used to determine the clotting factors of a patient's blood.

Code Brown: Term used when a patient doesn't make it to the bathroom in time.

Compazine: A drug (prochlorperazine) prescribed for severe nausea and vomiting and also for treatment of psychotic disorders and anxiety.

cordotomy: Surgical severing of the nerves in the spinal cord to relieve intractable pain in the pelvis and lower limbs.

Crasher: A person who passes out in the ER, often not a patient but a family member who is upset over what's going on with a loved one.

cricothyroidotomy: A procedure used to surgically establish an airway in the patient's throat when intubation isn't possible because of swelling or bleeding.

cricothyrotomy: See **cricothyroidotomy**.

crispy critter: Irreverent ER slang for a seriously burned patient.

Crit: Short for hematocrit.

CT scan: Same thing as a CAT scan.

CVA: Abbreviation for cerebrovascular accident, a.k.a. a stroke.

cyanotic: When a patient's skin and mucous membranes are bluish in color from an inadequate supply of oxygen in the blood.

cystic fibrosis: A lung disease that causes the production of thick mucus in the lungs, hampering breathing.

D5: The abbreviation for dextrose (glucose) given in a 5 percent normal saline solution.

Darvocet: A drug (propoxyphene hydrochloride) prescribed for pain.

DB: ER abbreviation for a dead body.

dead shovel: ER slang for a fat man who dies while shoveling snow.

debridement: Cleaning an open wound by removing foreign material and dead tissue. Debridement of burns is extremely painful.

decerebration: The progressive loss of cerebral function; advanced decerebration (and resultant deep unconsciousness) occurs with severe damage to the cerebrum, the largest part of the brain.

deep vein thrombosis: A blood clot in a deep vein.

defibrillation: The cessation of **fibrillation** of the cardiac muscle and restortaion of a normal rhythm.

defibrillator: Electronic device used to shock the heart out of **fibrillation** and back into a normal rhythm.

delusional: Having an irrational belief that cannot be changed by a rational argument, often found in schizophrenia and manic-depressive psychosis.

Demerol: Trade name for meperidine, a synthetic analgesic often used as a substitute for morphine.

diabetic ketoacidosis: Depletion of the body's alkali reserves due to diabetes, causing a major disruption in the body's acid-base balance. The breath smells fruity and the patient is usally comatose.

diagnosis: Determining what's wrong with a patient by using the patient's symptoms, signs, test results, medical background, and other factors.

diaphoresis: Sweating.

DIC: Abbreviation for disseminated intravascular coagulation (no blood clotting). (In many hospitals, ER personnel also interpret DIC to mean "death is coming" since disseminated intravascular coagulation usually means death is imminent.)

differential diagnosis: Diagnosis made by ruling out many disorders. The patient usually presents with symptoms that can be shared by many conditions. For example, chest pain can be caused by many diseases or conditions, and each one must be ruled out to arrive at the correct diagnosis.

digitalis: A drug prescribed for congestive heart failure.

Dilantin: An anticonvulsant drug used to prevent seizures.

diplopia: Double vision.

Disaster Protocol color coding: The following color tags are used to immediately triage patients during a mass casualty event: Green is Walking Wounded; Yellow is Urgent; Red is Critical; and Black is **DOA**.

distal pulse: The pulse farthest from the heart.

diuresis: The increased production of urine.

DNR: The abbreviation for do not resuscitate, which is requested or ordered for terminally ill patients.

DOA: Abbreviation for dead on arrival.

dopamine: A catecholamine neurotransmitter, similar to adrenaline. It is used during surgery to increase cardiac output and renal blood flow.

DTP: A tetanus toxoid injection.

dystocia: Difficult labor due to some fetal problem, such as dislocation of the shoulders. (See episode 19.)

ECG or EKG: Electrocardiogram.

eclampsia: A serious condition affecting pregnant women in which the entire body is affected by convulsions and the patient eventually passes into a coma.

ectopic pregnancy: The development of the fetus in the fallopian tube instead of in the womb.

edema: Excessive accumulation of fluid.

Elavil: Trade name for **amitriptyline**.

embolectomy: Surgical removal of an embolus (a blood clot).

EMT: Abbreviation for Emergency Medical Technician.

endocarditis: Inflammation of the inner lining of the heart.

epidural: An epidural block; an injection through a catheter of a local anesthetic to relieve pain during labor, usually done at the lumbar level of the spine.

epiglottitis: Inflammation of the epiglottis.

epinephrine: Synthetic adrenaline.

Esimil: A beta-blocking drug.

Feldene: A nonsteroidal anti-inflammatory drug (piroxicam) prescribed for arthritis and other forms of joint and bone inflammation.

fentanyl: A short-acting morphinelike narcotic analgesic of high potency, often used in conjunction with other drugs. Fentanyl can enhance the effect of certain narcotics (including morphine).

fetal distress: A term used to describe a number of critical conditions threatening the live delivery of a fetus.

FHT: Abbreviation for fetal heart tones.

fibrillation: An uncoordinated, quivering of the heart muscle resulting in a completely irregular pulse.

first-degree burn: A burn affecting only the epidermis, the outer layer of the skin. The color of the burn is red, capillary refill is present, the skin texture is normal, and the burn heals in five to ten days with no scarring.

Flexeril: A potent muscle relaxant.

Fluconazole: An antifungal drug used for infections of the mouth, blood, and throat. Fluconazole is often used by AIDS patients to combat oral thrush and other infections.

fluoroscope: An X-ray machine.

Focused H and P: A history and physical examination. *H and P* is the term used to describe an examination that results in a patient history and makes an assessment of his or her condition. The patient is physically examined and then talked to regarding his or her complaint, and the doctor then makes a probable diagnosis. *Focused* means do not examine a patient's feet or do a rectal if they're complaining of a headache and double vision.

Foley: A Foley (indwelling) catheter. This is a thin flexible tube inserted into the urethra in order to drain the bladder.

gangbanger: A gang member shot during gang warfare.

gastric lavage: Irrigation of the stomach when poisoning or bleeding is suspected.

GCS: See **Glasgow Coma Scale**.

Gentamicin: An antibiotic.

GGF1: An abbreviation for Grandpa's got a fever, which is shorthand for a battery of tests performed when an elderly male presents with a fever of unknown origin. The tests included in a GGF1 are a CBC, Chem 7, chest X-ray, U/A, and blood cultures times two.

GI cocktail: There seem to be as many definitions of this term as there are hospitals and emergency departments, although it is likely that since Dr. Greene ordered one for an ER patient, he was referring to a commonly-used mixture of liquid Donnatal (which stops gastrointestinal spasms), viscous Lidocaine (which anesthetizes the irritated gut), and Mylanta (which counteracts the stomach acid and soothes the stomach). This concoction (also known as a Green Lizard) is often given to patients presenting with severe heartburn, signs of an ulcer, or indications of an excess production of stomach acid. (If the brew works, then the problem is probably not cardiac.) An R.N. I spoke with told me that she gives GI Cocktails all the time to her patients (nonemergency) and that *her* "cocktail" consists of a mixture of milk of magnesia and cascara (both powerful laxatives). Other well-known medical "cocktails" are the Bellevue cocktail, given in the field by EMTs to suspected drug overdoses. This one consists of dextrose, Vitamin B1, and Narcan. And the Banana Cocktail (so called because the mixture is bright yellow) given to people who are extremely intoxicated. This one consists of dextrose, antinausea drugs (such as Compazine), and vitamins and electrolytes to replace depleted nutrients. (By the way, a doctor familiar with the Green Lizard told me it is the foulest-tasting mixture he's ever come across.).

giardiasis: Intestinal infection with the *Giardia* bacteria.

Glasgow coma scale (GCS): This scale is used to quickly determine the status and degree of injury of a trauma victim.

"Glove up and dig in.": See **bowel disimpaction**.

Golden Hour: Also known as the Golden Window. When treating a patient who has had a myocardial infarction, emergency personnel must be extremely careful during the first hour. The ventricles are very sensitive during this period and life threatening arrythmias can occur.

gorked: ER slang for unconscious (as in a "gorked patient"). Also used as a noun, as in "I've got a gork in 2."

Gram's stain: A stain test that identifies various forms of bacterial microorganisms.

granuloma: A tumor.

GSW: Abbreviation for a gunshot wound.

H and P (See Focused H and P): History and physical: The initial evaluation and examination of a patient.

Haldol: A drug (haloperidol) used for psychotic disorders, Tourette's syndrome, and hyperactivity in children.

heart/lung bypass: Using a machine to breathe and circulate blood for a patient for any number of clinical or surgical reasons.

The Heimlich maneuver: A first-aid measure used to dislodge something caught in a person's throat that is obstructing breathing. The person performing the Heimlich stands behind the victim and jerks his clenched fists into the area above the stomach and between the breastbone to forcibly expel the object out the mouth.

Hematocrit: The proportion, by volume, of red blood cells in a complete blood count.

hemiparesis: Paralysis or weakness on one side of the body

hemoperfusion: Dialysis of the blood to remove foreign substances such as poisons or drugs.

hemopneumothorax: Blood and air in the pleura, the membrane surrounding the lung. Also often referred to as a collapsed lung.

heparin: A blood anticoagulant.

hepatolenticular degeneration: Excessive accumulation of copper in the kidney, liver, and brain, which, if untreated, is invariably fatal.

holosystolic murmur: A heart murmur that begins with the heart sound S_1 and occupying all of systole, then reaching S_2. S_1 and S_2 refer to heart sounds noted during palpation.

Horner's syndrome: The term used to describe the clinical profile of **myosis, ptosis,** and **anhidrosis,** which usually follows paralysis of the cervical sympathetic nerves on one side of the body.

hydralazine: A synthetic compound that lowers blood pressure.

hyperaldosteronism: Overproduction of the adrenal hormone aldosterone, causing abnormalities in the sodium, water, and potassium levels in the body.

hypercalcemia: An abnormally high concentration of calcium in the blood.

hyperlipidemia: Excessive fat in the blood.

hypotension: Abnormally low blood pressure.

hypothyroidism: Subnormal activity of the thyroid gland.

hypovolemia: A decrease in the volume of circulating blood; also referred to as being in shock.

hypoxic: A severe deficiency of oxygen in the blood and tissues.

ileectomy: Surgical removal of the small intestine.

IM: Abbreviation for intramuscular (pertaining to injections).

infiltrate: An abnormal substance (e.g., a cancer cell) in a tissue or organ.

intubation: Insertion of an endotracheal tube to help an unconscious patient breathe.

irritable bowel syndrome: A chronic and unpleasant gastrointestinal condition marked by abdominal cramping, and diarrhea or constipation.

Isordil: An antianginal agent.

IV: Abbreviation for intravenous.

K-Y: K-Y Jelly. A widely used (both medically and sexually) water-soluble lubricant.

Kay Ciel: A potassium supplement.

K.U.B.: Shorthand for kidney, ureter, and bladder tests.

lac: Abbreviation for laceration (pronounced "lack").

laparotomy: Any surgery involving an incision in the abdominal wall.

laryngoscope: An instrument for examining the larynx.

larynx: The "voice box."

Lasix: A diuretic.

lidocaine: A local anesthetic.

lithium: A drug commonly used to treat manic-depressive illness.

lithotripsy: Breaking up renal calculi (kidney stones) with sound waves so they can be passed in the urine.

lumbar puncture: The withdrawal of cerebrospinal fluid through a hollow needle inserted into the lumbar region between the L4 and L5 vertebrae. Also referred to as a spinal tap.

lytes: Abbreviation for electrolyte analysis (pronounced "lights").

Macrodantin: An anti-infective antibiotic used to prevent and treat urinary tract infections.

macrosomic: Fetal weight of more than 4,000 grams.

magnesium sulfate: Epsom salts, a fast-acting laxative.

mannitol: A natural sugar that acts as a diuretic, used in cases of drug overdoses and cerebral swelling.

meningitis: An inflammation of the meninges, the membranes surrounding the brain and spinal cord.

meperedine: The chemical name for the narcotic painkiller **Demerol**.

metacarpal fracture: A fracture of one of the five bones that form that part of the hand between the wrist and the fingers.

methylprednisolone: An anti-inflammatory steroid.

mg: Abbreviation for milligrams.

MI: Abbreviation for a **myocardial infarction** (a heart attack).

MRI: Magnetic resonance imaging. Imaging by computer using a strong magnetic field and radio frequencies.

MVA: Abbreviation used in ERs for a motor vehicle accident.

myocardial infarction: A heart attack.

myosis: Excessive contraction of the pupil of the eye.

Narcan: Naloxone, a drug used to counteract drug overdoses.

necrotic: Dead, as in "necrotic tissue."

needle cricothyroidotomy: See **cricothyroidotomy**.

NG tube: Abbreviation for a nasogastric tube.

NICU: Abbreviation for the Neonatal Intensive Care Unit.

nitro drip: An IV infusion of the antianginal agent **nitroglycerin**.

nitroglycerine: An antianginal agent.

Norcuron: Vecuronium, a neuromuscular blocking agent used to paralyze for rapid-sequence intubation.

normal sinus rhythm: A normal heart rate, which is between 60 and 80 beats per minute in an adult.

nosocomial infections: Opportunistic infections contracted while in the hospital, e.g., a urinary tract infection a patient develops from his Foley catheter.

NPO: Abbreviation for nothing by mouth (from the Latin *Nil peros*).

NS: Abbreviation for normal saline solution.

NSAID: The abbreviation for a nonsteroid anti-inflammatory drug (e.g., Motrin, Advil, Naprosyn, etc.)

O neg: Type O, Rhesus negative blood; also called universal donor blood.

orbital fracture: A fracture of the bony socket that holds the eyeball.

osteosarcoma: Bone cancer.

otitis medea: An infection of the middle ear.

palp: (As in "60 palp.") This refers to blood pressure taken under emergency conditions when listening for the systolic and diastolic pressures with a stethoscope is impossible. Trained medical personnel can take a blood pressure by feel (*palp*ation) in which they can register by touch the beginning of the pulse. A blood pressure of 50 palp (Patient 3.52) or 60 palp (Patient 2.32) is extremely serious and critical and the patient is probably near death at this point.

pancreatitis: Chronic or acute inflammation of the pancreas.

papilledema: Edema of the optic disk, often indicative of increased intracranial pressure.

paresis: Partial or slight paralysis.

path urine: Urinanalysis.

Pavulon: Trade name for the muscle relaxant pancuronium bromide. Pavulon produces complete paralysis, but with no alteration of consciousness.

PCP: Phencyclidine. Also known as angel dust and crystal. PCP is a veterinary anesthetic that causes euphoria and hallucinations in humans. It is commonly used to "enhance" marijuana, amphetamines, and street hallucinogens, and can be snorted, smoked, injected, or ingested.

pedal: Related to the foot, as in "pedal edema."

pericardial centesis: The draining of fluid from the **pericardium**.

pericardial effusion: Blood or fluid leaking into the **pericardium**.

pericardium: The sac that envelops the heart.

peritoneal lavage: Irrigation of the **peritoneum**.

peritoneum: A transparent membrane enclosing the abdomenal cavity.

Pitocin: Synthetic oxytocin, a pituitary hormone that causes uterine contractions and is often used to induce labor.

placental abruption: The placenta separates from the lining of the womb too early, resulting in pain and bleeding.

PO$_2$: The oxygen tension in arterial blood.

PQRST: A mnemonic device used to quickly evaluate chest pain. *P* stands for "palliative and provoking": Does anything make the pain better or worse?; *Q* stands for "quality": What, precisely does the pain feel like? Is it stabbing and knife-like or dull and throbbing?; *R* stands for "radiation": Does the pain radiate anywhere beyond the chest, such as into the arm or jaw?; *S* stands for "severity": On a scale of 1 to 10, with 1 being almost no pain at all and 10 being the worst pain imaginable, what number does the pain rank?; *T* stands for "timing": What, specifically, were you doing when the pain began and how long have you had it?

preeclampsia: The physical condition of a pregnant woman prior to **eclampsia**. Symptoms include blood pressure greater than 140/90; persistent proteinuria (protein in the urine); and edema (swelling).

preemie: Slang expression for a baby born before full term, usually defined as a child born weighing less than five and a half pounds. Preemies usually have to spend some time in an incubator.

Procardia: A calcium channel blocker prescribed for angina and high blood pressure.

Prolixin: A drug (fluphenazine hydrochloride) used for psychotic disorders, moderate to severe depression, control of agitation, intractable pain, senility, and alcohol withdrawal symptoms.

ptosis: Drooping of the eyelid.

pulmonary edema: Fluid in the lungs.

pulmonary embolism: A blood clot in the lungs.

pulsatile: Beating, as in a pulsatile mass (a growth in which a pulse can be felt).

Puls/ox: Pulse oximetry. This is a measure of the saturation of hemoglobin by oxygen.

pulsus paradoxus: A condition in which the pulse pressure declines during respiratory inspiration.

PVCs: Premature cardiac ventricular contractions.

pyelogram: An X-ray of the kidneys using an intravenously inserted dye.

q 12: Every twelve hours.

rape kit: A package containing envelopes for the collection of hair, sperm, and blood samples of a rape victim; as well as the official reporting forms.

renogram: An X-ray of the kidneys.

respirations: Breaths; the act of inhaling and exhaling.

retrocecal: Behind the cecum, as in retrocecal appendix.

rifampin: An antibiotic used to treat meningitis, tuberculosis, Legionnaire's disease, leprosy, and staph infections.

Rifabutin: A drug used to help prevent mycobacterium avium complex (MAC) disease in patients with advanced human immunodeficiency virus (HIV) infection.

Ringer's solution: An intravenous solution consisting of salt, potassium, and calcium in boiled water used to treat dehydration.

schizophrenia: A mental disorder marked by hallucinations, delusions, and disintegration of the thought processes.

scoop and run: A term used by EMTs and ER personnel for a situation where no treatment is possible at an accident scene and all they can do is "scoop" up the victims and "run" with them to the ER (although some kind of emergency treatment will usually be attempted in the ambulance on the way to the hospital).

second-degree burn: There are two levels of **second-degree burn**: The first level is a burn in which both the epidermis and the underlying dermis are damaged. The color of the burn is red (and there may be blistering); capillary refill is present; the skin texture is edematous (filled with fluid), and the burn heals in ten to twenty-one days with no, or minimal, scarring. The second level is a damaging, deep partial-thickness burn that is pink or white in color; capillary refill might or might not be present; the skin texture is thick; and the burn heals in twenty-five to sixty days with a dense scar.

sed rate: Erythrocyte sedimentation rate, a red blood cell test used to determine inflammation and tissue destruction.

serum amylase enzyme test: A test for starch that helps determine kidney function.

shock: A circulatory disturbance marked by a severe drop in blood pressure, rapid pulse, clammy skin, pallor, and a rapid heart rate.

shunt: A "detour" passage (either congenital or surgically created) used to divert blood from one anatomical channel to another.

Solu-Medrol: Methylprednisolone, a form of prednisone, an adrenal corticosteroid.

spinal tap: See **lumbar puncture**.

splenectomy: Surgical removal of the spleen.

stasis: A slowing or stopping of blood flow.

sternotomy: Surgical opening of the breastbone.

streptokinase: An enzyme that can break up and liquefy blood clots.

stridor: What breathing sounds like when the larynx or trachea is obstructed.

sublingual: A medication that is taken by dissolving under the tongue.

succinylcholine: A short-acting muscle relaxant.

systolic murmur: A cardiac murmur that occurs between the first and second heart sounds.

T3, T4, etc: Third thoracic vertabrae; fourth thoracic vertabrae; etc.

tachycardia: An extremely rapid heart rate.

tamoxifen: The chemotherapy drug of choice for postmenopausal metastatic breast cancer.

tension pneumothorax: A collapsed lung.

tetralogy of Fallot: A surgically correctable congenital heart defect that consists of pulmonary stenosis, hypertrophy (enlargement) of the right ventricle, a ventricular septal defect, and a shift of the aorta to the right.

third-degree burn: A burn that damages (or destroys) the full thickness of the skin and the tissues underneath. The color of the burn is white, black, or brown; capillary refill is absent; the skin texture is leathery; and there is no spontaneous healing.

thoracotomy: Surgery on the thoracic (chest) cavity.

Thorazine: A multipurpose drug (chlorpromazine) that works as a sedative, an antiemetic, an antispasmodic, and a hypotensive. It is often used in the management of psychiatric and senile patients.

thrill: A vibration that a doctor or nurse can feel by touch, often used to describe cardiac murmurs that can be felt through the chest wall.

thrombosis: A blood clot.

Timoptic: A drug prescribed for high blood pressure and to reduce the possibility of another heart attack.

Toradol: Ketorolac, an injectable nonsteroid antiinflammatory agent often used as a substitute for morphine in intoxicated patients or for those patients suspected of seeking narcotics.

torsades de pointes: A type of polymorphic ventricular tachycardia in which the heart races at extremely high rates in an arrhythmia.

tox screen: Toxicological analysis of the blood, ordered when a drug overdose is suspected and the drugs need to be identified.

tPA: The abbreviation for tissue plasminogen activator, a drug used as an alternative to angioplasty to break up blood clots during a heart attack.

tracheal shift: A physical shift of the windpipe due to trauma.

triage: The system of prioritizing patients in an emergency situation in which there are a great number of injured or ill.

type and crossmatch: Blood typing to identify patient's blood type.

U/A: Urinalysis.

ulcerative colitis: An inflammatory and ulcerative condition of the colon.

ultrasound: A test similar to an X-ray, but which uses sound waves.

unstable angina: Angina pectoris in which the cardiac pain has changed in pattern.

uric acid: An acid formed in the breakdown of nucleoproteins in tissues; often tested when gout is suspected since a high uric acid content in the blood often causes gout symptoms and the formation of stones.

V/Q scan: A ventilation-perfusion scan, used to confirm a diagnosis of pulmonary embolism.

Valsalva maneuver: When a patient is instructed to blow on his or her thumb to maximize intrathoracic pressure. It is used when cardiac trouble is suspected.

Vecuronium: See **Norcuron**.

ventricular septal rupture: Rupture of the ventricular septum caused by mechanical failure of infarcted cardiac tissue.

Verapamil: A calcium channel blocker prescribed for angina pectoris, high blood pressure, asthma, and Raynaud's disease.

Versed: A benzodiazepine muscle relaxant used to sedate, often in conjunction with the paralyzing agent **Pavulon**.

Vitamin H: ER shorthand for **Haldol**.

wheezer: An asthmatic patient, or any patient having difficulty breathing.

Whipple procedure: A pancreatotomy, which is the technical term for surgical removal of the pancreas.

ABOUT THE AUTHOR

Stephen J. Spignesi is a Connecticut writer who specializes in popular culture subjects, including television, film, and contemporary fiction. He has written several authorized entertainment books and has worked with Stephen King, Turner Entertainment, the Margaret Mitchell Estate, Andy Griffith, Woody Allen, Viacom, and other entertainment industry personalities and entities on a wide range of projects.

Spignesi's books include:
- *Mayberry, My Hometown* (Popular Culture, Ink.)
- *The Complete Stephen King Encyclopedia* (Popular Culture, Ink; Contemporary Books)
- *The Stephen King Quiz Book* (Signet)
- *The Second Stephen King Quiz Book* (Signet)
- *The Woody Allen Companion* (Andrews and McMeel; Plexus; Popular Culture, Ink)
- *The Official "Gone With the Wind" Companion* (Plume)
- *The V.C. Andrews Trivia and Quiz Book* (Signet)
- *The Odd Index: The Ultimate Compendium of Bizarre and Unusual Facts* (Plume)
- *What's Your "Mad About You" I.Q.?* (Citadel Press)
- *The Gore Galore Video Quiz Book* (Signet)
- *What's Your "Friends" I.Q.?* (Citadel Press)
- *The Celebrity Baby Name Book* (Signet)
- *The Italian 100: A Ranking of the Most Influential Cultural, Scientific, and Political Figures, Past and Present* (forthcoming, Citadel Press)
- *Stephen King A to Z* (forthcoming, Popular Culture, Ink)

In addition to writing, Spignesi also lectures widely on a variety of popular culture subjects and is the founder and editor-in-chief of the small press publishing company, The Stephen John Press. He lives in New Haven, Connecticut, with his wife, Pam.